SPREADSHEET FUNDAMENTALS

EDWARD V. WEBER

Kendall Hunt
publishing company

Cover image © Shutterstock.com
Screen shots source: Ed Weber/Microsoft.

Kendall Hunt
publishing company

www.kendallhunt.com
Send all inquiries to:
4050 Westmark Drive
Dubuque, IA 52004-1840

Contents

Chapter 10 – Working with Macros   225

Introduction

Source: Shutterstock, Inc.

Why are we here?

I know why I am here: After having taught a course named *Spreadsheet Fundamentals* (or other similar titles) for over 20 years at different colleges and universities, I have known all along that this was a textbook that *needed* to be written! Ever since the first spreadsheet programs were developed for the first personal computers in the 1980s, students and business people have had a need to learn the fundamentals of spreadsheet programs and how to make spreadsheets become the "go-to" tool in their computing toolboxes.

But nearly every other year or so for the last three decades, software vendors have produced yet another new version of the spreadsheet application programs, whether a new version was really needed or not! As a result, textbook authors began to approach this topic by *not* writing about the fundamentals of working with a spreadsheet program, but rather by writing textbooks that were narrowly focused on just the latest single version of a single software from a single vendor. This meant that the shelf life and applicability of those textbooks were as limited as the version of the programs they were describing.

However, a well-kept secret is this: The fundamentals of working in a spreadsheet program have not really changed at all since those early programs in the 1980s! To clarify, while the newer versions of spreadsheet programs have often added many bells and whistles that the earliest versions did not have, there have not been any fundamental changes to the way spreadsheets work from those earliest days. In fact, I will suggest that there have been no fundamental changes to the way spreadsheets have worked for at least the last 10 years.

So *my* purpose for being here is clear: I wanted to write a textbook that would teach students how to perform all of the fundamental activities that you might want to do in a spreadsheet program – regardless of the version or vendor of the actual spreadsheet program you are using. In this manner, I will be able to continue to use this textbook for many years, regardless of what spreadsheet application program(s) the users might choose to use.

So that's why *I'm* here – but what about you? Why are *you* here?

I know that for some of you, the answer is that "this is the required text for a required course in my current program of study."

What I am hopeful that you will quickly discover is that this textbook can become an important ongoing reference tool for you. With this textbook, you will learn why we use spreadsheet programs and how to use spreadsheet programs (no matter which spreadsheet program!) to accomplish your goals – whether academic goals or work goals or personal goals.

At the successful completion of working through this textbook, you will be able to tell your peers, colleagues, and employers, that you are able to be productive working with **any spreadsheet program** that you may come across – including those that haven't even been released yet! This means that you will be able to use the most common business tool in use today after the word processor, email, and web browser.

Organization of this text

In each of the chapters of this text, you will find several sections. The first section always deals with the question *Why*? I have learned through the years that if you understand why you are doing something, you're much more likely to better grasp the *What* and *How* aspects about a topic.

After the *Why* section in each chapter, there will be a section that displays the outline of the *Learning Objectives* that will be covered in the chapter. Each of these objectives will be prefixed with an "LO" followed by the chapter initials or number followed by a sequence number. For example the first learning objective in the Computing Fundamentals chapter will be numbered "LO CF.1" and the third learning objective from Chapter 2 will be numbered "LO 2.3".

If you are using the electronic version of this textbook, then you can simply click on the links in the table of contents to easily jump to any section of the book that is outlined there.

The next section in each chapter will be a small table of key terms that are defined within each chapter. Each of these key terms will be found in bold text at the place in the chapter where the term is defined.

The next several sections will be individual sections for each of the individual learning objectives that are contained within the chapter.

Then finally, for most of the chapters, there will be a section containing assignments and projects for you to practice and reinforce the learned concepts from the chapter. Some of these assignments and projects will be *directed* in that the specific steps and desired outcomes will be fully described for you to follow. And some of these assignments and projects will be *creative* in nature such that only generalized instructions will be given and it will be up to you to come up with a creative solution to the task at hand. This approach reflects the typical ways in which assignments may be initiated in the "real world." Sometimes, there will be a very specific task to be accomplished working with some very specific materials as a starting point. Other times, there will be only a generalized task to be accomplished with no real details available as a starting point. By providing both types of assignments, you can really get a feel for the diverse ways in which spreadsheets are used in the "real world."

There are supplemental files available for use with this text that can be found at the following locations:

Student Data Files for Assignments and Projects: https://www.grtep.com/
Supplemental Video Files to Support Chapter Material: https://www.grtep.com/

The student data files will be required for you to be able to complete the projects and assignments at the end of the chapters. The supplemental video files are short explanations and demonstrations of the concepts that may be better reinforced with a visual display.

Which spreadsheet program to use?

Throughout this text, each concept will be presented using generic (non-vendor-specific or non-version-specific) terms as much as possible, and the figures throughout each chapter will be screenshots from various different spreadsheet programs. Generally speaking, you should be able to follow along with this text using practically any contemporary spreadsheet program that was designed intentionally to run as a desktop application. As of this publication, the spreadsheet applications that are designed to run as collaborative tools in the cloud space do not contain the full functionality of standard spreadsheet programs. Additionally, some online versions of contemporary spreadsheet programs are only available through a paid subscription and this is an unnecessary expense that the student should not need to incur.

Whenever there are known incompatibilities between particular versions of spreadsheet programs (in particular differences between desktop and online versions), this text will endeavor to indicate those peculiarities and, when applicable, provide "workarounds" for you to consider.

While many schools and employers will provide you with a spreadsheet program for your use, you may find yourself responsible for choosing your own programs to use at school, at work, or for your home. By becoming familiar with a variety of the different spreadsheet programs that are available to you, you will become significantly more marketable to potential employers and more able to adapt to changes within the programs as they arise.

The commercial versions of spreadsheet application programs that are available from Microsoft and Apple are good enough to work with, but being commercial software titles, there is a cost to license and use these programs. An alternative program that is available for no cost is the LibreOffice application suite. This suite includes a word processing program, a spreadsheet program, and a presentation application program. There are versions of this application suite that will run on Mac, Windows, or Linux operating systems. The LibreOffice suite can be downloaded from https://www.libreoffice.org/download/download/.

Acknowledgments and copyright information

Unless otherwise indicated herein, any third-party trademarks that may appear in this work are the property of their respective owners and any references to third-party trademarks, logos or other trade names are for demonstrative or descriptive purposes only.

Computing Fundamentals

Source: Shutterstock, Inc.

Why would you want to read this chapter?

The purpose of this chapter is to show you how computers work to allow you to create and save important information – not just spreadsheet information. This section is especially helpful if you have not worked with computers extensively in the past, or if you want some in-depth understanding of how the various software programs in computers work together.

Even if you are fairly comfortable with general computer operations, the paragraphs in this section that deal with the different file types may be of special importance to you. This section helps you understand how you can use any spreadsheet program to create and save files that anyone else can access – whether or not they have the same brand or version of the software that you might have! This section will also help you understand why you don't have to keep purchasing new versions of spreadsheet programs if you already have one that meets your needs.

LEARNING OBJECTIVES

In this chapter, we will explore these learning objectives:

Understanding the differences between an operating system and an application program and be able to identify examples of each.

Understanding how application programs and operating systems interact through the file system.

Understanding the three decisions that are necessary to properly save files for future use.

Learning how to create screenshots of your computer screen and then mark or highlight areas of interest within the captured picture.

LO CF.1 Operating Systems and Application Programs

The programs that are installed and run on computers are broken down into two primary categories: The first group of programs is called the operating system. The second types of programs are called application programs.

Key Terms
- application program
- cropping
- file extensions
- file locations
- file name
- file saving
- file system
- file type (version)
- folders
- highlighting
- operating systems
- screenshot

1

Operating systems for personal computers come from different software vendors. Two of the most commonly known vendors are Microsoft Corporation and Apple. Microsoft has created many versions of operating systems throughout the years, with the most common versions being the different versions of Windows. Apple has also created many versions of operating systems with the most common versions being versions of OS X.

Some examples of Microsoft operating systems through the years include DOS, Windows, Windows 2.0, Windows 3.1, Windows 3.11, Windows 95, Windows 98, Windows 2000, Windows XP, Windows Vista, Windows 7, Windows 8, and Windows 10, just to name a few. Some examples of Apple operating systems through the years include Mac OS, Mac OS 9, Mac OS X (with nine different versions), OS X (with four different versions), and now macOS.

Additionally, there are open source versions of operating systems that are mostly derivatives of a single operating system known as Linux. Most open source software can be downloaded and used *for free*, which make them appealing no-cost alternatives to name-brand commercial options.

Besides operating systems for personal computers, there are operating systems for other computing devices and platforms such as phones and tablets. Some examples of operating systems for these devices include iOS from Apple and Android OS from Google.

All operating systems from all vendors provide four specific functions:

1. **All operating systems allow the human to interact with the computing hardware.**
   It is because of the operating system that when a user types on the keyboard or moves a mouse or taps on a touch screen, the computer appears to respond. Type the letter Q on the keyboard; you see the letter Q show up on the screen . . . that is the operating system at work. When you move the mouse and you see the little arrow moving about the screen . . . that is also the operating system at work. When you click the play button on your music app and you suddenly hear your favorite song coming through the speakers of the computer . . . that is also the operating system. Every single interaction between you, the human, and the computer, is controlled by the operating system.

2. **All operating systems provide for user authentication and validation and provide access control to the computing resources.**
   When you first turn on a computer, before you can do anything else, the computer will typically prompt you for your username and password. This is called authentication and validation of your credentials. It is commonly known as "logging in" to the computer. In some newer computers, authentication is now being controlled by biometrics such as fingerprint scans, iris scans, voice recognition, and facial recognition. But it is still the operating system that is collecting the user's credentials and then validating that the user is authorized to use the system.

3. **All operating systems allow authorized users to run application programs.**
   Once you are logged into a computer, typically a computer user will run a program to do a particular task. The programs that you are running are called application programs. Each application program has a primary task that the program is designed to accomplish. An important point here: All application programs require an operating system in order to run! In other words, if your operating system isn't working first, you cannot run an application program.

   Some examples of application programs are word processing programs, spreadsheet programs, presentation programs, photo editing programs, web browsers, email programs, accounting programs, database programs, music and video programs, and the list goes on and on.

4. **All operating systems are responsible for maintaining the file system of the computer.**
   Computers have access to physical storage that can be thought of as an electronic filing cabinet. In order to properly store and retrieve digital information in this electronic filing cabinet,

the operating system creates and maintains a file system. The filing system of each computer is specific to the particular operating system that is running on that computer. In other words, the Windows filing system is different than the OS X filing system, which is different than the Linux filing system. But even though these filing systems are unique, they all share common attributes about the information that is being saved whenever a file is saved. We will explore these common features in the next section.

LO CF.2   How the File System Works

One of the responsibilities of every operating system is to maintain the file system of the computer. The file system of a computer is a collection of entries that represents information about every file that is known to the computer.

Every time a new file is created or accessed on a computer or anytime a file is updated on the computer, the file system for the computer is updated to reflect this new information. Some of the information that is maintained within the file system includes the following:

✦ the name of the file

✦ the file location within the file system

✦ the file type (file extension)

✦ the file size

✦ the date and time the file was created

✦ the date and time the file was last modified

✦ other pieces of information that each operating system deems to be important

Every operating system provides the user with some way to view the files within the file system. Figure CF-1 shows the file manager component of a Windows 7 operating system. This file manager component is called Windows Explorer.

In this figure, you can see the left pane is showing the locations where files and folders are stored. File locations are the named physical or logical locations where folders and files are digitally stored on a computer system. Physical locations, such as disk drives, can contain logical locations called folders, which are named containers for storing other folders and files. The indentions of the named locations in the left panel of the figure show which items are contained within each other container.

On the top of this window, you can see the location within the file system that is being viewed. In this example, in the location named *Computer*, there is a physical device named *OSDisk (C:)*, and in that location, there is a folder named *$000_Textbook_Samples*, and this is the location that is currently being viewed.

In the right pane of this example, we see the contents of this location. Here we see there are eight objects arranged in two rows.

The first object in the first row is a folder named *Ed's Work Folder*. The second file is a song file named *01 Sellé El Recuerdo*. The third file is a picture file named *A Very Cute Puppy*. The fourth file is a word processing document called *Ed's Biography*.

Then, beginning in the second row, there is the fifth file, which is a spreadsheet file called *Ed's Conference Budget*. Then the sixth file is a different kind of word processing file called *Ed's Spreadsheet Fundamentals Textbook*.

Next, there is seventh file, which is another different kind of spreadsheet file called *Ed's Vacation Travel Budget*. And finally, there is an eighth file, which is a presentation file called *Ed's Week 1 Presentation*.

The file system uses a file extension for each file to help control how the operating system will interact with each file. A file extension is from one to several characters that follow the last period in a file name and which correspond with known file types. For example, the music file shown in the example above has a file extension of *.mp3*. This file extension is a known file type for a music file. Likewise, the very cute puppy picture file shown above has a file extension of *.jpg*. This file extension represents a known file type for a digital photograph. Each operating system associates a file extension with a particular program so that it knows what type of information is contained within a file and what application program to use to open and process that file.

The file type (version) of a file is related to the file extension but is a different thing. The file type of a file is the internal structure of the file and is determined by the application program that actually saves the file. In most cases, the file type and the file extension will match as they are controlled by the application program during the save task.

Note: Simply changing the file extension (e.g. by renaming the file and typing a different file extension) *does not* change the file type (the internal structure of the file.) If you need to change a file's type and extension, you must open the file in an appropriate application program and then use the "Save As . . . " task to save the file with a different file type and extension.

In most operating systems, by default, the file extensions are hidden from the user. As a result, many users may never know that these file extensions even exist! But it is because of these file extensions that the operating system knows which icon or picture is used to represent that file graphically to the user. The user has the ability to tell the operating system whether or not you want to show or hide the known file extensions.

In Figure CF-1, we see there is a file that has a picture of a white capital-W on a blue background. You might recognize this icon as being representative of a Microsoft Word© word processing document. Likewise, you can see there is a file with a picture of a white capital-X on a green background. You might recognize this icon as being representative of a

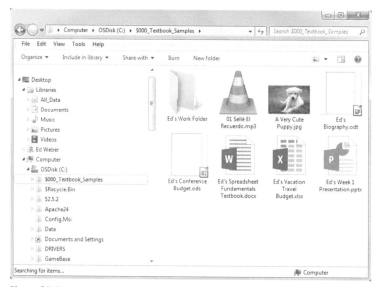

Figure CF-1

Microsoft Excel© spreadsheet document. It is because these two files have file extensions of *.docx* and *.xlsx* respectively that the operating system knows to show these icons. Understanding how file extensions represent the actual information that is stored in each file is very important and will be discussed in the next section.

LO CF.3 Three Decisions when Saving Files

In order for the operating system to do its task of maintaining the file systems, it needs your help. You, the user, must have an understanding of how the file system works so that you can provide the critical information that the operating system needs in order to save your work and then to locate and open your work at a later time.

Whenever you want to perform the task of File Saving, you will take an action to ask the application program to save your work. When this happens the operating system you are using will present you with a Save Dialog (a window) to ask you the three critical questions that it needs in order to accomplish this task:

1. What would you like this file to be named? (File name)
2. Where would you like this file to be stored? (File location)
3. What file type would you like this file to be stored as? (File type and extension)

In Figure CF-2, you will see a common dialog for the saving of a file in an application running in a Windows operating system.

In the top of this dialog and using the left pane of this dialog, you can answer the second question of *Where* do you want the file to be stored. This will become the file location in the file system.

Toward the bottom third of this dialog there is a data entry field with a label called "File name:" where you can type in the name for the file. A file name is the name that you, the user, give to any file that you create and save on your computer. Different operating systems have different rules regarding the length of your file names and which special characters can and cannot be used in a file name.

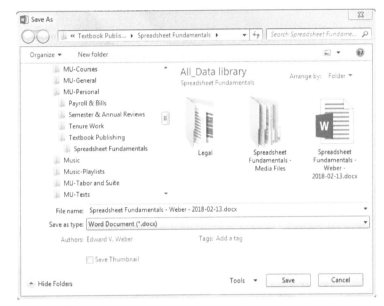

Figure CF-2

Directly below the file name area of the save dialog, there is a drop-down list where you can choose the file format, or file type, for this document.

By completing the information in this dialog, you are providing all of the critical information that the operating system needs to properly store your work within the file system. There are additional considerations that you will want to explore when thinking about the answer to these three questions when you save your work.

What's in a name?

When thinking about file names, you should remember that different organizations and different departments within organizations may dictate or specify the very specific naming conventions that you are to use when you are creating and saving files. For example, if you were to name a file something too generic like "file1", well then nobody (including yourself) will ever be able to know or remember what is contained within that file without specifically opening it up to inspect its contents. File names should always be meaningful and not just to yourself, but also to the next person who may be looking for that file on your machine in your absence.

The same holds true for file locations. You should intentionally create folders, which are named locations, to help you organize your digital filing cabinet with all of the various files and information that you will need to store over time.

But what about file types?

This last consideration is, perhaps, the most important part of this chapter. By understanding the different file types and file extensions, you will be empowered to create different versions of your work to satisfy the needs of multiple people who may need to access these files.

Whenever you attempt to save the file in an application program, that program will, by default, suggest that you save the file in its own, native file format and extension. And while this proposed file format would be fine if you are the only one who is ever going to work this file in the future, the reality is that in this day and age, most of the time, we need to exchange our files with other people in other departments or in other companies. And there is no guarantee that these other people will have the exact same version of the exact same software from the exact same vendor that you have on your machine!

This is why almost every application program today now allows you to save your work in a file format that is different than its own native file format. By choosing a different file format, you can save your work in an older version of the same application program or in a file format that was designed for a completely different application program. In other words, if you are using the latest version of the Microsoft Word© word processing program, it would want to save your work in its native file format using the *.docx* file extension. But what if you needed to send this document to your lawyer and they are not using the most current version of this word processor? In that case, you could save a copy of your work in the older version of Microsoft Word's© file format and it would then have the older file format and older *.doc* file extension.

It is by intentionally saving documents using other file formats that we are able to easily exchange documents among interested parties who are using different programs or different versions of the same program.

It is also because of your ability to save your work in any file format that you will be able to use any contemporary spreadsheet program to complete all of the work that is contained within this book. Additionally, being able to save your work in different file formats will enable you to very easily share your files with your colleagues in other areas of your work setting or with other interested parties like customers or vendors or other business partners.

LO CF.4   Taking and Manipulating Screenshots

Oftentimes when you are working on your computer system, you will have a need to show and discuss something that you are seeing on your computer screen. Fortunately, all contemporary operating systems have the ability for you to create a screenshot of your current desktop view, of a single window within your active desktop, or of a partial selection of any part of your active screen. A screenshot is a picture of the actual contents of your computer screen that can be saved as a picture file and then can also be further manipulated.

There are quite a number of different ways that screenshots can be captured. Some of these mechanisms are embedded into the operating system itself while others utilize independent screen capture programs to accomplish the task. The easiest way to discover the correct process for your particular machine is to utilize an online search engine to look up the keywords "screen capture" along with your particular operating system name and version.

Many of the screen capture commands will utilize the print screen key on the keyboard along with some combination of the control key, the alt key, or the command key.

Some screenshot methods allow you to select or highlight the particular area that you want to capture while others simply capture the entire active window or the entire active screen.

Once you have captured an image of your screen, there are several other tasks that you may want to accomplish with this image. To accomplish these tasks, you may need to use another program to help you out. The captured screenshot can be pasted into a word processing document, or into an image manipulation program, or pasted directly into an email message, etc. If the screenshot will not need any additional manipulation, then you can simply paste the image directly into the location where you want the image to appear. But if you need to manipulate the image further, then you will want to paste the image into some image manipulation program so that you can make your adjustments. A free, open-source image manipulation program that will run on Windows, Mac, and Linux is called **Gimp** and can be downloaded from this location: https://www.gimp.org/downloads/

Two types of image manipulation you might want to achieve before using your screenshot might be *cropping* and *highlighting* your image.

For example, Figure CF-3 is a screenshot that I took while I was composing this very section. As you can see, the original screenshot shows the entire screen including this word processing document as well as the spreadsheet program in the upper right corner of the window. But what if all I was interested in was the window in the upper right corner of the desktop screen? In this case, I can crop this captured image so that it only contains the information I need.

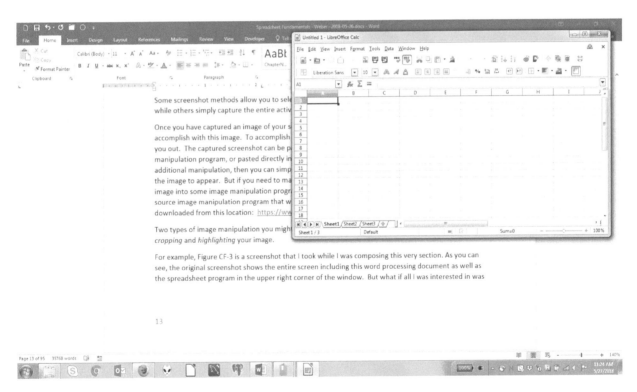

Figure CF-3

Cropping an image is the process of using a cropping tool to cut away all of the extraneous portions of an image file that you don't want so that you only leave the remaining portion of the image that you do want to keep. By cropping a screenshot, you can reduce the total file size of the image and reduce the content to only the information that you want to focus on.

Figure CF-4 shows the same screenshot after the cropping was completed. Notice that all of the rest of the extraneous information has been removed from the original screenshot. By cropping the image, you are able to reduce the total file size of the image that you will be sharing and you are able to bring specific attention to the information that you want your audience to focus on.

Next, after an image is cropped, you may want to highlight one or more pieces of information contained in the screenshot to help the viewer focus on the critical information that you want them to see. Highlighting is the process of drawing additional new information onto a screenshot so as to call the viewer's attention to a particular area of the screenshot.

Figure CF-4

There are several tools that can help with this task. Figure CF-5 shows the same cropped screenshot after some highlighting has been applied.

Some highlighting tools behave very much like a physical ink highlighter. You simply select the tool (and optionally the tool color) and then *paint* the area that you want to highlight. In Figure CF-5, the menu bar and the sheet tabs have been highlighted in yellow. We will be defining the terms *menu bar* and *sheet tabs* in Chapter 2.

Another highlighting tool includes the ability to draw shapes (e.g. boxes, circles, ovals, diamonds, and free-form shapes) around the particular areas that you want to highlight. In Figure CF-5, the column letters G, H, and I have been highlighted with a free-form red circle.

Yet another highlighting tool includes the ability to add text boxes to your image. By doing this, you can type a specific message right next to a particular area that you want to be highlighted and annotated in your screenshot.

Once you have captured a screenshot, cropped it to the desired size, and then highlighted the important areas, you can then possibly save this altered image as its own file for future use, or you could copy and paste this updated image and use the image directly in a document or an email, etc.

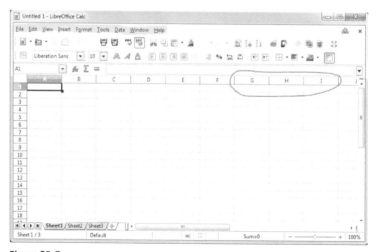

Figure CF-5

Please note: Several of the assignments in this text will instruct you to create a screenshot of your active program and then highlight your captured screenshot to annotate specific areas of interest.

Computing Fundamentals – Assignments and Projects

Directed Assignments

DA CF-1. For this directed assignment, you will be creating a word processing document that contains information that you will look up and supply about your own computing environment.

Required student data file: None. Use a new, blank word processing document.

1. Create a new, blank word processing document in your favorite word processing program.
2. Save this blank document by using the following specifications:
   a. File name: Name the file **_YourName_DA_CF-1_**
   b. File location: Place this file in any location you choose, but make a note of the location as you will need it later.
   c. File format: Because this file will be sent in to your professor, you must check with him or her to see what format **_he or she_** will want this file to be saved in. Don't just assume that the default file format for your computer will be acceptable!
3. Once the blank file is saved, update the document to contain the following information on the inside at the top of the document:
   a. Your name
   b. Your professor's name
   c. The course number and course name
   d. This assignment number (**DA CF-1**)
   e. The current date
4. Next write a single paragraph that answers all of the following questions:
   a. What is the operating system (vendor, name, version, etc.) that you are using to complete this assignment?
   b. What is the word processing program (vendor, name, version, etc.) that you are using to complete this assignment?
   c. What is the final name of this file that you are creating?
   d. What is the file location of where this file is saved on your machine?
   e. What file format and file extension did your professor tell you that they wanted your work to be saved as?
5. Finally, write a single paragraph that describes what, if anything, you already knew about operating systems, application programs, file names, file locations, and file formats **_before_** you worked through this chapter.
6. Check the spelling and grammar of your final work and then save it and submit it in accordance with your class instructions.

DA CF-2. For this directed assignment, you will be creating a word processing document that contains two screenshots: The first will be an original screenshot of your entire desktop and the second will be a cropped and highlighted version of the original screenshot.

Required student data file: None. Use a new, blank word processing document.

1. Create a new, blank word processing document in your favorite word processing program.

2. Save this blank document by using the following specifications:

   a. File name: Name the file *YourName_DA_CF-2*

   b. File location: Place this file in any location you choose, but make a note of the location as you will need it later.

   c. File format: Because this file will be sent in to your professor, you must check with him or her to see what format *he or she* will want this file to be saved in. Don't just assume that the default file format for your computer will be acceptable!

3. Once the blank file is saved, update the document to contain the following information on the inside at the top of the document:

   a. Your name

   b. Your professor's name

   c. The course number and course name

   d. This assignment number (**DA CF-2**)

   e. The current date

4. Next, using any of the screen capture mechanisms that are available for your operating system and machine, create a screenshot of your entire desktop screen. Make sure that the original screenshot includes the entire desktop from the upper left corner down to the lower right corner.

5. Paste this original screenshot into your word processing document. Underneath this picture, type the caption "**Original Screenshot**".

6. Next, use an image manipulation tool to crop the original screenshot image. You can use any image manipulation tool that is available on your machine, but you can also use the open-source, free image manipulation tool called Gimp that was described in this chapter.

   Crop the original screenshot so that it only shows a much smaller portion of your original screen. This could be a single window or a portion of a window or any part of the screen that you want.

   Once the original screenshot has been cropped, paste this cropped image into your document and the type the caption "**Cropped Screenshot**" beneath this image. Do not worry if the images do not all fit on the same page; that is not a requirement.

7. Next, use an image manipulation tool to add some highlighting to the cropped screenshot image. The highlighting can be anything of your own choosing. However, whatever highlighting you complete, you will describe this highlighting as the caption beneath the highlighted, cropped image.

8. Paste the final cropped and highlighted image into your document and then add an appropriate caption underneath the image that describes the highlighting that was performed.

9. Check the spelling and grammar of your final work and then save it and submit it in accordance with your class instructions.

Creative Projects

CP CF-1. In most contemporary operating systems, the file extensions for known file types are *hidden* from the user by default. For many users, this is not a problem. But when users have to concern themselves with the file type and file extensions for files that they create and intend to share with others, this can be quite a hassle and can cause problems.

Required student data file: None. Use a new, blank word processing document.

For this creative project, you will use your own computer and online resources to investigate the steps that are necessary to show or hide the file extensions for the known file types in your own operating system. Then, you will create a new, blank word processing document and save it with the file name of ***YourName_CP_CF-1***. In this word processing document, you should thoroughly describe your machine including the name and version of your operating system. Then, you should describe how you found the technique to show or hide the known file extensions on your machine. This might be the help system of your operating system or this might be an online resource, which you should properly cite.

And finally, you should include a screenshot that shows a view of some files on your own machine with their file extensions visible in the image. You will check your final work for spelling and grammar correctness and submit your file in the manner prescribed for your class.

CP CF-2. In preparation for our continued work in spreadsheet programs, you will create a word processing document that describes the spreadsheet program that you intend to use for the majority of your coursework. This may be the spreadsheet program already installed on your own machine, but it may also be a different program that is available to you on a work machine or a school machine, etc.

Required student data file: None. Use a new, blank word processing document.

For this creative project, you will create a new, blank word processing document and save it with the file name of ***YourName_CP_CF-2***. In this word processing document, you should thoroughly describe the machine you will be using to complete your spreadsheet work. You should include the name and version of the machine operating system as well as the vendor name, program name, and program version of the spreadsheet application program that you will most often be using.

Next, you will provide two screenshots in this document. The first screenshot will be a picture of the version information screen that the spreadsheet program provides for you. In some programs, this can be located by using the ***Help*** menu followed by the ***About . . .*** command. In other programs, this information will be located by using the ***File*** menu followed by the ***Account . . .*** command. You may need to look up online how to find the specific version of your own spreadsheet program.

The other screenshot will be a picture of all of the different file formats that you will be able to use to save your spreadsheet files. To accomplish this, you will open up a new, blank spreadsheet file and then you will begin the process of saving the blank file. When you have the ***Save As . . .*** dialog open, you will want to use the drop-down list to show all of the various file types that you could possibly use. Then, you will want to create a screenshot that shows this extended menu of the various file types that are available in your spreadsheet program. Remember to check your final work for spelling and grammar correctness and then submit your file in the manner prescribed for your class.

Source: Shutterstock, Inc.

Why do we use spreadsheets?

As was discussed in the Computing Fundamentals chapter, application programs exist to perform a specific task on behalf of the computer user. For example, a word processing application program is designed to allow the user to capture text on a page and then save and/or print the document for future use. One could say that the purpose of a word processing program is to accept text input into a document, format it in a particular way, and then store the document for future use.

Each application program was designed to perform its own primary task. The purpose of a photo editing program is to allow the user to open digital images, make alterations to the image (e.g. color correction, resizing, and applying filters) and then store the manipulated image. The purpose of a web browser application program is to allow the user to enter addresses (URLs) and navigate to a resource that is accessible via the Internet. The purpose of an email program is to allow users to send and receive emails, organize and process their inbox collection of emails received, and organize the email contact information for each of their email correspondents.

Each application program has its own primary task.

So what is the primary task of the spreadsheet application program?

Many new users who have dabbled with spreadsheet programs might answer that the primary purpose of using a spreadsheet program is to help organize rows and columns of information. And while this is a task that spreadsheet programs are capable of doing, this isn't the spreadsheet program's primary purpose. In fact, if all you need to do is organize some information in a series of rows and columns, then the correct tool you should be using is a table in a word processor program.

No, the primary purpose of a spreadsheet program is not just to organize information into rows and columns. **The primary** purpose of a spreadsheet program **is to perform calculations on data.**

LO 1.1   Similarities between Spreadsheets and Word Processing Programs

As we will quickly discover in the next chapter, spreadsheet programs are primarily used to perform calculations on some known data to derive information that is originally unknown. A secondary purpose of the spreadsheet program is to format and organize the data into meaningful arrangements and to create aesthetically pleasing representations of the data.

The spreadsheet programs should be considered extensions of word processing programs. In fact, the vast majority of the functionality that exists in a word processing program can also be found in spreadsheet programs. For example, all of the things that can be done in a word processing program with regards to manipulating the font (typeface), size, color, alignment, and spacing of text and numbers can also be done in a spreadsheet program.

Likewise, many of the other concepts from word processing can be found in spreadsheet programs. Shared functionality like page set up, orientation, margins, headers and footers, borders, inserting graphics, inserting hyperlinks, are all available in spreadsheet programs.

LO 1.2   Spreadsheets as Extensions of Word Processing Tables

In most contemporary word processing programs, there are features which enable you to enter tables to organize information in a document. These tables are represented by a grid-like structure of rows and columns.

When you first open a spreadsheet program, you will quickly see that the entire document appears to be structured like a large word processing table. And when you start working with your first spreadsheet, you will also see that the spreadsheet has inherited nearly all of the features of a word processing table.

Figure 1-1 is a word processing table example. As you can see, this table allows for text to flow above, below, and around the table. The information that would be entered within the table would be arranged in rows and columns.

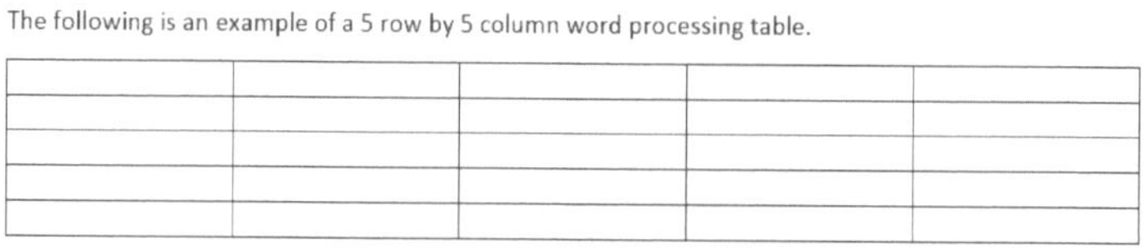

The following is an example of a 5 row by 5 column word processing table.

Figure 1-1

Similarly, Figure 1-2 is a spreadsheet example. With the exception of the column headings (A, B, C, ...) and the row numbers (1,2,3, ...) you can see that the structure of a spreadsheet document is nearly identical to that of a word processing table.

Figure 1-2

But the single most significant difference between spreadsheets and word processing tables is that spreadsheets allow you to very easily perform calculations on the data that exists in the rows and columns. Word processing tables provide the primary function of organizing and aligning data into rows and columns. Spreadsheets do all of that but also provide the greater functionality of being able to perform calculations on the data that is entered into the rows and columns.

LO 1.3   Ubiquitousness of Spreadsheets in Businesses and Organizations

People who use spreadsheet programs on a regular basis will probably tell you that the functionality of a spreadsheet program is one of *the most important tools available to a business or organizational professional*. The functionality of spreadsheet programs allows a user to create both simple and advanced calculations on both small and large sets of data with extreme ease and efficiency. Using spreadsheet programs reduces the total amount of time and the total cost in resources that would be necessary to calculate required information. And the information that is derived through spreadsheet programs help businesses and organizations make informed decisions to better manage their efforts and activities.

Spreadsheets can be found in almost every area of businesses and organizations. From accounting, to marketing, to operations, to human resources, to sales, to distribution, to recruiting, to research and development, to purchasing, to finance, to logistics . . . well . . . you get the idea! Spreadsheets can be found almost everywhere within an organization.

But spreadsheets aren't only useful in businesses and organizations. Spreadsheets can also be used by individuals for a variety of personal tasks as well. Everything from creating a personal budget, to tracking information about your favorite sports teams, to creating information about your savings or investments, to planning out your vacation or your work schedule or your wedding, to . . . well . . . once again, you get the idea here!

Spreadsheets are *everywhere* and the people who can master them are in very high demand!

LO 1.4   Spreadsheets as Precursors to Database Applications

Would it surprise you to know that spreadsheets can store and process **millions** of rows of data in a single file? It's true!

However, we will also discover that spreadsheets have practical usability limitations and constraints that must be considered. And it is for this reason, that just as spreadsheets are a natural extension of the functionality found in word processing tables, we will see that spreadsheets are actually precursors to *database* applications. And database applications are a natural extension of the functionality of spreadsheet programs.

Similar to the fact that much of the word processing functionality can be found in spreadsheet applications, much of the spreadsheet functionality can be found in database applications. These office applications were built upon the functionality found in each other. So learning about the fundamentals of spreadsheet applications becomes a significant skill set in high demand for anyone working with office application tools.

Chapter 1 – Assignments and Projects

Directed Assignments

DA 1-1. For this directed assignment, you will be creating a word processing document that contains a couple of paragraphs and a single table of data with some very general formatting of the paragraph and table contents.

Required student data file: None. Use a new, blank word processing document.

1. Create a new, blank word processing document in your favorite word processing program.
2. Save this blank document by using the following specifications:
   a. File name: Name the file **YourName_DA_1-1**
   b. File location: Place this file in any location you choose, but make a note of the location as you will need it later.
   c. File format: Because this file will be sent in to your professor, you must check with him or her to see what format **he or she** will want this file to be saved in. Don't just assume that the default file format for your computer will be acceptable!
3. Once the blank file is saved, update the document to contain the following information on the inside at the top of the document:
   a. Your name
   b. Your professor's name
   c. The course number and course name of your course
   d. This assignment number (**DA 1-1**)
   e. The current date
4. Next write a single paragraph that answers all of the following questions:
   a. How much have you used word processing programs to create documents?
   b. Describe at least five different types of formatting changes that you have made to text or paragraphs in word processing documents.
   c. Have you ever created tables in word processing documents? What are some things you already know about word processing tables?
5. Next, create a word processing table that has 3 rows and 4 columns and contains the following information:

Program Type	Program's Primary Purpose	Can Organize Data in Rows and Columns	Can Perform Calculations
Word Processors	Create text documents	Yes – by using tables	Very limited
Spreadsheets	Perform Calculations	Yes – basic structure	*Primary Function!!!*

6. Complete the following basic formatting to make your table look nearly identical to the sample above:
   a. Center all of the information in each cell of row 1 and make them all **bold**.

  b. Make sure that the height of row 1 allows the text to properly wrap and not be cut off.

  c. Change the background color of row 1 to be some similar shade of gold.

  d. Change the background color of the rows 2 and 3 to be some similar shade of green.

  e. Change the font color and style of the very last cell to be some similar shade of red, **bold**, and *italics*.

  f. Change the alignment of the last cell of rows 2 and 3 to be aligned to the right side of the cells.

7. Finally, write a single paragraph that describes what, if anything, you already knew about general word processing formatting and word processing tables *before* you worked through this chapter.

8. Check the spelling and grammar of your final work and then save it and submit in accordance with your class instructions.

Creative Projects

CP 1-1. It is one thing to have a textbook tell you that "*spreadsheets are really important*" and are used in almost all businesses and organizations. It is quite another thing for you to discover this reality for yourself.

In this creative project, you will seek out and interview an individual or two who use spreadsheet files on a regular basis as a part of their work or home activities. This could be a family member, or a friend, or a work colleague, or a classmate, or a professor, or someone in the administration of your school, or just about anyone at all. You will then create a new, blank word processing file to document your findings.

Required student data file: None. Use a new, blank word processing document.

The person(s) that you interview should use a spreadsheet program at least a few times a week or more frequently. You will then ask the person to share information about their use of the spreadsheet programs. Some questions you might include:

> "What different spreadsheet program(s) have you worked with?"
> "How frequently do you find yourself working with a spreadsheet?"
> "What type of data do you currently work with or have you previously worked with in spreadsheets?"
> "What are some of the formulas or functions that you use in your spreadsheets?"
> "Who are some other people or departments or areas in your business/organization that you think might also use spreadsheets?"
> "How important do you think spreadsheets are to your business/organization?"

After you have asked the previous questions and any other questions that you might find interesting, create a new, blank word processing document and save it with the file name of *YourName_CP_1-1*. In this word processing document, you should thoroughly describe the person(s) that you interviewed including things like the job or tasks that they perform with the spreadsheet programs and how you came to know that they use spreadsheets on a regular basis. You should also include all of the information that you gathered from your interview.

Check your final work for spelling and grammar correctness and submit your file in the manner prescribed for your class.

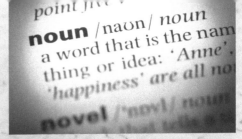

Source: Shutterstock, Inc.

Chapter 2

The Basic "Nouns" and "Verbs" of a Spreadsheet

Why should we think of "nouns" and "verbs" when working with a spreadsheet?

Throughout my experiences teaching various technology subjects to a myriad of audiences, I have discovered a technique that often helps people grasp the concepts more easily: I break the topics down to the "nouns" and "verbs" that make the concepts work.

For example, we all remember when we first learned to speak, read, and write, that language is composed of nouns and verbs. The nouns were the things (people, places, and things to be precise) and the verbs were the action words. I have discovered that this analogy works very well when talking about technology-based concepts.

LEARNING OBJECTIVES

In this chapter, we will explore these learning objectives:

The Major Nouns (Things) of a Spreadsheet Program

The Major Verbs (Actions) of a Spreadsheet Program

Key Noun Terms (Things)

- accounting format
- alignment
- argument or parameter
- borders
- cell
- cell reference
- chart
- clipboard
- column
- column separator
- colors
- currency format
- data – known
- data – unknown

- date / time format
- dollar sign
- decimal precision
- errors
- fill handle
- font
- formatting
- format painter
- formula
- formula bar
- function
- hashtags
- horizontal
- indention
- labels

- literal value
- menu
- merging
- number
- octothorpes
- operators
- order of operations
- parenthesis
- percentage format
- pound signs
- predictable series
- range
- resulting value
- ribbon
- row

- row separator
- scrollbars
- shading
- spanning
- symbols
- syntax
- text
- tools
- toolbars
- truncation
- vertical
- workbook
- worksheet

Key Verb Terms (Actions)

- applying formatting
- auto-fitting rows and columns
- calculating unknown data
- changing alignment
- creating a workbook
- editing a workbook

- entering formulas
- entering functions
- entering known data
- entering labels
- inserting charts
- inserting objects
- manipulating worksheets

- planning worksheet layout
- referencing cells
- resizing rows and columns
- reviewing formulas and functions
- saving a workbook

- selecting adjoining cells
- selecting disjointed cells
- sorting and filtering data
- using tool and command dialogs

If we first list out the nouns of our topic – the *things* that are part of a spreadsheet program – we will then have all of the terminology that we need to appropriately discuss the concepts. Then, if we next start listing out the verbs of our topic – the *actions* that we will take and perform using the nouns of the spreadsheet program – we will then start to appropriately assemble the language of all of the terms, the nouns and the verbs, to accurately describe how to use the spreadsheet program.

We will be covering the majority of the nouns and verbs of a spreadsheet program in this chapter. In subsequent chapters, however, additional terms will be introduced that are specific to those particular chapters.

LO 2.1   The Major Nouns (Things) of a Spreadsheet Program

The nouns, or things, that are part of a spreadsheet program can be broken into various categories. The first category we will look at are the nouns that are common to many other programs. You may already have familiarity with these nouns from having worked with other programs on your computer. You will find definitions of these nouns in Table 2-1.

Common Nouns Found in Many Programs		
Nouns (Things)	**Where Found**	**Definition or Use**
Menu [a]	Nearly all application programs	Commands that allow the user to take some action, use a tool, or select a different ribbon
Ribbon [b]	Later versions of Microsoft products	Location where tools reside within the program
Toolbars [c]	Earlier versions of Microsoft products and most open source products	Location where tools reside within the program
Tools [d]	Nearly all application programs	Icons or commands that allow the user to take some action
Scrollbars [e]	Nearly all application programs	Structures that allow the user to change the current area of visibility within a document

Table 2-1

Also, you will find highlighted visual representations of these nouns in Figures 2-1 and 2-2 (the letter boxes in each figure corresponds to the letter markings for each term that is defined below.)

The two figures below show screenshots of two popular spreadsheet programs. The first figure (Figure 2-1) is a screenshot of Microsoft Excel 2016 ©. The second figure below (Figure 2-2) is a screenshot of LibreOffice Calc 4.2©.

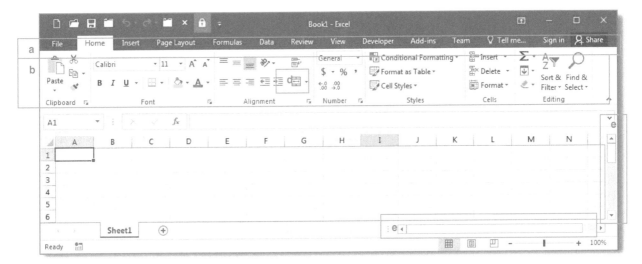

Figure 2-1

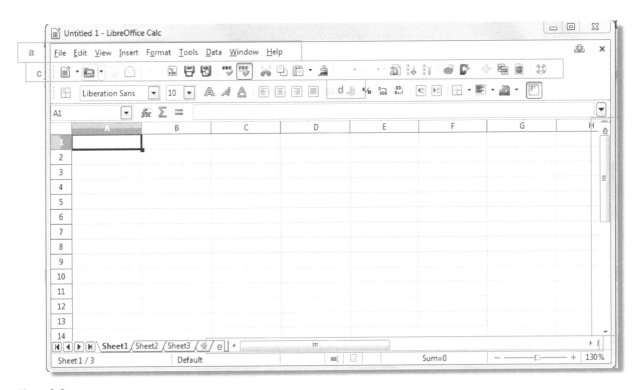

Figure 2-2

As you can very quickly see, these two programs share quite a number of visually similar attributes. Throughout the remainder of this text, we will see screenshots of various programs and will begin to recognize the patterns of consistent design and functionality between all of these similar programs.

Common Nouns Originating in Word Processing But Also Found in Spreadsheets	
Nouns (Things)	**Definition or Use**
Font	The typeface (font name), style (normal or italics), weight (normal or bold), size, color and decoration (underline, strikethrough, subscript, superscript, etc.) of the text and numbers contained within a document.
Alignment – word processing	The positioning of information relative to other information around it. Alignments include top, bottom, left, right, center, middle, and justified (spread across evenly.) Alignment was originally created to adjust text positioning within a word processing document and then was enhanced to include table alignment. Tables will be discussed in the upcoming section. Additionally, alignment is enhanced even further in spreadsheets, which will be discussed in the spreadsheet-specific nouns section below.
Indention	The positioning of some information such that it is aligned more directly toward the center of the paragraph or page as compared to other information that is above or below. Indention can occur on the left or right side of information so as to offset this information from other surrounding information.
Horizontal and Vertical	These are more adjectives than nouns as they are typically used in conjunction with either Scrollbars (see Table 2-1) or with Alignment as defined above. These are the descriptors that reflect movement (as in with scrollbars) or positioning (as in with alignment) that is either up-and-down (Vertical) or left-and-right (Horizontal).
Colors	Originally defined to allow more than just black text on a white page, colors were introduced first in word processors to change the color of text on a page. Colors are now applicable to foregrounds (text and numbers), backgrounds, borders, shadows, objects, and many other components within a program.
Shading	The color and/or pattern of typically the background of some piece of information. Originally used to change the background color of a page, a paragraph, a sentence, or a word, shading evolved to include changing the color of tables. This table has three different color shadings. Tables will be discussed in detail in the next section.
Text	The basic information that can be keyed into a document using a standard keyboard. The alphabet, numbers, symbols, and other special characters that you might want to put into a document.
Numbers	The non–text and non–special characters that are available from the keyboard. Specifically, the digits 0–9, the minus sign, and the decimal point are all considered valid numeric characters.
Formatting	The collection of all of the characteristics described above which, all together, represent how a particular piece of information appears within the document.
Format Painter	A tool that was introduced in word processors to copy the Formatting (see above) of the information you currently have selected and then subsequently allow you to "paint" that copied formatting to any new information that you choose to drag your mouse across. This tool typically looks like a paintbrush in many programs.

Table 2-2

The previous table (Table 2-2) shows a collection of nouns that were originally introduced in word processing programs, but then were fully incorporated into spreadsheet programs and other advanced programs while maintaining their basic concepts and behaviors. We will be exploring all of these nouns in much greater detail in the upcoming chapters.

The next collections of nouns (Table 2-3) were originally introduced in word processing programs when word processing programs introduced the concept of **tables**. A table in a word processing program was a way to create additional organization of information above and beyond simple paragraphs. The basic concepts and behaviors of these table items continues on into spreadsheets and other advanced programs.

The final collection of nouns (Table 2-4) is specific to spreadsheet programs and represent the significant extension above and beyond simple word processing tables. Whereas word processing tables were conceived to allow you to organize your information into basic rows and columns and then format and decorate the information and the layout of these tables, the additional concepts introduced here are what allow the spreadsheet programs to take on their primary function: the ability to perform calculations on the information contained within the document.

Common Nouns Originating in Word Processing TABLES But Also Found in Spreadsheets	
Nouns (Things)	**Definition or Use**
Row	For word processing tables and spreadsheets, this is the collection of all contiguous horizontal cells exactly one cell high. In spreadsheets only, these are labeled down the leftmost edge with row numbers.
Column	For word processing tables and spreadsheets, this is the collection of all contiguous vertical cells exactly one cell wide. In spreadsheets only, these are labeled across the topmost edge with column letters.
Cell – word processing tables	A cell is the intersection of exactly one row and one column. In both word processing tables and spreadsheets, cells can have content (text or numbers) and cells can have their contents formatted (font, color, alignment, etc.) and can also be formatted themselves (shading, borders, etc.) In spreadsheets only, however, cells have "names" and cell references, which will be defined in the next section.
Row and **Column Separators**	The lines in between rows and columns that allow the user to resize the heights of rows and the widths of columns. In word processing tables, these are typically located directly within the table itself. In spreadsheets, however, these are located *in between* the column headings (lettered column names beginning with A, B, C . . .) and *in between* the row headings (numbered row names beginning with 1, 2, 3 . . .)
Merging	The combination of two or more cells to behave as a single merged cell instead of remaining as the individual, separate cells that were originally present. Looking at this table, you can see that the very first row has its two individual cells spanned or merged together.

Table 2-3

The final collection of nouns (Table 2-4) is specific to spreadsheet programs and represent the significant extension above and beyond simple word processing tables. Whereas word processing tables were conceived to allow you to organize your information into basic rows and columns and then format and decorate the information and the layout of these tables, the additional concepts introduced here are what allow the spreadsheet programs to take on their primary function: the ability to perform calculations on the information contained within the document.

Common Nouns Existing within Contemporary Spreadsheets	
Nouns (Things)	**Definition or Use**
Workbook	This is the basic document that is created using a spreadsheet program. A "workbook" is synonymous with a "spreadsheet file." The workbook name will be the file name as it is saved within the operating system. The workbook will have a file name, a file location, and a file type and extension (e.g. .xlsx, .xls, and .ods). Please see the Computing Fundamentals chapter for more discussions about file name, file locations, and file types and extensions. A workbook can contain one to many worksheets (defined below).
Worksheets	Originally called a spreadsheet, a worksheet represents a single collection of rows and columns within a workbook. There can be one to many worksheets within a workbook. Specifically how many worksheets can exist within a workbook varies by spreadsheet program and version. Suffice to say that contemporary workbooks *can* contain upwards of thousand(s) of worksheet within a single file. But practically speaking, having more than 20 or so worksheets in a single file would not be considered "best practices." Having too many worksheets make finding and working with information contained therein very cumbersome. Worksheets can be added and removed from a workbook. Worksheets can **and should** be renamed to provide a meaningful name for the data that it contains. Worksheets can be colored and rearranged in different orders within the workbook. The worksheets are tabbed at the bottom of the spreadsheet program.
Cell Reference	In spreadsheets, the intersection of a single row and a single column is a cell. To refer to a particular cell, you will use its cell reference. A cell reference is defined by using the column letter followed by the row number of the intersecting column and row. Examples of cell references include A1, F14, and C57. There are several variations to cell references known as relative references, absolute references, and mixed references. These will be discussed in detail in Chapter 4.
Cell – spreadsheet-specific features	In addition to basic text and numbers that can be entered into cells like within a word processing table, spreadsheets allow you to enter formulas and functions and provide enhanced formatting beyond what can be done in a word processing table. Formulas, functions, and enhanced cell formatting are defined below.

Table 2-4 (Continued)

| Common Nouns Existing within Contemporary Spreadsheets ||
Nouns (Things)	Definition or Use
Range	A range is a collection of one to many contiguous (touching) cells. Ranges are always described from the upper-left cell through the lower-right cell with a colon separating the two corner references (e.g. A4:C15 or D37:F44) Ranges can be named and these names can be used in calculations.
Layout	The overall design of a worksheet. This includes the page layout (e.g. portrait vs. landscape), possible headers and footers (e.g. just like within word processors), column and row labels (defined below), and the placement of known data and unknown data (also defined below.)
Labels	Typically, labels are text data that are entered into the first couple of rows of a worksheet and in the first column of a worksheet to help describe ***the rest*** of the known data. Known data is defined below.
Alignment – spreadsheet cells	In spreadsheet cells, there is a default "general" alignment that is set for each cell, which affects the way data becomes positioned within the cell. General alignment specifies that **text data is aligned to the left within a spreadsheet cell**. General alignment also specifies that **numeric data is aligned to the right within a spreadsheet cell**. This is important to remember because simply looking at the default alignment can tell you what type of data is entered in each cell. Numeric calculations can only be performed on numeric data. We will look into these concepts in more detail in Chapter 4.
Data – Known	This is the data that is entered into the main portion of each spreadsheet; this could be text or numbers or dates, etc. This data could represent quantities, dollar values, or text information . . . the possibilities are endless. This known data is typically entered as either literal values (defined below) or as cell references.
Octothorpes or **Hashtags** or **Pound Signs**	Octothorpes or hashtags or pound signs are the names for the symbol "#". When a cell is displaying a number of these, the spreadsheet is telling you two things: (1) This cell contains numeric data; and (2) The width of this numeric data as formatted is wider than the width of this cell. This is telling you that in order to properly see this value, you must either expand the width of this cell or change the number format so that this value will fit in the current cell width.
Literal Values	Text, numbers, or dates that are entered into a cell or a formula or function (defined below). Literal values are typically entered as known data into a spreadsheet. When literal text values are used in formulas or functions (defined below) they must be surrounded in quotation marks.

Table 2-4 (Continued)

Common Nouns Existing within Contemporary Spreadsheets	
Nouns (Things)	**Definition or Use**
Truncation	When a cell contains text data, either a literal text value or a text resulting value (defined below) and the width of that data as it is formatted is wider than the cell's width, *and* there is any kind of data in the cell immediately adjacent to the right of this cell, then the displayed data will be "cut off" to the limit of the cell width. This is known as text truncation.
Spanning	When a cell contains text data, either a literal text value or a text resulting value (defined below) and the width of that data as it is formatted is wider than the cell's width, *and* the cell immediately adjacent to the right of this cell is *empty*, then the displayed data will span or bleed over into the subsequent empty adjacent cells.
Data – Unknown	This is why spreadsheets exist – to discover unknown data by performing calculations using the known data. Unknown data usually shows up in the bottom rows or the rightmost columns of a spreadsheet. They are created by using calculations like formulas and functions (defined below and explored in detail in Chapter 4).
Formula	The combination of one or more values or cell references to calculate a new resulting value. All formulas and functions (defined below) begin with the equal sign (=). Formulas will contain one or more literal values, cell references, operators (defined below), or other functions. Whenever possible, it is most often better to use a function instead of direct formulas. Whenever possible, it is most often better to use a cell reference instead of literal values in formulas or functions. Formulas and functions follow the order of operations (also defined below). Formulas will be fully discussed in Chapter 4.
Function	These are named, predefined specific calculations. There are hundreds of available functions to accomplish different types of calculations. These functions are grouped into categories to help the user find specific functions for specific tasks. Most of these functions use one or more parameters or arguments (defined below) but some have no parameters or arguments. To use a function, you start with the equal sign and then follow with the exact spelling of the function name, following with parentheses that surround the required and/or optional parameters or arguments. An example of a function is =SUM(B2:B14) Functions will be fully discussed in Chapter 4 and Chapter 6.
Argument or **Parameter**	An argument or parameter is usually a cell or range reference, but may also be literal values. These are the specific pieces of information that are required by the named function in order for the function to perform its calculation. These may be required or they may be optional based on the needs of each specific function.

Table 2-4 (Continued)

Common Nouns Existing within Contemporary Spreadsheets	
Nouns (Things)	**Definition or Use**
Operators, Parenthesis, and Symbols	Operators, parenthesis, and symbols are the characters that are used within the syntax (defined below) of formulas and functions to perform the calculations in a spreadsheet. Some of the commonly used symbols and operators are:

Name	Symbol	Meaning
Asterisk	*	Multiplication of numeric data
Forward Slash	/	Division of numeric data
Caret	^	Exponentiation (raised to a power)
Plus sign	+	Addition of numeric data
Minus sign	–	Subtraction of numeric data
Percent sign	%	Modulo division (the remainder after division)
Ampersand	&	Text concatenation (joining together)
Parenthesis	()	Forces a preliminary order of operations
Dollar Sign	$	Represents absolute cell references (defined below)
Brackets	[]	Used for workbook referencing
Exclamation	!	Used for worksheet referencing
Equal sign	=	Used to begin every formula and function

Nouns (Things)	Definition or Use
Order of Operations	The order of operations is the same that you learned in your grade school or high school math courses: **P**lease **E**xcuse **M**y **D**ear **A**unt **S**ally – **P**arenthesis are evaluated first, then **E**xponentiation, then **M**ultiplication, then **D**ivision, then **A**ddition, then **S**ubtraction. All cell references are evaluated before the mathematical operations are completed.
Syntax	The syntax in a spreadsheet includes the specific keywords (function names), symbols and operators (defined below), and sequence of parameters and arguments that are used to tell the spreadsheet how to perform its calculations.
Formula Bar	The formula bar is an area just above a worksheet that shows you the precise contents of the currently selected cell. If the cell contains a literal value, you will see that value in the formula bar as well. If the cell contains a formula or a function, then the cell will show the resulting value (defined below) of the calculation, however the formula bar will show the exact contents of the cell (before the calculation is performed).
Resulting Value	A resulting value is the data that is shown in a cell after the completion of a calculation of either a formula or function.
Errors	An error occurs when the spreadsheet is unable to understand or calculate a cell. Errors are identified by showing a resulting value of a single octothorpe (#) followed by an error name. Some examples of errors are #REF!, #DIV/0!, #NAME?. A spreadsheet should never be allowed to have errors that are uncorrected.

Table 2-4 (Continued)

Common Nouns Existing within Contemporary Spreadsheets	
Nouns (Things)	**Definition or Use**
Decimal Precision	One of the kinds of formatting that can be applied to numeric values (either literal values or resulting values) that specifies the number of decimals after the decimal point. Decimal precision can be either increased (e.g. more decimal digits) or decreased (e.g. less decimal digits).
Accounting Format	One of the kinds of formatting that can be applied to numeric values (either literal values or resulting values) that specifies that the numeric values will be represented with financial formatting (e.g. dollar sign, comma for thousands separator, and two decimal points of precision). The accounting format aligns the dollar sign to the far left side of the cell, and pads spaces up to the numeric value, and shows zero values as a dash.
Currency Format	One of the kinds of formatting that can be applied to numeric values (either literal values or resulting values) that specifies that the numeric values will be represented with financial formatting (e.g. dollar sign, comma for thousands separator, and two decimal points of precision). The currency format aligns the dollar sign immediately to the left of the numeric value with no padding, and shows zero values as $0.00.
Percentage Format	One of the kinds of formatting that can be applied to numeric values (either literal values or resulting values) where the value is first multiplied by 100 and the shown with a percent symbol (%). For example the number .0475, when formatted with percentage formatting, will have a resulting displayed value of 4.75%
Date/Time Format	One of the kinds of formatting that can be applied to numeric values (either literal values or resulting values) where the resulting value is formatted to appear like a date and time. There are numerous date/time format styles including long date, short date, date only, date and time, time only, and others.
Fill Handle	The fill handle is a small square that is shown at the lower right corner of the currently selected cell or range. When this small handle is used to drag the contents of a cell or range either across or down the worksheet, then the contents of the cell(s) will be either copied to the new cells or, if there is a known predictable series (defined below) then the new cells will be filled with the next data in the predictable series.
Predictable Series	A predictable series is any series that is known to the spreadsheet program. For example, if one cell contains the literal text value of "Monday", then the next cell either immediately below this cell or immediately to the right of this cell can be said to be known to be part of a predictable series. The next predictable value would be "Tuesday". Whenever a predictable series is known to the spreadsheet program, you can use the fill handle (defined above) to fill contiguous (touching) cells with the next value(s) in the predictable series.
Chart	A chart is an aesthetically pleasing way to visualize data and to obtain insights about the data via a graphic representation. Charts will be fully explored in Chapter 5.

Table 2-4 (Continued)

These nouns, or things, that are found in a spreadsheet program represent the majority of the items that you will interact with as you create and modify your spreadsheet files. In the next section, we will be defining the verbs or actions that you will typically take when using a spreadsheet program.

LO 2.2   The Major Verbs (Actions) of a Spreadsheet Program

In the previous section, we looked at the "nouns," or things, that make up a spreadsheet program. Now, we will look at the "verbs," or actions, that you will take as you use a spreadsheet program to complete various tasks. The following Table 2-5 shows the common verbs, or actions, that can be taken in many programs – not just spreadsheet programs.

Common Verbs (Actions) Taken in Many Programs		
Verbs (Actions)	**Where Found**	**Definition or Use**
Creating a File (Workbook)	Nearly all application programs – found on a toolbar and/or on a file menu – also typically uses the keyboard shortcut of Ctrl+N on Windows or ⌘+N on Mac	Creating a new, blank document of the specific type and format that the program is designed to work with.
Saving a File (Workbook)	Nearly all application programs – found on a toolbar and/or on a file menu – also typically uses the keyboard shortcut of Ctrl+S on Windows or ⌘+S on Mac	Saves a file that has been previously saved by overwriting the existing file with the current document contents. Alternatively, prompts the user with the *Save As . . .* dialog if the file has not yet been saved initially.
Editing (Opening) a File (Workbook)	Nearly all application programs – found on a toolbar and/or on a file menu – Also typically uses the keyboard shortcut of Ctrl+O on Windows or ⌘+O on Mac	Opens an existing file that has been previously saved. Allows the user to be able to make changes to previously saved work.

Table 2-5

Now, the following Table 2-6 will outline the majority of the remaining verbs or actions that can be taken in any contemporary spreadsheet program. While the terms are being defined initially here, many of these terms will be more fully defined in their respective upcoming chapters.

Common Verbs (Actions) Taken in Spreadsheet Programs		
Verbs (Actions)	**Where Found**	**Definition or Use**
Manipulating Worksheets	At the bottom of workbook documents, worksheets are also called tabs or sheets.	These sheets can be manipulated in several ways: Sheets can be added, deleted, moved (rearranged), renamed, and colored.
Planning Worksheet Layout	Can be drawn with pencil and paper before working in the spreadsheet program or can be worked out directly in the worksheet.	The preliminary work of imagining how the data labels, known data, and unknown data will be arranged within a worksheet. Planning the sheet in advance can help identify any problems before they arise.
Entering Labels	Typically found in the first one or two rows across the top of a spreadsheet. These become column heading labels. Also found in the first one or two columns down the left side of a spreadsheet. These become row heading labels.	Labels are typically text data fields that are entered across the top and down the side of a spreadsheet to help describe the rest of the known data on a worksheet.
Entering Known Data	Typically found below the column header labels and to the right of the row header labels.	This data may be text but is often numeric values that will be used in numeric calculations.
Calculating Unknown Data	Typically found below the known data or to the right of the known data.	This is typically derived by entering formulas or functions while referencing cells in the known data area to calculated new, unknown data values. This is the main reason why spreadsheets are used – to derive meaningful new information based on previously known data.
Entering Formulas	Typically found in the rows and columns where previously unknown data is to be calculated.	After first entering an equal sign (=), formulas are entered by typing in cell references, operators, or other functions to create a calculation that will return a resulting value.
Entering Functions	Typically found in the rows and columns where previously unknown data is to be calculated.	After first entering an equal sign (=), functions are entered by typing in the specific named function to perform a predefined calculation using cell references, operators, or other functions. The result of a function is some new resulting value of previously unknown data.

Table 2-6 (Continued)

Common Verbs (Actions) Taken in Spreadsheet Programs		
Verbs (Actions)	**Where Found**	**Definition or Use**
Selecting Adjoining Cells	This can happen anywhere within the worksheet.	With the keyboard, you can navigate to the first active cell you would like to select. Then, you can use the shift key along with any combination of the arrow-keys, page-up or page-down keys, ctrl-key, home-key, or end-key to select or de-select the cells that are touching each other. With the mouse, you can simply click once and hold and then drag to create a selection of adjoining or touching cells. You must make sure that you first click in the middle of a cell to begin your selection. Clicking on the border of a cell and dragging will not select adjacent cells, but rather will *move* the selected cell to a new location. Likewise, clicking on the lower right corner of a cell and dragging will not select adjacent cells, but rather will *fill* the adjacent cells with predictable values based on the original cell. We will be going over this in more detail in Chapter 3.
Selecting Disjointed Cells	This can happen anywhere within the worksheet, but it is *very common* to use this technique when creating certain types of charts.	This technique is used to select multiple cells when they are not touching each other. A common use of this technique is selecting the labels in the first column and the calculated unknown data in the last column while intentionally skipping the known data in the middle columns. This technique is frequently used with certain chart types. We will go over this concept and how to perform this action in more detail in Chapter 5.
Referencing Cells	This can happen anywhere within a spreadsheet, but is most commonly used in cells that are calculating unknown data by using (referencing) known data in other cells.	This is accomplished by using the cell's reference, which is typically its column and row designation. Examples of cell references are A5, F13, AX91 where A, F, and AX represent column names and 5, 13, and 91 represent row numbers respectively. There are actually three different kinds of cell references called *relative, absolute,* and *mixed* cell references. We will go over this in more detail in Chapter 4.

Table 2-6 (Continued)

Common Verbs (Actions) Taken in Spreadsheet Programs		
Verbs (Actions)	**Where Found**	**Definition or Use**
Reviewing Formulas and Functions	The entire worksheet is affected when performing this action.	This is a keystroke or command that "toggles" the view of the spreadsheet from either showing the resulting values of formulas and functions or showing the actual formulas and functions that are keyed into each cell. This technique should be used frequently to make sure that the spreadsheet calculations are being set up correctly.
Applying Formatting	Any selected cells can have any aspect of the formatting changed.	Formatting such as number formats, decimal precision, alignment (both vertical and horizontal), font, size, color, borders, decorations, backgrounds, and more can all be set to change the aesthetic appearance of the worksheets.
Changing Alignment	Any selected cells can have the alignment changed from the default alignment.	By default, text-based data is aligned to the left of a cell and numeric-based data is aligned to the right of a cell. Alignment can be changed to any desirable format without changing the type of data that is contained within the cells.
Auto-fitting Rows and Columns	This technique is achieved by first selecting the desired rows or columns to be auto-fitted and then double-clicking between the selected rows or columns.	This technique will automatically adjust the column width(s) or row height(s) to reflect the widest or tallest data values that are found within that selection. This is a way to quickly make sure that all of the relevant data is visible to the user.
Resizing Rows and Columns	This technique is achieved by first selecting the desired rows or columns to be resized and then manually dragging to adjust the size of the selected rows or columns.	This technique will adjust the column width(s) or row height(s) to reflect the specific size that you want by the way you drag the mouse. This is a technique to force multiple rows or columns to all be the exact same size.

Table 2-6 (Continued)

Common Verbs (Actions) Taken in Spreadsheet Programs		
Verbs (Actions)	Where Found	Definition or Use
Sorting and Filtering Data	This technique is typically used by selecting a single row of column heading labels and all of the known detail data that follows below while *excluding* any calculated unknown data that may follow the known detail data. Properly selecting the correct data before applying the Sort and Filter commands is a **very important** concept that will cause undesirable results if performed incorrectly.	Very often, it will be necessary to sort the data based upon some particular column of information. Additionally, especially with larger collections of data, it will be necessary to Filter the data to exclude or hide rows of data that do not match a particular value that you are interested in focusing upon. The concepts of Sorting and Filtering data will be further explored in Chapter 7.
Inserting Charts	Typically, small charts may appear on the same worksheet as a small amount of data, but more often, charts are placed on their own worksheets so that they can be sized large enough to show an easy-to-read visual representation of the selected data.	The action of inserting charts is accomplished by three steps: 1. First verify that the labels, known data, and unknown data calculations are all correct. 2. Select all of the data that you want to show up in the chart. This may involve selecting disjointed cells. 3. Use the toolbar or menu command to insert the desired chart type based on the type of data selected. Charting will be covered in detail in Chapter 5.
Inserting Objects	Similar to charts, other objects may be inserted into a worksheet and the placement of these objects will likewise depend on the object type and the amount of data already on a worksheet.	Objects that may be inserted include audio clips, video clips, or other types of embedded documents like word processing documents, presentation files, picture files, or practically any other type of file or document.

Table 2-6 (Continued)

Common Verbs (Actions) Taken in Spreadsheet Programs		
Verbs (Actions)	**Where Found**	**Definition or Use**
Using Tool and Command Dialogs	Everywhere throughout the spreadsheet program.	In order to accomplish all of the other aforementioned actions, there are tool and command dialogs that will allow you to specify numerous related parameters to help the program accomplish your desired tasks. The specific nature of these tool and command dialogs is as unique as the commands themselves, and many of them have keyboard shortcuts, which can help you quickly work with your files. But oftentimes, you will only be able to **fully** complete a particular task by using the tool or command dialog because not all of the commands have their own, unique keyboard shortcut! The important thing to remember is that by fully exploring the tool and command dialogs, you will be able to learn more of the details of what your particular program can do for you!

Table 2-6 (Continued)

Now armed with the fundamental terminology of the "nouns" and "verbs" of the typical contemporary spreadsheet program, you are ready to begin setting up and using spreadsheets to accomplish your desired goals.

Chapter 2 – Assignments and Projects

Directed Assignments

DA 2-1. For this directed assignment, you will be using the student data file named **DA_2-1.xls** to complete the required information. This file is in Microsoft Excel 97–2003 format and should open in any contemporary spreadsheet program.

Required student data file: *DA_2-1.xls*

You will be filling in information into this file based on observations you will make as you look at the several annotated screenshots over the next several pages.

1. Open the student data file named **DA_2-1.xls**.
2. Immediately save a copy of this file using the following specifications:
   a. File name: Rename this file using the filename *YourName_DA_2-1*

   b. File location: Place this file in any location you choose, but make a note of the location as you will need it later.

   c. File format: Because this file will be sent in to your professor, you must check with him or her to see what format **he or she** will want this file to be saved in. Don't just assume that the original file format or the default file format for your own computer will be acceptable!

3. Once the original file is saved, you will update the document to fill in the data for the cell range B3:D15 according to the following specifications.

   a. For the cell range B3:B15, (column B) you will use the screenshot below labeled **DA_2-1_Excel_Screenshot** to identify the highlighted items.

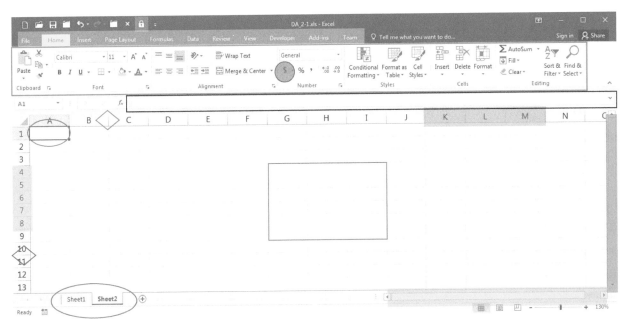

DA_2-1_Excel_Screenshot

   b. For each spreadsheet "nouns" that are listed in column A in your data file, describe the screenshot highlighting that was used to indicate each particular noun within the screenshot. Make sure you include the color and the shape of the specific highlighting. These descriptions should include the color of the highlighting (e.g. yellow, red, green, blue, black, or white) as well as the highlighting effect (e.g. "coloring," "circle," "rectangle," or "diamond"). Cell B3 has already been filled in for you to show that the Menu Bar or Ribbon Tab for MS Excel 2016 was **colored yellow** in the screenshot.

   c. Repeat steps 3a and 3b above to fill in the answers for the range C3:C15. For this range, however, use the screenshot below labeled **DA_2-1_LiberOffice_Screenshot** to answer the questions. Cell C10 has already been filled in for you to show that the Formula Bar for LibreOffice Calc was highlighted with a **red rectangle** in the screenshot.

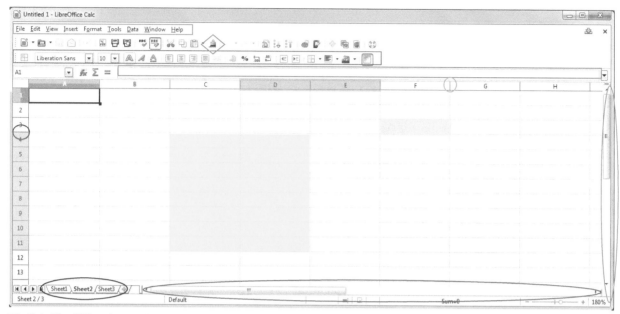

DA_2-1_LibreOffice_Screenshot

d. Repeat steps 3a and 3b above one final time to fill in the answers for the range D3:D15 in your spreadsheet file. For this range, however, use the screenshot below labeled *DA_2-1_ GoogleSheets_Screenshot* to answer the questions. Cell D5 has already been filled in for you to show that the Worksheet Tabs for Google Sheets was highlighted with a **purple oval** in the screenshot.

4. Double-check to make sure that you have filled in entries for all of the cells in the range B3:D15. Also make sure that you did not, inadvertently, make any changes to the pre-existing labels that were already filled in for you.

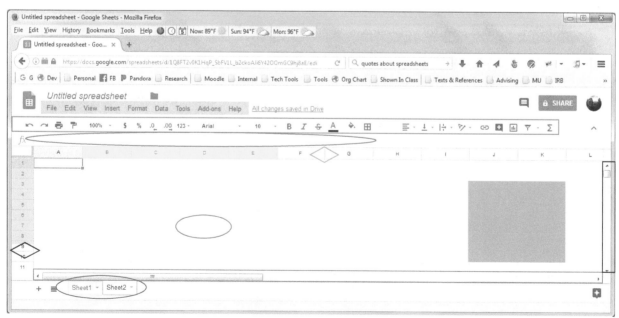

DA_2-1_GoogleSheets_Screenshot

5. Finally, double-check the spelling of your new data entry to make sure you have created good quality final work. When everything is correct, save your work and then submit it in accordance with your class instructions.

Creative Projects

CP 2-1. Tables 2-1 through 2-4 in this chapter define over 40 "nouns" or things that are the basic components that are found and used within a spreadsheet program. Tables 2-5 and 2-6 in this chapter define over 20 "verbs" or actions that one could take when working within a spreadsheet program.

Required student data file: None. Use a new, blank word processing document.

In this creative project, you will create a new, blank word processing document and save it with the file name of *YourName_CP_2-1*. Review the lists of spreadsheet nouns and verbs and create a short report (no more than one page) that describes some of the terms that you were already familiar with, some of the concepts that you may have already used, and some of the concepts that were completely foreign to you before working through this chapter.

Identify any terms that you may feel still unsure about and list out any questions you may have about these terms in preparation for the next class session.

Remember to check your final work for spelling and grammar correctness and then submit your file in the manner prescribed for your class.

Chapter 3

Setting Up and Using Spreadsheets

Source: Shutterstock, Inc.

Why should you think about and plan the layout of your spreadsheets before actually building them?

It may be very tempting just to dive right in to working with a spreadsheet program, but there is a lot to be said for doing some preliminary planning of your work before you start. Specifically, you will want to ask yourself a number of questions before you begin and make sure you have good answers for your questions to help you make the most efficient use of your development time.

Some of the questions you will ask yourself include:

✦ What is the purpose of this spreadsheet and who is the primary target audience for this information?

✦ Will someone else, other than yourself, need to open up and use this spreadsheet? If so, what file format(s) will they be able to work with?

✦ What are the labels and the known data that will be entered into the spreadsheet and where will that data come from?

✦ What are the desired calculations that will process the known data to derive new, unknown information? What formulas or functions will be needed to complete these calculations?

LEARNING OBJECTIVES

In this chapter, we will explore these learning objectives:

Creating and Saving a Workbook

Manipulating Worksheets in a Workbook

Planning a Worksheet Layout

Performing the Data Entry of Labels

Performing the Data Entry of Known Data

Performing Minimal Formatting of Labels and Known Data

Preparing for Calculating the Unknown Data

Key Terms

- auto-fit column widths
- auto-fit entire worksheet
- auto-fit row heights
- change column widths
- change row heights
- color worksheet tabs
- create a new workbook
- create additional worksheets
- delete worksheets
- file location
- file name
- file type or format
- merge cells
- planning a worksheet layout
- rearrange worksheets
- rename worksheets
- saving a workbook
- using the fill handle
- wrapping text

✦ Will there need to be any charts or graphs to help convey the information about the spreadsheet data for the target audience?

By thinking about and answering these questions *before* actually beginning to work in the spreadsheet program, you will be much better prepared to efficiently create the desired output.

LO 3.1   Creating and Saving a Workbook

The first action we should consider is the fundamental task of how to Create a New Workbook. This task is similar to the creation of any other kind of document that you may have accomplished in any other program. Typically, when creating a new document in any program, you will use either the mouse or the keyboard to execute the *File... New...* series of commands. When issuing commands to any program via the mouse, you will either click on a tool icon found in a toolbar or ribbon, or you will click on a command found in a menu.

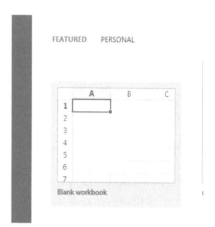

When you first start a spreadsheet program, depending on the vendor and version of the program, you may be presented with a new, blank workbook and you are already, immediately ready to start working. In other versions, however, you have to create a new workbook from a template. We will be discussing templates in detail in Chapter 9. At this time, it is enough to know that there is a template called "Blank Workbook" or "Blank Document" that will, as you can imagine, create a new, blank workbook file for you to begin working with. Figure 3-1 shows an Excel 2016 template for a Blank workbook.

Figure 3-1

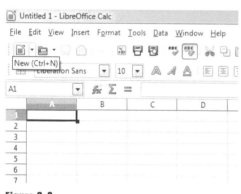

Figure 3-2

Additionally, nearly all contemporary programs allow you to use keyboard shortcuts to execute a variety of common commands and tasks. There are many ways that you can begin to learn these shortcuts to make your work in these programs more efficient. For example, please observe the details of Figure 3-2. This image shows the Libre Office Calc program as the user has simply rested her mouse pointer on the toolbar icon to create a new spreadsheet document. Notice how a tool tip has popped up to describe the tool as being the "New" command and then, in parenthesis, the tool tip is showing that the keyboard shortcut of "Ctrl+N" would also create a new workbook document.

Additionally, when using the menus for issuing commands in a program, most contemporary programs also show the keyboard shortcuts for the menu commands in the same fashion. Figure 3-3 shows a series of menus expanded. These menus appeared when the user clicked the *File* menu followed by the *New* command. As you can see, the keyboard shortcuts for many of the available commands are shown right alongside the actual commands. This becomes an easy way for you to begin to discover all of the keyboard shortcuts that can make working in any program more efficient.

Now, at this point, you might be asking yourself, "Why are there so many different ways to accomplish the exact same task?" And true enough, for every one way that there is to accomplish a task in a contemporary program, there are often 2, 3, 4, or more ways of accomplishing the same task!

The goal of the software authors is ***not*** to intentionally try to confuse you or overwhelm you with too many options. But rather, the intention is to provide you with numerous avenues to accomplish your work so that you can begin to discover your own preferences, which make working in a program easy and efficient and well-matched to your own working style.

OK – so whichever method you choose to create a new workbook file, the end result will be the same: You will now have a new, blank workbook pulled up in your spreadsheet program and you are now ready to work on the next task: **Saving a Workbook**.

But wait! You may be asking yourself, "Why would I want to save a workbook at this point? It's completely blank?" To answer that question, I'd like to paint a picture for you and then ask you a question: Imagine you've been working on a really important document for the past two hours and the deadline is approaching very soon. Now imagine that there is a severe storm kicking up outside of your building and the power in the building starts to flicker on and off! Would you rather have your incomplete work saved – at least at the point it is now – prior to losing all power to your computer –

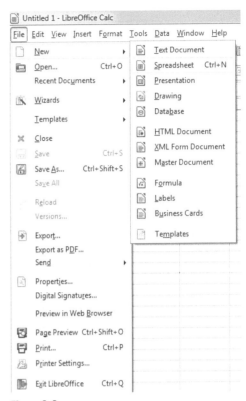

Figure 3-3

or would you rather have to start over from scratch when the power goes out and all of your hard work is lost?

Saving a workbook file (or any file for that matter) is one of the most important fundamental computing skills that you should master right away. When saving a workbook file, the operating system will prompt you for three pieces of information:

1. **File name** – this is the name that you give to your workbook file. It should be something meaningful for you and anyone else who may work with this file. While it is *possible* to name a workbook file "Workbook1", this file name is not meaningful. Anyone who needs to work with this file in the future will have to open up the file just to see if it is the file they are looking for. Rather, a workbook file with a name of "Marketing Budget – 2018" immediately tells anyone looking at this workbook what is going to be on the inside. Many businesses and organizations will have specific file-naming conventions that they will want you to use when naming your spreadsheet files

2. **File location** – this is the combination of physical and logical locations within a computer system where files could be stored. Physical locations are the internal hard drives (e.g. C: drive on Windows, harddisk: on Mac) and removable devices (e.g. external hard drives, flash drives) where digital information can be stored. Logical locations are the series of folder names (also known as the path) of logical named containers where digital files are stored. For example, on a Windows machine, you may have a folder on your internal C: drive that you created and named "MyWorkBooks". And then in that folder, you may have another named folder that you called "2018 Budgets". If you were to save your file in this location, then the final file location or path would be "C:\MyWorkBooks\2018 Budgets\". Notice that there will be either a backslash "\" or a forward slash "/" character that will separate the logical locations (folders) within the path location for a

file. The forward or back slash characters are determined by the operating system of the physical device you are working with.

A final note about file locations is that besides using your own, local machine for saving your work, you may also save your work to shared file locations such as a network server or an internet server location. There are many pros and cons to saving your work in remote locations, which we will not get into now. But it is important to know that when you save your work, you must always be mindful of the location to where you save your files . . . so that you can find them again when you need them!

3. File type or format – this is the internal file format and external file extension that will be given to your file when your work is saved. The file type and format of a document represents the version of the workbook program that created the file. Generally speaking, newer programs can open the newer file formats as well as older file formats, but older programs can only open the older file formats and **cannot** open newer file formats.

   But this is the most important part of this discussion: Most contemporary programs have the ability to save the files that they create in multiple different file formats. The reason for this is because, quite often, you will find yourself in a situation where you need to share your work with someone else – maybe a coworker, or maybe a customer, or maybe a business partner like an accountant or a lawyer, etc. And oftentimes, these other folks will **not** have the exact same software programs and versions that you have! Therefore, you may need to save your work in some file format that will be compatible with the programs that *they* will use to open the work back up!

   When you save your work, if you do not intentionally change the file format, then whichever program you are using will save your file in its own, native file format. You can recognize what file format a file was saved with by looking at the file extension that is suffixed to the file name that was given to the file. For example, in Microsoft Excel versions 2007 and higher, this will be a file extension of **.xlsx**. For Microsoft Excel versions prior to 2007, the extension will be **.xls**. For Open Office or LibreOffice spreadsheet files, the extension will be **.ods**.

4. Figure 3-4 shows how you can change the file type of your work by simply choosing one of the other file types at the time you save your work.

When you have successfully chosen and typed your new file name, chosen and navigated to your new file location, and chosen your desired file type, then your new workbook file will be saved and you can continue working.

Now, once you have successfully saved your workbook, then whenever you make subsequent changes to your workbook and click or execute the save command, the program will simply save the updated version of your file right over the top of the old document. In other words, the program will not prompt you again for a new file name, location, or file format on subsequent "saves." Rather, it will just keep updating your work in the same location. If you *need* to have a different copy or a different version of the same document, then you can optionally use the *Save As...* command to save a *new copy* of the active file with either a new name, or in a new location, or in a different file format, etc.

Once you have created and saved a workbook, very often you will need to update or make changes to a spreadsheet file. Opening an existing workbook is as simple as navigating to the location where the file is stored, selecting the file name to be opened, and then clicking the "Open" button. Once opened, the task of editing a workbook is simply making changes to the content in the workbook and then saving the file – either in place and overwriting the existing file or by saving a copy of the new, updated file as described above.

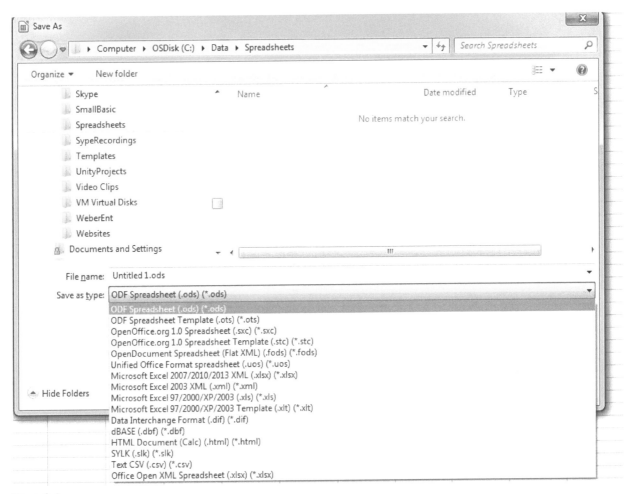

Figure 3-4

LO 3.2 Manipulating Worksheets in a Workbook

Now that you know how to create, save, and update a workbook file, it is now time to put our focus onto working within a single workbook file. To help with this next section, please look carefully at the bottom of the workbook file.

Figure 3-5 shows two different spreadsheet programs, layered one on top of the other. Both of these programs are showing the bottom of the program and the bottom of the spreadsheet documents that are open in each program.

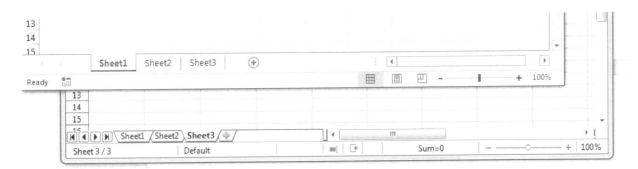

Figure 3-5

Here you can see that both documents currently are showing three (3) different worksheets. These worksheets are currently named Sheet1, Sheet2, and Sheet3 respectively. Did you notice how on the top spreadsheet program, Sheet1 appears white and on top of the other two sheets? But in the bottom program, Sheet3 appears white and on top of the other two sheets? This is showing you that the sheets can be selected independently of each other and, when you select a sheet, it will become the "active" sheet and you can continue to work with the contents on that sheet.

So now we know we can select one of the many worksheets that are in a workbook. But what else can we do with a worksheet. Here are the various verbs or actions you can take when manipulating worksheets:

✦ You can Create Additional Worksheets – by clicking the "+" next to the existing sheet(s) you can add another sheet to your workbook. How many sheets can you add to a workbook? That answer varies with each program and version, but most contemporary programs will allow over 1,000 worksheets in a workbook! Now, that being said, the real question shouldn't be how many sheets *can* you add to a workbook, but rather how many sheets *should* you add to a workbook? Generally speaking, once you get more than about 10 sheets in a single workbook, the workbook becomes generally more difficult for others to work with. Please always remember that " . . . just because you *can* do something, doesn't necessarily mean that you *should* do that thing!"

✦ You can (and should) Rename Worksheets – by simply double-clicking on a worksheet, you can change the name of your worksheets. And just like having a meaningful filename for your workbook, *all* of your worksheet should be given meaningful names to tell the users, at a glance, what each worksheet contains.

✦ You can Rearrange Worksheets – by simply clicking and dragging a worksheet, you can move the sheets to a different position in the workbook.

✦ You can Color Worksheet Tabs – by right-clicking on a sheet tab, you can change the background color of the tab.

✦ You can Delete Worksheets – by right-clicking on a sheet tab, you can delete a worksheet. ***Use caution when deleting worksheets*** – not all programs will allow you to "undo" the deletion of a worksheet! Make sure you really want to delete a sheet before executing this command!

LO 3.3   **Planning a Worksheet Layout**

Once you have created a worksheet and have given it a meaningful name, the next thing you should do is figure out what information you want in this worksheet. This concept is called Planning a Worksheet Layout. When planning your worksheets it is often helpful to think about the three primary types of data that will be found on a typical spreadsheet:

1. **Labels** – these are the text values that typically are found across the top one or two rows of the spreadsheet and down the first one or two columns as well. These labels are used to describe the data that is found below and to the right of the labels.

2. **Known Data** – these are the text or numeric values that are typically found below the column heading labels and to the right of the row heading labels. This information can be entered through data entry or may be imported from an external source.

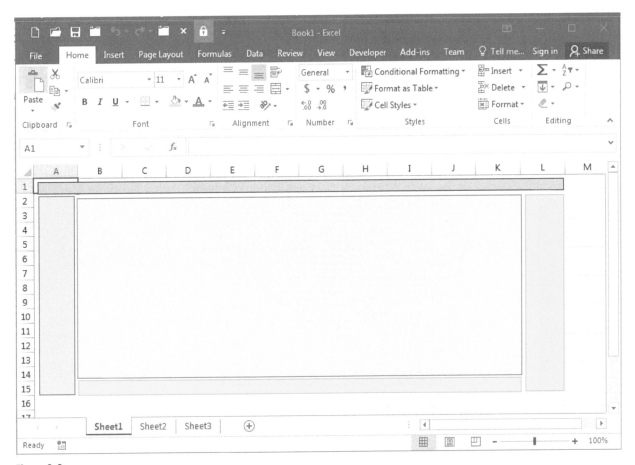

Figure 3-6

3. **Calculated Data** – these are the unknown values that are derived from the known data. These are the main reason why you are using a spreadsheet: to perform calculations that will process the known data to deliver previously unknown information about the known data. The calculated data are the resulting values that are achieved from calculations involving formulas and functions. Formulas and functions will be covered in detail in Chapter 4.

In Figure 3-6, you can see a blank worksheet with five colored rectangular areas highlighted. The blue rectangle represents where column heading labels would typically be entered. The green rectangle represents where row heading labels would typically be entered. The red rectangle represents where the known data would typically be entered. And the orange rectangles represent where the calculated data would typically be found.

Please note that this is just a general description of the layout of a typical worksheet but is, by no means, an absolute requirement. Sometimes you may have more than one row at the top of the spreadsheet to serve as headings for the data. Likewise, it is very common to have multiple rows or columns of calculated data. This layout is just presented to show a generalized layout of typical spreadsheet documents.

Figure 3-7 shows a sample worksheet representing some sales data for ten divisions of a fictitious company for the first six months of 2018. The information in this spreadsheet has been highlighted with the same coloring as the descriptions in Figure 3-6. Here you can see two rows (blue) at the top that have labels to define the rest of the data that is below the first two rows. These labels tell the viewer that this whole sheet is the First Six Months Sales data for 2018 and also individual column labels that describe the rest of the data in each column. Then, you can also see the first column (green) is filled with labels that describe that the rows will each contain sales data for each division. This sales data will be entered to the right of these row labels. The main center of the spreadsheet (red) contains the known sales figures for each division in each month. These dollar amounts would be data entered and validated to make sure that there were no data entry errors. Then finally, at the bottom and far right of the spreadsheet (orange) are the calculated cells that total up the values of known data.

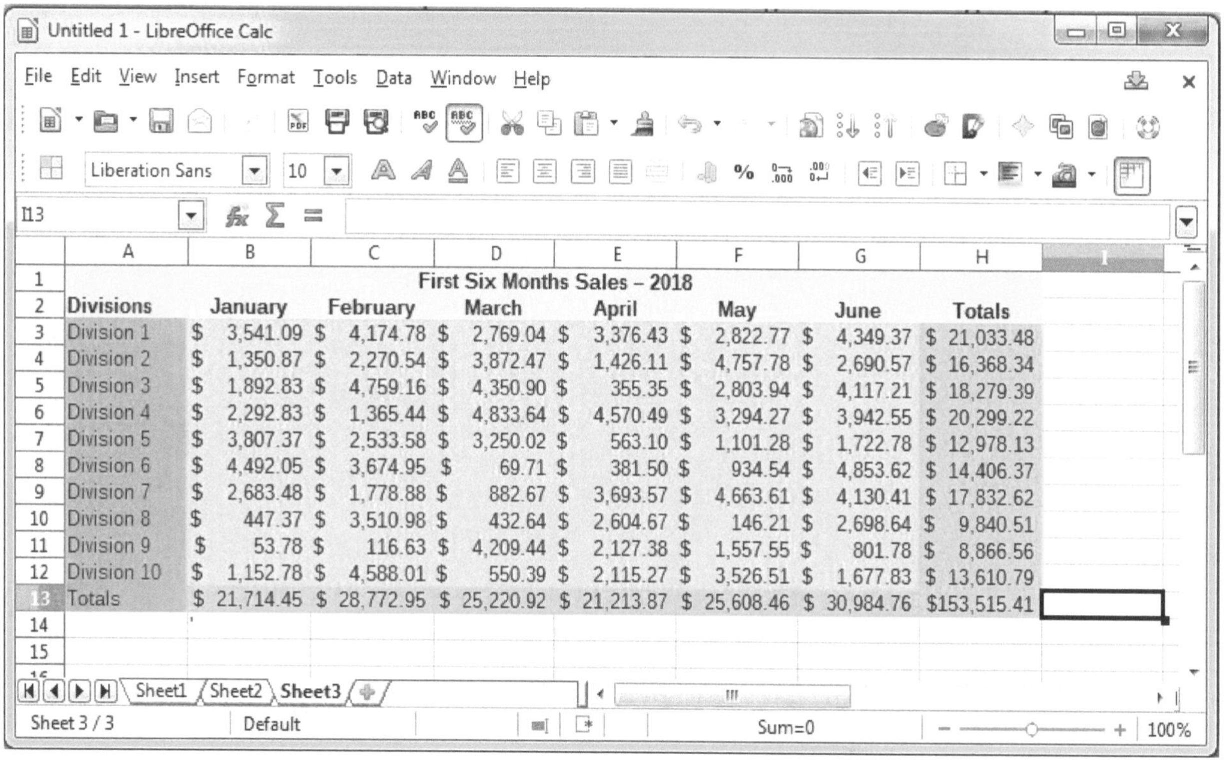

	A	B	C	D	E	F	G	H
1	First Six Months Sales – 2018							
2	Divisions	January	February	March	April	May	June	Totals
3	Division 1	$ 3,541.09	$ 4,174.78	$ 2,769.04	$ 3,376.43	$ 2,822.77	$ 4,349.37	$ 21,033.48
4	Division 2	$ 1,350.87	$ 2,270.54	$ 3,872.47	$ 1,426.11	$ 4,757.78	$ 2,690.57	$ 16,368.34
5	Division 3	$ 1,892.83	$ 4,759.16	$ 4,350.90	$ 355.35	$ 2,803.94	$ 4,117.21	$ 18,279.39
6	Division 4	$ 2,292.83	$ 1,365.44	$ 4,833.64	$ 4,570.49	$ 3,294.27	$ 3,942.55	$ 20,299.22
7	Division 5	$ 3,807.37	$ 2,533.58	$ 3,250.02	$ 563.10	$ 1,101.28	$ 1,722.78	$ 12,978.13
8	Division 6	$ 4,492.05	$ 3,674.95	$ 69.71	$ 381.50	$ 934.54	$ 4,853.62	$ 14,406.37
9	Division 7	$ 2,683.48	$ 1,778.88	$ 882.67	$ 3,693.57	$ 4,663.61	$ 4,130.41	$ 17,832.62
10	Division 8	$ 447.37	$ 3,510.98	$ 432.64	$ 2,604.67	$ 146.21	$ 2,698.64	$ 9,840.51
11	Division 9	$ 53.78	$ 116.63	$ 4,209.44	$ 2,127.38	$ 1,557.55	$ 801.78	$ 8,866.56
12	Division 10	$ 1,152.78	$ 4,588.01	$ 550.39	$ 2,115.27	$ 3,526.51	$ 1,677.83	$ 13,610.79
13	Totals	$ 21,714.45	$ 28,772.95	$ 25,220.92	$ 21,213.87	$ 25,608.46	$ 30,984.76	$153,515.41

Figure 3-7

Please note that the coloring shown in the previous two figures is simply to highlight areas where the different types of information are generally placed within a spreadsheet. You do not need to specifically color any aspects of your own spreadsheets. This is just done to make it easier for you to visualize the different types of data that will be entered into a spreadsheet.

One additional consideration that is considered "best practices" when it comes to spreadsheet layouts: In general, **you should not leave blank rows or columns in your spreadsheet files**. Often, some people leave blank rows and columns in their worksheets as a means to try to control the "white space" or visual separations between elements in the file. While this visual separation is often desirable, the better way to control the desired "white space" is to use extended row heights or column widths to provide the additional white space. This latter method is preferred to the former method because blank rows and columns can cause significant problems later on when you want to create charts based on your data. Blank rows and columns will be treated as "0"s or "missing data," which can negatively impact your charts. We will be going over this in more detail in the next several chapters.

LO 3.4   Performing the Data Entry of Labels

The data entry of labels is usually as simple as selecting a desired cell and then typing in the label. When you type a text label, by default, this text data will automatically align to the left side of the cell and will extend across the cell to the right. Numeric data that is used as a label will automatically align to the right side of the cell and will extend "backwards" to the left of the cell. On the surface, this seems simple enough, however, what you will actually see in the cell when you hit the enter key after typing in the label will depend on several different factors.

First let's focus on text labels. If the size of the text label that you entered is smaller than the width of the column, then that text label will align to the left and the rest of the cell will appear blank.

If, however, the size of the text label you enter is larger than the width of the column, then what you will see when you hit the enter key will depend on the contents of the cell immediately to the right of this active cell. There are two possibilities of what you will see if the text that you enter is larger than the column width:

1. **If there is no data** in the cell immediately to the right of the active cell, then the extra-long text of your label will simply "bleed-over" into the visual space of the empty cells to the right. Those extra cells are actually empty, but the long text will just "appear" to be in those extra cells.

2. **If there is already some data present** in the cell immediately to the right of this active cell, then your extra-long text will be truncated or cut off by the end of the column width.

Figure 3-8 shows examples of two cells that each has very long text in cells A1 and A2. As you can see in row 1, because there is no

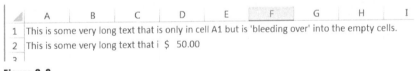

Figure 3-8

data in any of the cells B1 through I1, the long text simply "bleeds over" into those adjacent, empty cells. But in row 2, the exact same long text is in cell A2. This time, however, there is a data value in cell D2 of $50. Because cell D2 is not empty, the long text from cell A2 can only "bleed over" into the blank cells of B2 and C2 but then the text gets truncated or cut off at the nonblank cell D2. Notice that once the text is truncated, it will not re-appear after the nonblank cell! Also, please note that this behavior is only for text-base labels that are longer than the width of the column in which they reside.

Next, let's focus on what happens when you enter numeric data that is too large for a column width. First, as mentioned before, numeric data will automatically align to the right of the cell and will take on a general numeric format (until you change the number format.) But what happens if you attempt to enter a very large number in a very small column width? When you hit the enter key after doing the data entry, what you will see is a number of octothorpes (a.k.a. hashtags or pound signs). Depending on the version of spreadsheet program you are using, you might see just three of these (###) or you might see the entire cell filled with these octothorpes (###########).

Whenever you see three or more octothorpes in a cell, the spreadsheet program is trying to tell you two things:

1. The cell that contains these octothorpes actually contains a numeric value (either a literal value or a numeric result of a calculation) and

2. The current format of this numeric value is such that it is too wide to be fully represented within the confines of the current column width.

So, unlike long text values, long numeric values will neither "bleed-over" nor get truncated if the column width is too small. Rather, the displayed value will simply be repeating octothorpes.

Figure 3-9 shows some numeric data in columns A and B. The actual values in both columns are identical. But as you can see, column B is wide enough to show the entire numeric value as it is formatted. But in column A, the cell is not wide enough to show the entire data so octothorpes are shown instead. Also, please note that the highlighted cell (A2) shows you what the actual value of the cell is if you look at the formula bar (the red circled area).

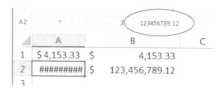

Figure 3-9

When entering data values as labels or known data (whether text or numeric values) you must always be mindful of how the data will display if the columns are too narrow for the formatted data. The most common way to handle data that does not properly show up in the cells is to increase the column width of the columns that are too narrow. To change column widths you can simply drag the column separator that is between the two columns. For example, if we wanted to fix the column A in Figure 3-9 so that the data in cell A2 can be fully seen, then you would simply click-and-hold on the line between column letter A and column letter B and then drag this separator to the right. Alternatively, you can use the auto-fit actions to automatically adjust a column width. The technique to Auto-Fit Column Widths is to select the column(s) that you would like to adjust by clicking on the column letter(s), then double-click the separator between the columns. This will tell the spreadsheet program to automatically adjust the column widths to the largest width needed to fully view the longest data element that is within each column respectively.

When performing the data entry for labels and known values, it is very common that you will need to adjust the column widths to prevent undesired visual truncation, bleeding-over, or octothorpes.

This same technique can be used to change row heights. You can manually change a row's height by dragging the row separator between the row numbers. Optionally, you can Auto-Fit Row Heights by double-clicking the separator between the rows.

Additionally, you can Auto-Fit the Entire Worksheet by clicking on the single gray square in the upper left-hand corner of the worksheet (where the row numbers and the column letters intersect.) This will select the entire worksheet. With the entire worksheet selected, you can double-click between the row and column separators to Auto-Fit the entire worksheet at one time.

Another activity that you might choose to do when you are entering data labels is you might choose to Merge Cells. Merging cells is a technique that takes multiple contiguous (touching) cells and merges them into a single cell. By doing this, you can create a visual representation of a larger grouping of information. In Figure 3-7 above, you can observe this effect if you look at the single text label in row 1. You can see that this single text cell appears to be spanning the cells A1 through H1. These cells have all been merged together and are now treated as a single cell.

Figure 3-10 shows three different examples of merged cells. As you can see, any number of contiguous (touching) cells can be merged together into a single cell. Then, once the cells are merged, you can fully control the other aspects of the cell formatting, which will be covered in more detail later on. In this example, 4 cells are merged together in row 2 (cells B2 through E2) and the text is formatted to be aligned in the center with a yellow background color. Also, 9 cells from 3 rows and 3 columns (cells B3 through D5) are all merged together to form a single block. The text in this block is aligned to the left, has been colored with a reddish background color, and has been configured to have the text wrap within the confines of the newly merged cell. We will discuss text wrapping in the next section. And finally, the three cells in column E (cells E3 through E5) have been merged, colored blue, and then aligned to the right with text wrapping as well.

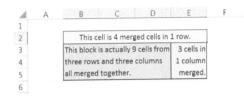

Figure 3-10

As you can quickly see, the ability to merge cells gives you significant control of the overall look and feel of your spreadsheets!

In the last example, we mentioned the concept of wrapping text. Wrapping Text is the technique of telling the spreadsheet program that the text value in a cell that is longer than the width of the column should be allowed to wrap to a second line (or more if needed) but still remain within the same row. By doing this, a particular row height may become larger to allow for the wrapped text to show up without being truncated.

Figure 3-11 shows several examples of wrapped text. As you can see, row one and row two have data labels that are wrapping within the cells so that longer text can still show up without being truncated. The row heights were adjusted to allow the wrapped text to become fully displayed.

Additionally, you can see that cell A1 through cell G1 have also been merged together as well as having the text wrapping turned on. Likewise, cells A2 and B2 were also merged together. Here, however, even though text wrapping is turned on for this merged cell, because the text is small enough to fit within the cell, no default text wrapping occurs.

In LO 3.6, we will look into more details as to how you will format your worksheet with minimal formatting to help you better work with your labels and your known data.

Our School Basketball Team (Season Conference Games Only)						
Player Full Name		Primary Position	Height (in Feet & Inches)	Weight (in Pounds)	Total Points in this Season (after 14 games)	Average Points in this Season
Chris	Cayman	C	6' 7"	204	266	19
Pat	Peterson	F	6' 2"	198	182	13
Jamie	Johnson	F	6' 1"	201	84	6
Lou	Lewis	G	5' 11"	187	154	11
Sydney	Samson	G	5' 9"	180	28	2
Taylor	Thomson	G	5' 8.5"	182	98	7
Totals					812	9.7

Figure 3-11

One final technique that can be used when entering in data labels is the concept of using the fill handle to fill a predictable series. Using the Fill Handle is a technique whereby you select the lower right-hand corner of a single cell or a range of cells and then drag in a direction. There is a small uniquely shaped square mark in the lower corner of the selected cell or range of cells. This small square-shaped corner of the selection indicator is called the fill handle.

When you click and hold the fill handle and then drag in a direction (either across to the right or down), you are indicating that you would like the spreadsheet program to fill the new cells with the data values that can be predicted from the currently selected cell or cells.

Figure 3-12 shows ten rows of data values that were created by using the

	A	B	C	D	E	F	G
1	January	February	March	April	May	June	July
2	Wed	Thu	Fri	Sat	Sun	Mon	Tue
3	Dept. 1	Dept. 2	Dept. 3	Dept. 4	Dept. 5	Dept. 6	Dept. 7
4	Qtr. 1	Qtr. 2	Qtr. 3	Qtr. 4	Qtr. 1	Qtr. 2	Qtr. 3
5	Item 004	Item 005	Item 006	Item 007	Item 008	Item 009	Item 010
6	1	1	1	1	1	1	1
7	1	3	5	7	9	11	13
8	15.5	16.5	17.5	18.5	19.5	20.5	21.5
9	15.5	11.33	7.16	2.99	-1.18	-5.35	-9.52
10	5/6/2018	5/7/2018	5/8/2018	5/9/2018	5/10/2018	5/11/2018	5/12/2018
11							

Figure 3-12

fill handle. If you look closely at Figure 3-12, you will see that two cells A7 through B7 are currently both selected. The fill handle is shown as the small square in the lower right-hand corner of cell B7.

The following describes how each row of data was created:

✦ For row 1, the word "January" was typed into cell A1 and then the enter key was pressed. Then, cell A1 was selected and then the fill handle was clicked and dragged to cell G1. Because "January" is part of a predictable series (namely, the names of the months), the rest of the cells were automatically filled with the consecutive month names through "June".

✦ For row 2, the word "Wed" was typed into cell B2. When the fill handle was used, the predictable series of the days of the week were filled in.

✦ In cell A3, the label "Dept. 1" was keyed in. Then, when using the fill handle, the spreadsheet program recognized that the numeric value that followed the text was probably an incrementing numeric label, so it filled in the next labels in the predictable sequence.

✦ In A4, the label "Qtr. 1" was entered. But even though this is similar to the previous example, the spreadsheet program knows that quarters (whether fully spelled out or abbreviated) only have 4 values. So using the fill handle, the program correctly predicts that cell E4 should "start over" again at "Qtr. 1" and not proceed incorrectly to "Qtr. 5"!

✦ In row 5, we see once again how item numbers could be a predictable series even if we didn't start at Item 001.

✦ In row 6, we see an interesting difference. In cell A6, only the number 1 was keyed in. Then, when using the fill handle, the spreadsheet doesn't really know if this number is part of any predictable series. Therefore, if the spreadsheet program doesn't recognize a predictable series, then the fill handle will simply act like the "copy-and-paste" function and just copy the original data to all of the filled cells.

✦ In row 7, the data entry was the number 1 in cell A7 and the number 3 in cell B7. Then, both *cells* A7 *and* B7 were selected at the same time as shown in the example. Then, when using the fill handle, since two cells were selected, the spreadsheet program could determine that there was, in fact, a predictable pattern between these two cells. Specifically, the program recognized a pattern of increasing by a value of 2. That is how the rest of the predicatble series was then filled.

✦ In row 8, another technique was used. Cell A8 was entered with a value of 15.5. Now, similar to row 6, no additional data was directly entered into this row. Therefore, if we were to use the fill handle, the single value of 15.5 should have been merely copied to the other cells. But I wanted the other cells to reflect an increase of 1. So, while holding down the control-key on the keyboard, and then using the fill handle, the spreadsheet program knows to change from being a simple "copy" command to become a "fill and increment" command. Therefore, holding the control-key while using the fill handle will change the behavior of the fill handle.

✦ In row 9, the first two cells were keyed in. Then, using the fill handle, the spreadsheet correctly determined that the predictable pattern was a *decrease* in value by 3.17. The result is a continuous decreasing pattern even into negative numbers.

✦ The final example in row 10 shows that date values (which are actually numeric values) are also recognized as predictable series and can be used with the fill handle as well. We will be discussing more about date values in the next section.

Please remember that the fill handle can be used in either the across direction or in the downward direction. This is a very powerful way to rapidly enter large series of data values without having to type each item independently.

LO 3.5 Performing the Data Entry of Known Data

After planning the overall layout of your spreadsheet and adding the labels, the next step is to perform the data entry of the known data for your spreadsheet. Very often, this data will be numeric data that can be used in calculations. Looking back at Figure 3-7, for example, the data that was known was the data that was entered in the red section of the spreadsheet. It is important to note that the actual data entry of numeric data should not include any special formatting characters.

In other words, cell B3 in Figure 3-7 shows a final displayed value of $ 3,541.09. However, this is **not** what was entered into the cell! The actual value that was keyed into the cell was 3541.09. Notice how when you perform data entry, you should not key in any of the special formatting characters. Rather, these characters are added by the spreadsheet program when you format the cells to stipulate that the numeric data should be formatted as currency or with accounting formatting, etc.

When performing data entry into a large range of cells, it is often very helpful to select the range of cells where you are going to be entering data before you begin typing. By doing so, you are telling the spreadsheet program that you will be doing data entry into these selected cells.

When performing data entry in a cell, when you have finished entering the data, you can either press the enter key or press the tab key (or the shifted-enter key or the shifted-tab key) to signify that you have completed the data entry for that cell. If you press the enter key in a range of selected cells, then the current data entry is completed and the next lower cell in the selected range becomes the newly active cell. If you keep pressing the enter key, you will see that the active cell will keep moving down and then across all of the selected cells. Holding the shift key when pressing the enter key causes the active cell to move in the reverse direction.

Likewise, pressing the tab key after performing a data entry will cause the active cell to move across the selected cells and then down. The shift key when used with the tab key will also reverse directions. These key combinations are intended to help make the task of large amounts of data entry just a little bit easier.

It is often best to simply do all of the data entry that you can to just get the raw known data into the spreadsheet. Then, after the raw data is input, you will then be able to perform some minimal formatting to make the labels and the raw known data easier to work with.

Some additional considerations about the data entry of the known data:

✦ **Do not put multiple data values into a single column.** For example, if you create a column with a label of "Student Name", you may be intending to have rows with student names in that column. But you have to ask yourself this question: Will I ever want to sort these rows so that they are arranged by the students' last names (i.e. in alphabetical order by last name)? If so, then I will need to have the first name in a separate column from the last name – otherwise, I won't be able to sort solely on the students' last names!

✦ **Do not mix data values and labels in a single column.** For example, if you had a column labeled "Peanuts Sold" and then your rows of data beneath that label showed weekly values of something like "6 bags" and "14 bags" for the first two weeks, then this will cause problems later on when we want to perform calculations on this data. This is a mixture of numeric data values (e.g. the **number** of bags sold) along with a text label (e.g. the **text** word "bags").

✦ *Numeric* values like 6 and 14 can be mathematically added together to derive a total of 20. But *text* values like "6 bags" and "14 bags" **cannot** have mathematic calculations performed on them.

✦ The correct way to do this would be to label this column something like "Peanuts Sold (*in bags*)" and then simply performing data entry of the number 6 and 14 into the cells beneath the label.

This way, when it comes time to perform the total calculation, you will simply be adding the number 6 and number 14 and will get the result of 20 that you are expecting.

After the data entry of the known data is complete, you will now be ready to format this initial data to make the remaining tasks in the spreadsheet easier to manage.

NOTE: Don't forget to periodically save your work as you go so that you are never at risk of losing too much of your work should there be a power outage or some other, unexpected system or program crash!

LO 3.6 Performing Minimal Formatting of Labels and Known Data

Once the data labels and known data have been keyed into the spreadsheet, now is a good time to perform some minimal formatting of the labels and the known data. All of the formatting commands are available via the tools in the toolbars and ribbons and via the menus in the spreadsheet programs.

Some of the specific kinds of formatting that you will want to consider at this point are as follows:

+ Adjust the column widths and row heights to make sure that there are no truncated or hidden data values. Doing this right up front will make working with the rest of the data easier.

+ Select any numeric data that should be represented as currency and change the formatting accordingly. Please note that you can select more than one cell at a time to perform formatting changes to all of the selected cells all at one time.

+ Select any numeric data that should be formatted with decimal precision and specify the number of decimal points to display. Please note – changing the number of decimal places and decimal precision may result in automatic rounding of your numeric data, which may not be what you want to occur. You have to always be mindful of the effects of rounding on numeric data!

+ Select any numeric data that should be formatted as percentages and format those data values accordingly.

+ Select any date values and make sure that these numeric values are properly formatted as dates or dates and times.

+ Select the text labels and determine if these values should have their text wrapped or spanned across multiple cells and adjust them accordingly.

+ Select any of the desired cells and change the alignment from the default alignment if it will make the data easier to read. For example, column heading labels are often centered within the cells.

Once this basic formatting of your spreadsheet is completed, it should now be much easier to review your work so far and to get ready to begin adding the calculations and formulas and functions to derive the unknown data for your spreadsheet.

Don't forget to save your work!!!

LO 3.7 Preparing for Calculating the Unknown Data

By this point, you will have a spreadsheet that is generally laid out in a very organized fashion and which contains all of the needed text labels and known data values. But all of this work so far could have been equally accomplished using a simple table in a word processing document! So now we are at the point of actually utilizing the spreadsheet program to accomplish its primary purpose in life – to perform calculations!

To prepare for entering the desired calculations, the first step is to think about what additional information you want to know about your data and then what calculations you will want to use to help you determine the unknown information.

For example, in Figure 3-7, the blue, green and red sections would have been created by this point, but the orange sections would still be yet to be completed. So at this point, you would be saying to yourself that you want to know the totals of the sales for each Division and you will want those totals to be calculated into column H in the spreadsheet. Likewise, you may want to know what the total sales were for each month in the first six months of the year. These totals, you will want to be calculated into the row 13. And then finally, you may decide that you want to see a grand total of all sales for all divisions in the first six months of the year and this calculation will end up in cell H13.

Now you know **what** calculations you want the spreadsheet to perform for you. In the next chapter, we will look at **how** you make the spreadsheet perform calculations on your known data to produce some new, unknown information.

Chapter 3 – Assignments and Projects

Directed Assignments

DA 3-1. For this directed assignment, you will be using the student data file named **DA_3-1.xlsx** to complete the required information. This file is in Microsoft Excel 2007 or newer format and should open in any contemporary spreadsheet program.

Required student data file: *DA_3-1.xlsx*

In this file, you will see information about a University's Sports Teams. The information includes the type of teams, which genders play on which teams, the number of players on each team, the number of coaching staff for each team, and the average GPA for the players for each team. There are no calculations in this spreadsheet. Rather, your task will be to simply clean up the layout of the overall spreadsheet, add and correct labels and known data, and provide basic manipulation and basic formatting to the worksheets.

1. Open the student data file named **DA_3-1.xlsx**.
2. Immediately save a copy of this file using the following specifications:
   a. File name: Rename this file using the filename *YourName_DA_3-1*
   b. File location: Place this file in any location you choose, but make a note of the location as you will need it later.
   c. File format: Because this file will be sent in to your professor, you must check with him or her to see what format **he or she** will want this file to be saved in. Don't just assume that the original file format or the default file format for your own computer will be acceptable!
3. Rename sheet1 to "Blank Worksheet" and move it to the last position in the workbook.
4. Delete the worksheet named sheet2.
5. Rename sheet3 to "University Sports" and make sure it is in the first position in the workbook.
6. Select the range A1:E1 and merge and center these cells.

7. Select the range A2:E2 and format the cells so that the text wraps within the cells. Adjust the row height to make sure there is enough (but not too much) space to show the wrapped text.

8. Select cell A3 and use the fill handle to copy this cell's contents to the range A4:A6.

9. Cut the contents of cell A8 and paste the cut label into cell A7.

10. Use the fill handle in cell A7 to copy the contents to the range A8:A10.

11. Select cell A1 *and* the range of cells A2:E2. With these cells selected, change the formatting to bold and centered.

12. Change cell A1 to have a tan background color and red font color with a font size of 20pt.

Figure DA_3-1_Completed

13. Resize column B so that none of the data is truncated.

14. Find and fix the two spelling mistakes that can be found in the text-based data.

15. The numeric value in cell C6 is a data entry error. There are not 177 Men's soccer players. Rather, there are exactly 17 players. Correct this error.

16. Select the range C3:D10 and format these numeric values to be centered within their cells.

17. Select the range E3:E10 and format these numeric values to decrease the decimal precision so that there are only two decimal places of precision for each value. (Notice that rounding will occur and that will be OK for this assignment.)

18. Insert a row between rows 6 and 7 so that you can add a new row of data that was forgotten when the original spreadsheet was created.

19. In the newly created row, perform data entry in cells A7:E7 by typing in each of these literal values that are separated by commas. One value should go into each of the five cells in the range A7:E7. The values you should enter are: **Co-Ed**, **Track and Field**, **28**, **3**, **3.45**

20. Make any final necessary adjustments to ensure readability and correctness of your work. Then, once you are sure that everything is correct, you should save your work and then submit it in accordance with your class instructions.

At the completion of this directed assignment, your final work should look very similar to Figure DA_3-1_Completed found here.

DA 3-2. For this directed assignment, you will be using the student data file named **DA_3-2.ods** to complete the required information. This file is in LibreOffice Calc version 4.2 or newer format and should open in any contemporary spreadsheet program.

Required student data file: *DA_3-2.ods*

In this workbook, you will find stock market information about some Selected Tech Stocks including things like the company name, the stock ticker symbol, the last stock price, the 52-week high and low prices, and some calculations based on those data. There are some predefined calculations in this spreadsheet that you will want to make certain that you don't change it in any way. Rather, your primary task will be to simply clean up the layout of the overall spreadsheet, add and correct labels and known data, and provide basic manipulation and basic formatting to the worksheets.

1. Open the student data file named **DA_3-2.ods**.

2. Immediately save a copy of this file using the following specifications:

   a. File name: Rename this file using the filename **YourName_DA_3-2**

   b. File location: Place this file in any location you choose, but make a note of the location as you will need it later.

   c. File format: Because this file will be sent in to your professor, you must check with him or her to see what format **he or she** will want this file to be saved in. Don't just assume that the original file format or the default file format for your own computer will be acceptable!

3. Rename Sheet1 to have the name "Blank Worksheet", color the tab color to be some shade of green, and move this worksheet to the last position in the workbook.

4. Delete the worksheet named Sheet3.

5. Rename Sheet2 to have the name "Selected Tech Stocks", color the tab to be some shade of red, and then make sure that this worksheet is positioned as the first worksheet in the workbook.

6. Select row 1 and format the row alignment so that the text wraps automatically in the cells and so that all of the text is bold and centered.

7. Adjust the column widths and row height so that the text in row one looks appropriate.

8. Select the range F2:G10 and format these numeric values to be formatted as percentages with 3 decimal places of precision.

9. Change the label in cell H1 to read, "Last Price was Closer to 52-Week High or 52-Week Low".

10. Change the formatting of the resulting values in the range H2:H10 to center.

11. Insert two blank rows above row 1.

12. Merge and center the cells A2:E2 and enter the label "Known Data For Tech-Related Stocks".

13. Merge and center the cells F2:H2 and enter the label "Calculated Data For Each Stock".

14. Merge and center cells A1:H1 and enter the label "Tech Stock Information as of May 27, 2018".

15. Change the formatting of the merged cells in row 1 to be colored some background shade of blue, have a 14pt font size, and have a solid border around the cell.

16. Format the range A2:E3 to have a background color of some shade of green and format the range

A1		fx Σ =	Tech Stock Information as of May 27, 2018					
	A	B	C	D	E	F	G	H
1			Tech Stock Information as of May 27, 2018					
2		Known Data for Tech-Related Stocks				Calculated Data for Each Stock		
3	Company	Stock Symbol	Last Price	52-Week Low	52-Week High	Last Price as Percentage Above Low	Last Price as Percentage Below High	Last Price was Closer to 52-Week High or 52-Week Low
4	Google	GOOG	$1,075.66	$894.79	$1,186.89	20.214%	9.372%	High
5	Apple	AAPL	$188.58	$142.20	$190.37	32.616%	0.940%	High
6	Microsoft	MSFT	$98.36	$68.02	$98.98	44.605%	0.626%	High
7	Oracle	ORCL	$47.00	$43.74	$53.48	7.453%	12.117%	Low
8	IBM	IBM	$143.64	$139.13	$171.13	3.242%	16.064%	Low
9	Facebook	FB	$184.92	$144.56	$195.32	27.919%	5.325%	High
10	Snapchat	SNAP	$10.71	$10.50	$21.75	2.000%	50.759%	Low
11	Twitter	TWTR	$33.63	$15.67	$36.80	114.614%	8.614%	High
12	Cisco	CSCO	$43.26	$30.36	$46.37	42.490%	6.707%	High
13								

Selected Tech Stocks / Blank Worksheet

Sheet 1 / 2   Default

Figure DA_3-2_Completed

F2:H3 to have a background color of some shade of light yellow. Also make sure that each cell has a solid border around it.

17. You suddenly realize that the information for the Disney company was included in your Tech stock spreadsheet. Completely delete the row that contains the Disney information.

18. Now you also see that one of your stocks is missing. Add a row at the bottom of your existing data with the following known data: **Cisco, CSCO, 43.26, 30.36,** and **46.37.** Make sure that the new data is formatted the same as the data directly above the new data.

19. There are accurate formulas and functions in cells F11:H11, which we will be learning about in the next chapter. But for now, since we know they are correct, simply copy-and-paste the contents of the range F11:H11 into the range F12:H12.

20. Make any final necessary adjustments to ensure readability and correctness of your work. Then, once you are sure that everything is correct, you should save your work and then submit it in accordance with your class instructions.

At the completion of this directed assignment, your final work should look very similar to Figure DA_3-2_Completed found here.

DA 3-3. For this directed assignment, you will be using the student data file named **DA_3-3.xlsx** to complete the required information. This file is in MS Excel version 2007 or newer format and should open in any contemporary spreadsheet program.

Required student data file: *DA_3-3.xlsx*

In this workbook, you will find information about some students in a class including the students' names and IDs, five quiz grades, and some predefined calculations that calculate the student and quiz averages. You will want to make certain that you don't change any of the predefined calculations in any way. Rather, your primary task will be to simply clean up the layout of the overall spreadsheet, add and correct labels and known data and provide basic manipulation and basic formatting to the worksheets.

1. Open the student data file named **DA_3-3.xlsx**.

2. Immediately save a copy of this file using the following specifications:

   a. File name: Rename this file using the filename *YourName_DA_3-3*

   b. File location: Place this file in any location you choose, but make a note of the location as you will need it later.

   c. File format: Because this file will be sent in to your professor, you must check with him or her to see what format *he or she* will want this file to be saved in. Don't just assume that the original file format or the default file format for your own computer will be acceptable!

3. Rename worksheet 1 to have the name "Student Grades".

4. Merge and center cell A1:I1 and insert the label "First Half Quiz Grades and Averages" and make the text bold and 14-point size.

5. Clear the contents of cells A2:B2 and then merge and center those two cells and insert the label "Student Name".

6. Select Cell D2 and then use the fill handle to fill the predictable series from cell D2 through cell H2.

7. Select row 2 and format the cell alignment to wrap the text in the cells, make the text bold, and center the text within the cells.

8. Select cells A16:C16 and merge and center these cells.

9. Change all of the averages in column I and row 16 to have one single digit of decimal precision.

10. Change column I and row 16 to be bold and centered for all cells.

11. Change the general coloring of the spreadsheet so that cell A1 is a shade of green, cells A2:I2 and cell A17 are a shade of red, cells I3:I6 and D17:H17 are a shade of tan, and cell I17 is a shade of yellow. Make sure all of the cells that you colored in this step are also bold and centered.

12. While working on the data, you recognize that your own student information is missing from the spreadsheet. Imagine that you have a student ID that is some 6-digit number between 800000 and 900000. Notice now that all of the students are currently sorted in ascending Student ID order! Insert a new row *in the proper location* for you to enter your own data. Because you will choose a student ID number somewhere between 800000 and 900000, your inserted row will be somewhere between rows 12 and 14. In this row you will enter your own first name, your own last name, and your fictitious student ID. Your scores for the five quizzes were **92, 90, 99, 88,** and **97.** Make the data in this new row bold so it can be easily found.

13. There are accurate functions in the cells I3:I15 that we will be learning about in the next chapter. But for now, you can copy any one of those cells into the new blank cell in column I in the same row where you just entered your own data for step 12 above. This should complete the entire new row that you just created.

A1			f_x	First Half Quiz Grades and Averages					

	Student Name		Student ID	Quiz 1	Quiz 2	Quiz 3	Quiz 4	Quiz 5	Overall Student Averages
1	**First Half Quiz Grades and Averages**								
3	Yuli	Clay	100040	77	100	81	88	72	83.6
4	Scott	Hunt	239939	96	83	99	94	89	92.2
5	Winter	Vaughn	348154	96	91	85	85	98	91.0
6	Macy	Walton	377211	84	79	92	98	87	88.0
7	Fuller	Schultz	403023	78	77	100	95	89	87.8
8	Reuben	Hall	422422	76	92	73	89	83	82.6
9	Nigel	Hopkins	511068	97	93	80	93	60	84.6
10	Violet	Manning	535532	94	87	81	79	68	81.8
11	Wylie	Bullock	662332	97	88	74	86	66	82.2
12	Larissa	Sosa	774313	100	82	98	66	69	83.0
13	*Your First*	*Your Last*	**800001**	**92**	**90**	**99**	**98**	**97**	95.2
14	Molly	Zebryn	877213	60	98	98	84	72	82.4
15	Sawyer	Best	943092	75	98	99	88	71	86.2
16	Donovan	Odonnell	958901	88	68	86	90	100	86.4
17	**Overall Class Averages**			86.4	87.6	88.9	88.1	80.1	86.2

Student Grades

Figure DA_3-3_Completed

14. Inspect the overall quiz averages in the cell range D17:H17 and then highlight the quiz with the best overall average so that it is dark green text with a light green background and a black border. Apply this same formatting by using the format painter to highlight the highest individual student average in range of cells I3:I16.

15. Make any final necessary adjustments to ensure readability and correctness of your work. Then, once you are sure that everything is correct, you should save your work and then submit it in accordance with your class instructions.

At the completion of this directed assignment, your final work should look very similar to Figure DA_3-3_Completed found here.

Creative Projects

CP 3-1. For this creative project, you will be making improvements to a file that was begun by one of your colleagues who is now currently on vacation. This file is in LibreOffice Calc version 4.2 or newer format and should open in any contemporary spreadsheet program.

Required student data file: *CP_3-1.ods*

When you open this file, you should immediately save a copy of this file with the name *YourName_CP_3-1* in the file format as instructed in your class. In this file, you will see that column A contains a list of beverages that were sold at your concession stand over the first three days of last week. You also notice that some calculations of totals and averages have already been entered into the spreadsheet in columns I, J, and in row 14.

There are several tasks that your boss wants you to accomplish while your colleague is out on vacation:

1. First, you need to fill in the number of cups sold for each of the remaining four days of last week into the appropriate cells. Those numbers are here:

a.	Cola	189	57	140	70
b.	Diet Cola	162	156	101	144
c.	Root Beer	45	57	108	38
d.	Diet Root Beer	123	122	72	88
e.	White Soda	175	17	198	28
f.	Diet White Soda	108	58	123	56
g.	Sweetened Tea	153	98	194	174
h.	Unsweetened Tea	48	23	10	80
i.	Lemonade	150	146	149	130
j.	Coffee	183	98	122	97
k.	Decaf Coffee	62	102	137	153
l.	Hot Tea	87	42	128	27

2. Next, you need to add appropriate column labels that specify the day and the date of each of the days for last week.

3. Next, you need to reformat the entire sheet to make sure that the text is all readable and to make sure that the numeric calculations "make sense"(e.g. not too many decimal places).

4. Also, there should be an overall heading for the entire sheet that shows that this is the weekly sales of soft drinks from Concession Stand #1.

5. Also, this worksheet should be named "Week 1" because after it is all cleaned up, the boss wants you to copy the entire sheet and paste it into a new, second sheet that will be named "Week 2".

6. Finally, on the Week 2 sheet, the boss wants you to clear out all of the known data for the actual cups that will be sold next week and update the dates to be next week's dates. What will be left in the file at the end then will be a completed Week 1 sheet and a Week 2 sheet that is just an open shell for the new week to be filled in when your colleague returns from vacation. There should be no other "leftover" sheets in your workbook.

Remember to check your final work for spelling, grammar, and overall correctness and then submit your file in the manner prescribed for your class.

CP 3-2. For this creative project, you have just been hired as an intern at the local animal shelter and they have just gotten swamped with a large number of new intakes into the shelter. Your new boss has asked you to create a spreadsheet to help track all of the new animals that have arrived recently. Since this is a brand new task, you have nothing to start with, you are on your own!

Required student data file: None. Start with a new, blank workbook file and name the file *YourName_CP_3-2*.

Here is the type of information that the boss wants you to track:

✦ The date that the animal showed up at the shelter (usually called an "Intake Date")

✦ The type of animal (e.g. dog, cat, bird, reptile, etc.)

✦ The breed of the animal (if known)

✦ The color of the animal

✦ The age of the animal (if known or else an educated guess)

✦ A "yes-or-no" field if the animal needs medical attention

✦ A "yes-or-no" field if the animal is adoptable right away

✦ Make sure you add in the information for the last 10 animals that were brought in last week (*for this data, you will just make up typical data for animals in your local animal shelter*)

Make sure that all of the columns have meaningful text labels. Also, make sure that there is an overall label for the entire contents of the worksheet and that the worksheet tab itself has been properly named.

There are no calculations to be made in this worksheet yet. At this time, all the boss wants is just the overall layout for the worksheet and the data entry of the appropriate labels and the known data. Once you have completed setting up the worksheet, apply appropriate basic formatting to the entire sheet.

Remember to check your final work for spelling, grammar, and overall correctness and then submit your file in the manner prescribed for your class.

CP 3-3. For this creative project, you have been asked by a friend to set up a new spreadsheet to track a little-league sports team for the twelve (12) games of their season. Your friend doesn't know how to work with spreadsheets so there is nothing for you to start with except your own spreadsheet skills!

Required student data file: None: Start with a new, blank workbook file and name the file _YourName_CP_3-3._

Here is the type of information that the friend would like to see tracked:

+ The number of the game in the season, (e.g. 1, 2, 3, and so on)
+ The name of the opponent team
+ The date of the game
+ The weekday of the game
+ Whether the game was played at Home or Away
+ Our team's final score
+ The opponent team's final score
+ Whether the game ended in a "Win", "Loss", or a "Tie"
+ Make sure you add in the information for the first 5 games that have already been played (_for this data, you will just make up typical data for whatever sport you chose_)
+ Make sure that you complete as much of the remaining data that can be filled in (e.g. you can fill in the rest of the schedule for the games that haven't been completed yet and just leave the scores and the win/loss/time columns blank)

Make sure that all of the columns have meaningful text labels. Also, make sure that there is an overall label for the entire contents of the worksheet and that the worksheet tab itself has been properly named.

There are no calculations to be made in this worksheet yet. At this time, all that your friend wants is just the overall layout for the team schedule and the data entry of the appropriate labels and the known data. Once you have completed setting up the worksheet, apply appropriate basic formatting to the entire sheet.

Remember to check your final work for spelling, grammar, and overall correctness and then submit your file in the manner prescribed for your class.

Source: Shutterstock, Inc.

Chapter 4

References, Calculations, Formulas, and Functions

Why are references, calculations, formulas, and functions so important?

Now that we understand the basic terminology that is associated with spreadsheets, and we understand how to plan a spreadsheet and set up the basic known data within a spreadsheet, we now are ready to perform the most important activities that you will do in a spreadsheet: Calculate the unknown data!

As your recall from Chapter 1, this is the primary reason why we use spreadsheets. The spreadsheet program will perform calculations to derive previously unknown data from the known data that you have entered into the worksheet.

In this chapter we will discover how spreadsheets will allow you to perform calculations on numeric and text data and appropriately leverage all of the known data that you have entered into your spreadsheet.

Key Terms

- absolute cell references
- arguments or parameters
- cell ranges
- comparison operators
- equal sign
- formula bar
- formula
- function categories
- functions
- insert function dialog
- mathematical operators
- mixed cell references
- optional
- relative cell references
- required
- resulting value
- rounding
- showing all formulas
- text operators

LO 4.1   Simple Formulas to Complete Calculations

In the previous chapter, we learned about entering data into a spreadsheet. To enter simple text or numbers, you simply begin typing the information in the cell where you want that information to appear and then press the enter key.

Now, however, we want to perform a calculation. To perform any calculation in a spreadsheet, you must let the spreadsheet know that you intend for it to do this work. This is accomplished by typing an equal sign (=) before typing the rest of the desired calculation.

In Figures 4-1 and 4-2, we see the process of typing a simple formula into a spreadsheet in cell A1. In Figure 4-1, we see that the formula starts out with an equal sign, and then is followed by the equation "3 + 4". (**Note:** you do not need to type spaces in between the values and the operators, but it does aid in readability. This will be discussed in more detail later on in this chapter.)

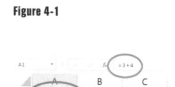

Figure 4-1

To think about what is happening in this cell, you can consider reading this newly typed formula as though it was saying the following to you:

> "The resulting value in cell A1 will equal the calculation of the number three plus the number four."

Figure 4-2

Now, we all know from grade school math that 3 + 4 = 7, but observe what happens when the formula in cell A1 is completed by pressing the enter key on the keyboard. Figure 4-2 shows that cell A1 now *seems* to have two different things going on! In the cell A1 within the worksheet area, we see the resulting value of the calculation – the number 7. This is indicated with a green circle. The resulting value of a cell is the final result after all calculations have been completed for a cell. This is what is eventually displayed within the cell.

But we also notice a second thing is going on here: In the formula bar, we see the actual contents of the cell is the formula that was typed: "= 3 + 4". This is indicated with the red circle. The formula bar will always show the *actual cell contents* regardless of what the resulting value of a cell may be.

Over time, as a spreadsheet is developed, there will eventually be as many formulas and functions contained within a spreadsheet as there are raw data values. As a result, it is often helpful to be able to see exactly which cells have raw data values (e.g. the known data that was keyed in) vs. which cells have calculations (e.g. the formulas or functions that were keyed in to derive the unknown data.)

All contemporary spreadsheet programs allow you to change the view of a spreadsheet to change what is displayed in the spreadsheet. This is known as showing all formulas. By changing the view, you can *toggle* between the normal view and the formula view of a spreadsheet. In the normal view, the spreadsheet displays the resulting values of the calculations, along with all of their formatting, in the content areas of the cells. But in the formula view, the spreadsheet will display the actual cell contents in the cell area itself. That way you can quickly see which cells have literal values and which cells have calculations.

Figures 4-3 and 4-4 show the same spreadsheet in these two different views. This is a spreadsheet showing the sales of pizzas for the month of July for Patty's Pizza Parlor. Figure 4-3 shows the normal view of the spreadsheet. Here we can see some interesting information for the store. We can see that the cheese pizza is the lowest costing item and the Hawaiian pizza is the most expensive pizza. We

	A	B	C	D
1		Patty's Pizza Parlor		
2		July's Monthly Sales		
3	Pizza	Unit Price	Quantity Sold	Total Revenue
4	3-Cheese	$ 7.99	453	$ 3,619.47
5	Pepperoni	$ 9.99	398	$ 3,976.02
6	Sausage	$ 9.99	324	$ 3,236.76
7	Canadian Bacon	$ 9.99	289	$ 2,887.11
8	Vegetarian	$ 8.99	403	$ 3,622.97
9	Hawaiian	$ 10.99	348	$ 3,824.52
10	Totals		2215	$ 21,166.85

Figure 4-3

	A	B	C	D
1		Patty's Pizza Parlor		
2		July's Monthly Sales		
3	Pizza	Unit Price	Quantity Sold	Total Revenue
4	3-Cheese	7.99	453	=C4*B4
5	Pepperoni	9.99	398	=C5*B5
6	Sausage	9.99	324	=C6*B6
7	Canadian Bacon	9.99	289	=C7*B7
8	Vegetarian	8.99	403	=C8*B8
9	Hawaiian	10.99	348	=C9*B9
10	Totals		=SUM(C4:C9)	=SUM(D4:D9)

Figure 4-4

can also see that the total number of pizzas sold was 2,215 and the total revenue brought in for the month was $21,166.85. We can also see the individual totals for each of the pizza types sold in the month. In other words, we can see a lot of valuable information about the sales in the store for this month.

But now, in Figure 4-4, we see the same spreadsheet information but displayed using the formula view. Here we can see that the formatting has been removed from the values in columns B and D. We can also see that the values in row 10 are not literal values but rather are actual calculations. Likewise, we see that the values in column D are actually the results of calculations as well.

All of the versions of the different spreadsheet programs will allow you to toggle between these two views, but the specific keyboard shortcuts or commands that you will use to switch between the views are not always the same. In most versions of spreadsheet programs, the keyboard shortcut of Ctrl+` will switch these views. This is accomplished by pressing the control-key at the same time as the grave key (which is a backwards-facing single tic-mark.) Pressing this key combination will allow you to quickly toggle back and forth between these two views.

You may have noticed that in Figure 4-4, the calculations in column D and in row 10 did not use literal values, but rather seemed to refer to specific cells. This concept is called cell referencing and this will be discussed in detail in the next three sections.

LO 4.2   Cell Referencing – Relative References

In Chapter 2, we learned that a range is a collection of one-to-many contiguous (touching) cells. Cell Ranges are always described from the upper-left cell through the lower-right cell with a colon separating the two corner references (e.g. A4:C15 or D37:F44). When speaking about cell ranges, typically the range will be spoken by stating the first cell (the upper-left cell) and then saying the word "through" and then stating the last cell (the lower-right cell). So the cell range A4:C15 would be read aloud as "A4 through C15".

The designations of "A4" and "C15" are relative cell references. Relative cell references are indicated by using the column letter followed by a row number with no other prefix characters. Examples of relative cell references are F11 (column F row 11), X349 (column X row 349), and AA2732 (column AA row 2732).

To help understand why these cell references are called *relative* cell references, it may help to imagine yourself sitting in a classroom on three different days. Figure 4-5 represents the first day. Now, ask yourself this question and observe your answer: "Who is the person sitting immediately to my right?" Well, the answer to this question might be very simple – you

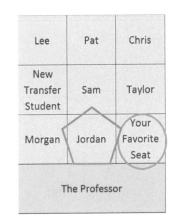

Figure 4-5

might say, "The person sitting to my right is my best friend, Jordan, who takes all of the same classes that I take and who helps me out with my homework!" In all of the examples, your seat is circled with green and the person to your right is indicated with red.

But then, what if during Tuesday's class, Sam takes your favorite seat and now you have to sit in a different seat? Figure 4-6 shows the seating chart on Tuesday. This time, your answer to the question of "Who is the person sitting immediately to my right?" becomes a little more interesting. Now, you might have to say, "The person sitting to my right is a new transfer student whose name I don't know! I need to introduce myself before class starts!" When you do introduce yourself, you discover that the new transfer student's name is "Skylar".

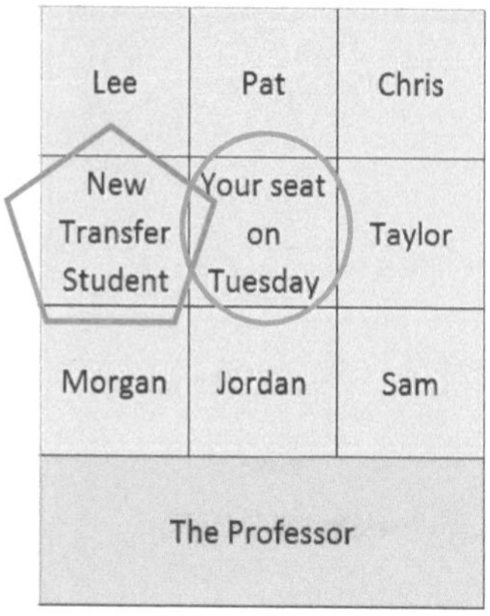

As we are starting to see, the answer to the question "Who is the person sitting immediately to my right?" is not just a simple question that has one, and only one, correct answer! Rather, the answer to this question is variable and changes based on the current circumstances. Specifically, the answer to the question is dependent upon the *location of the data relative to the location of where the question is being asked.*

This type of relative referencing can also have some other unexpected results. For the final example, please observe what happens to the seating chart on Friday. Figure 4-7 represents what happens on Friday when your favorite seat is taken because you overslept and you were almost late for class. Now, if you answer the question, "who is the person sitting immediately to my right?", your answer may be "There is nobody sitting to my right because the only open seat was the one next to the wall in the back corner."

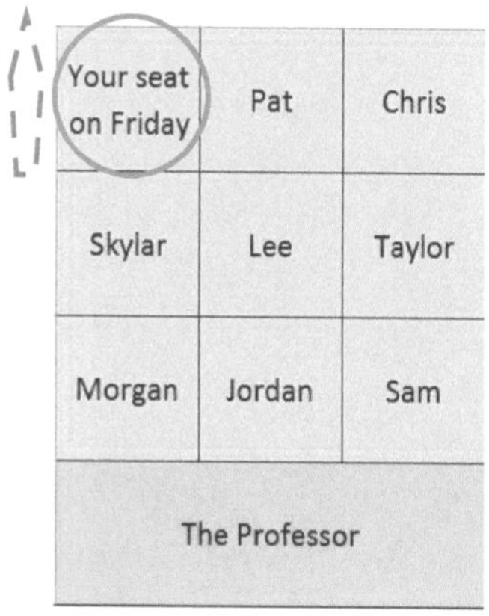

What we see here is that the answer to the simple question is not a constant answer because the answer depends upon the location of where you are sitting to begin with. The answer is, therefore, **relative** to where you are sitting when you ask and answer the question.

Now let's apply this concept of relative references to spreadsheets.

One of the simplest ways to create a relative reference to a cell is to simply select a cell and then type the equal sign (=), then select some other cell, and then press the enter key. Figure 4-8 shows a spreadsheet where the user is in the process of creating a relative reference. Here, the user is typing in

Figure 4-6

Figure 4-7

Figure 4-8

cell B10. The user typed the equal sign and then clicked on the cell C3. There are several things that you can observe here. First, the referenced cell has been colored blue and the cell reference in the formula is colored with the same corresponding color of blue. Please note that the specific colors that are used will vary with each spreadsheet program, but there will be some form of coloring that will be used to help you recognize which cells are being referenced.

When the user hits the enter key, the resulting value in cell B10 will be the same resulting value of the referenced cell. Since the resulting value in cell C3 is $25.79, the resulting value in cell B10 will also be $25.79.

To think further about how this cell reference is a relative reference, think about the *locations* of each cell involved. The destination cell B10 is referencing a cell that is 7 rows up above itself and one column to the right of itself.

This concept becomes significant when we think about what happens when we copy-and-paste cells from one location to another.

In Figure 4-9, we see the user in the process of copying the contents of cell B10, to the destination cell C8.

	A	B	C	D	E	F	G
1		January	February	March	April	May	June
2	Dept. 1	$ 438.41	$ 470.02	$ 209.36	$ 186.51	$ 274.95	$ 353.48
3	Dept. 2	$ 397.51	$ 25.79	$ 297.99	$ 252.32	$ 279.63	$ 431.01
4	Dept. 3	$ 76.45	$ 476.70	$ 283.54	$ 259.98	$ 58.25	$ 127.85
5	Dept. 4	$ 194.76	$ 65.62	$ 410.81	$ 247.02	$ 65.79	$ 440.56
6	Dept. 5	$ 123.03	$ 293.00	$ 1.75	$ 90.28	$ 487.40	$ 385.24
7							
8			=D1				
9							
10		$ 25.79					
11							
12							

Figure 4-9

In this example, the user copied the contents of the cell from B10 to C8, which means that the content was copied up two rows from where it started and over to the right one column from where it started. As we recall, the actual cell contents of cell B10 was "=C3" before the user copied-and-pasted the cell to the new location of cell C8. Because this cell contained the relative reference, this *relative reference is automatically updated to reflect the new location*. So the new contents in cell C8 becomes "=D1" and when the user completes the copy-and-paste, the ending resulting value in cell C8 displays the label "March".

To recap – A relative cell reference occurs by simply typing the column label followed by the row number of a cell. The majority of the cell references in spreadsheet calculations are relative references. Additionally and most importantly, anytime a cell contains a relative cell reference to another cell, these relative references will be automatically updated whenever these references are copied-and-pasted to some other, new location.

LO 4.3   Cell Referencing – Absolute References

Absolute cell references are indicated by prefixing both the column letter and the row number of a cell reference with the prefix character of a dollar sign ($). Examples of absolute cell references are $F$11 (absolutely column F and absolutely row 11), $X$349 (absolutely column X and absolutely row 349), and $AA$2732 (absolutely column AA and absolutely row 2732).

The purpose of prefixing the column or row reference with the dollar sign is to force the particular reference to become permanent and non-changing. As opposed to relative cell references, **absolute cell references are not updated or changed in any way** whenever these references are copied-and-pasted to new locations. In LO 4.6 and 4.8, we will be exploring examples of why you would want to use absolute references instead of relative references in some calculations.

LO 4.4   Cell Referencing – Mixed References

Mixed cell references are indicated by prefixing **either** the column letter or the row number of a cell reference with the prefix character of a dollar sign ($). Examples of mixed cell references are $F11 (absolutely column F and relative row 11), X$349 (relative column X and absolutely row 349), and $AA2732 (absolutely column AA and relative row 2732).

The purpose of using mixed cell references is to *lock down* the absolute portion of a cell reference while leaving the relative portion of the cell reference to be able to be updated when you copy-and-paste the mixed reference. This type of referencing is probably used the least frequently but can be beneficial in some circumstances.

LO 4.5   Simple Formulas Using Cell Referencing

Now that we have explored the different ways in which you can reference cells, our next objective is to use cell references in some simple formulas to perform some simple calculations. A formula is a simple calculation that contains the following things:

1. All formulas start with an equal sign (=) as the first character in the cell.
2. All formulas will contain one or more of the following:
   a. . . . zero or more literal values. Numeric examples of literal values include values like 415.87 and 52 and 0.01457. Text examples of literal values include values like "Pizza" and "Department 001" and "Participant #". Notice that text literal values are always surrounded in quotation marks!
   b. . . . zero or more cell references. Cell reference examples include things like F11, and X349 and AA2732.
   c. . . . zero or more operators. Operators include all of the Mathematical Operators (^, *, /, +, –,), Text Operators (&), and/or Comparison Operators (<, >, <=, >=, =, <>) that were defined in chapter 2.
   d. . . . zero or more functions. Functions are named calculations that will be more fully discussed in LO 4.6.
3. All formulas, after the equal sign as described in item #1 above, **must contain at least one** of the items listed in items 2(a) through 2(d) above.

For this discussion on basic formulas, let's imagine we are creating a shopping list to purchase some fresh fruit for an upcoming picnic. Figure 4-10 shows this shopping list with labels and known data already entered. The user is just now beginning to type in the first formula.

As we can see in the example, the user has begun to enter a formula to calculate the first item's Extended Cost in cell D3. Here are the steps that the user has taken to begin this formula:

1. The user selected cell D3 to make it the active cell.

2. The user typed the equal sign (=) to tell the spreadsheet that she was beginning to create a calculation.

3. The user clicked on cell A3 to create a relative reference to that cell which contains the quantity to be purchased (2).

4. The user entered the asterisk (*), which is the operator that is used to perform multiplication.

5. The user clicked on cell C3 to create a relative reference to that cell which contains the unit price of the items to be purchased ($2.99).

C3	▾	✕	✓	fx	=A3*C3	
	A	B			C	D
1		Picnic Fresh Fruit Shopping List				
2	Quantity	Description			Unit Price	Extended Price
3	2	Large Bag of Apples			$ 2.99	=A3*C3
4	5	Pounds of Bananas			$ 0.89	
5	2	Large Bags of Oranges			$ 3.97	
6	4	Pounds of Strawberries			$ 2.49	
7	5	Pounds of Green Grapes			$ 0.99	
8	3	Whole Pineapples			$ 2.59	
9	4	Whole Watermelons			$ 2.99	

Figure 4-10

6. The user is now ready to hit the enter key. When she does, the resulting value will be displayed in cell D3 ($5.98).

By using the combination of relative cell references and the mathematical operation of multiplication, the user was able to quickly calculate the line item price for each item that she will be getting from the produce stand.

Now, let's discuss why this particular way of creating calculations is so important. First off, could you imagine the user typing the following into cell D3 instead of typing the formula as it was described above:

= 2 * 2.99

Wouldn't we end up with the exact same answer by using literal values instead of the cell references?

The short answer is, yes, 2 times 2.99 will always equal 5.98 whether we use literal values or relative cell references. So then, why is it always better to use the cell references?

Well, there are actually two reasons why using cell references is better than using literal values in formulas. For the first reason, let's imagine that we learn that the number of people attending our picnic is going to double and so we now need to double our shopping list! When we change all of the known values in column A to reflect the new, larger quantities that we will need to buy, what else do we want to change as well?

The unit price of the items (column C) won't change just because we are buying more quantities, but what about column D – the Extended Price? We would want this column to automatically reflect the new calculation by using the new quantities! Now, if we use cell references in our formulas, then when the value of a cell changes, then all of the other cells that reference the changed cell will also automatically be updated!

The second reason why using cell references is better than using literal values in formulas comes into play when the user wants to complete the other calculations in cells D4:D9. While it is true that the user could simply re-key in all of the individual formulas in each of those cells, that becomes a lot of typing with a lot of opportunity to make errors!

But what about using the copy-and-paste function that we are already familiar with? By copying the completed formula from cell D3 and pasting that formula in cells D4:D9, the relative cell references will automatically become updated to reflect the new cell locations. In other words, the user only had to type the formula in once and then because of the relative cell references, she could simply copy-and-paste the formula to all of the other desired locations and the new resulting values will all be instantly updated to the correct answers! This would not happen if the user typed in literal values instead of cell references for the first formula in cell D3.

Literal values used in calculations cannot be automatically updated and should therefore be avoided most of the time! Generally speaking, calculations in spreadsheets should use cell references instead of literal values.

LO 4.6   Functions as Compared to Formulas

Now that we understand that we can complete simple calculations by entering formulas into our spreadsheets, it may be pretty tempting to begin to tackle larger projects with this newfound power! After all, isn't that why we use spreadsheets – to perform calculations?

While it is true that simple calculations can be used easily within a spreadsheet program, we will quickly discover that there are some limitations to using simple formulas exclusively within spreadsheets. To discover some of these limitations, let's continue and expand our shopping list example used above.

In Figure 4-11, we see that the individual line items have had their extended prices calculated when the formula in cell D3 was copied down to the cells D4:D9. The next unknown piece of information that the user wanted to know was, "what is the total amount that we are planning to spend for fresh fruit for this picnic?"

In order to calculate this unknown value, the user knows that she has to add up all of the individual line items' extended costs. As an initial attempt to create this calculation, we can see that in cell D10, a simple addition formula is being entered to add up all of the extended prices that exist for each line item in cells D3:D9.

Figure 4-11

While this formula will, in fact, give the correct answer at this particular point in time, what we will discover is that there is a problem with this type of simple formula.

When the user hits the enter key, the spreadsheet appropriately calculates the resulting value and shows the user that the total of the shopping list, at this moment in time, is $53.01.

But what happens to the spreadsheet in the following scenario? What if the user decides that she also wants to buy 5 Pounds of Red Grapes to go along with the 5 Pounds of Green Grapes? In Figure 4-12, we see the results when the user inserts a new line item in between rows 6 and 7 for the red grapes.

Figure 4-12

The total calculation in cell D11 is noticeably *missing* the newly added cell in its calculation! As a result, the total calculation in cell D11 now needs to be manually updated to include the addition of the newly added cell D7!

This is the problem with using simple formulas exclusively to perform calculations in spreadsheet: As the data in the spreadsheet changes with rows and columns be added and removed, the cell references will be updated but will **not** automatically include any new rows or columns that are added!

Additionally, our example includes less than 10 rows of data – a very small number of rows. But this is not the reality of most spreadsheets! In the "real world," spreadsheets typically have hundreds or thousands, or even tens of thousands or more rows of data! When this is the reality, nobody is going to enter a formula to add up all of those rows by typing "=A1 + A2 + A3 + A4 . . . " and continuing on for several hundreds or thousands of rows! There had to be a better way of accomplishing this kind of task!

From the earliest versions of spreadsheet programs, there was a recognized need to be able to quickly perform some common actions on large collections of data without having to manually type in the very verbose formulas with individual cell references. This concept and its implementation came to be known as functions.

A function in a spreadsheet is a uniquely named, predefined calculation that will return a specific value when it is given its appropriate required and/or optional parameters or arguments.

The following table lists some of the more commonly used functions:

Function Name	Function Syntax	Function Parameters or Arguments	Purpose and Results of Function
SUM	=SUM(*arg1*, *arg2...*)	At least one required argument must be supplied	This function will perform addition on all of the values, references, or ranges that are included in the comma-separated argument list and will return a numeric value.
AVERAGE	=AVERAGE (*arg1*, *arg2...*)	At least one required argument must be supplied	This function will calculate the average of the values, references, or ranges that are included in the comma-separated argument list and will return a numeric value.
TODAY	=TODAY()	No arguments	This function takes no parameters or arguments but returns the current computer system date.
PMT	=PMT(*periodic_ interest_rate, total_ loan_periods, present_ value*, *future_value, payment_type*)	Three required arguments or parameters and two optional parameters	This function takes a periodic interest rate, the total number of payments for a loan, and the original value of the loan and calculates a loan payment based on those three values and returns a negative value representing the payment amount to be paid back during each periodic payment.

Table 4-1

Function Name	Function Syntax	Function Parameters or Arguments	Purpose and Results of Function
MIN	=MIN(*arg1*, arg2...)	At least one required argument must be supplied	This function will return the smallest value in the argument list.
MAX	=MAX(*arg1*, arg2...)	At least one required argument must be supplied	This function will return the largest value in the argument list.
COUNT	=COUNT(*arg1*, arg2...)	At least one required argument must be supplied	This function will return the count of all numeric values in the argument list.
COUNTA	=COUNTA(*arg1*, arg2...)	At least one required argument must be supplied	This function will return the count of all non-blank values in the argument list.

Table 4-1 (Continued)

Note that for some functions, the parameters or arguments may be a single cell reference or a literal value while for other functions, the parameters or arguments may be cell ranges. So let's return to our previous example of the Fresh Fruit Shopping List.

In Figure 4-13, we see the total calculation for the shopping list has now been replaced with the **SUM** function with a cell range as its one required parameter. By using the range of cells D3:D10, the SUM function will now add up all of the values in that range and return the sum of all of those cells in the resulting value in cell D11.

As you can imagine, being able to perform an operation on all of the cells in a large range of cells makes the spreadsheet program an extremely powerful tool to use. With the spreadsheet and functions, you can perform calculations on very large collections of data with extreme ease!

	A	B	C	D	E
1		Picnic Fresh Fruit Shopping List			
2	Quantity	Description	Unit Price	Extended Price	
3	2	Large Bag of Apples	$ 2.99	$ 5.98	
4	5	Pounds of Bananas	$ 0.89	$ 4.45	
5	2	Large Bags of Oranges	$ 3.97	$ 7.94	
6	4	Pounds of Strawberries	$ 2.49	$ 9.96	
7	5	Pounds of Red Grapes	$ 0.99	$ 4.95	
8	5	Pounds of Green Grapes	$ 0.99	$ 4.95	
9	3	Whole Pineapples	$ 2.59	$ 7.77	
10	4	Whole Watermelons	$ 2.99	$ 11.96	
11		Total Shopping List Budget		=SUM(D3:D10)	
12					

Figure 4-13

As we consider using ranges as the arguments or parameters of functions, we should probably define these items in a little more detail.

Arguments or Parameters are literal values, cell references, cell ranges, or other formulas or functions that are placed in specific positions within a function (and separated by commas) to allow the function to perform its preprogrammed calculation. Some arguments or parameters may be Required in order for the function to work and other arguments or parameters may be Optional and may be omitted if desired. Additionally, some functions actually take **no arguments or parameters**. These functions will still have an open and close parenthesis but with nothing in between to show that there are, in fact, no parameters being supplied. The TODAY() function and the NOW() function are two examples of functions that take no parameters or arguments.

LO 4.7 Simple Functions Using Cell Referencing

In Learning Objective LO 4.6, we saw that a user could use the simple SUM function to total up all of the line items for the Fresh Fruit Shopping List. This was our first example of using a simple function with cell references. Now, we will look at another example of a calculation using a different simple function but also using the same cell references.

In Figure 4-14, we see that the user has decided to add another calculation to the bottom of the spreadsheet to calculate the *average* fresh fruit cost for this shopping list. Here, you can see that the average function is using the same range of cells (D3:D10) as the argument or parameter that was used in the SUM function in cell D11.

By using cell references, any changes to the underlying values will automatically update the resulting value in both of these calculated cells.

But there is another feature of spreadsheets at work here that needs to be further explored. Consider the differences between the two values in cell D12 in Figures 4-15 and 4-16.

In Figure 4-15, the user has completed the average function and the default formatting for currency values automatically shows dollars and cents. As a result, the average fresh fruit cost *appears* to be $7.25 in cell D12.

But what we are seeing as the resulting value of $7.25 isn't exactly completely accurate! As we can see in Figure 4-16, the highlighted tool has been used to increase the decimal precision of the displayed value in cell D12. As a result, we can see that the actual average cost for the fresh fruit is $7.245!

The effect that we are observing here is the effect of rounding. Rounding is the default behavior in spreadsheet programs

	A	B	C	D	E
1		Picnic Fresh Fruit Shopping List				
2	Quantity	Description	Unit Price	Extended Price	
3	2	Large Bag of Apples	$ 2.99	$ 5.98	
4	5	Pounds of Bananas	$ 0.89	$ 4.45	
5	2	Large Bags of Oranges	$ 3.97	$ 7.94	
6	4	Pounds of Strawberries	$ 2.49	$ 9.96	
7	5	Pounds of Red Grapes	$ 0.99	$ 4.95	
8	5	Pounds of Green Grapes	$ 0.99	$ 4.95	
9	3	Whole Pineapples	$ 2.59	$ 7.77	
10	4	Whole Watermelons	$ 2.99	$ 11.96	
11		Total Shopping List Budget		$ 57.96	
12		Average Fruit Cost		=AVERAGE(D3:D10)	
13					

Figure 4-14

D12   ƒx   =AVERAGE(D3:D10)

	A	B	C	D	E
1		Picnic Fresh Fruit Shopping List				
2	Quantity	Description	Unit Price	Extended Price	
3	2	Large Bag of Apples	$ 2.99	$ 5.98	
4	5	Pounds of Bananas	$ 0.89	$ 4.45	
5	2	Large Bags of Oranges	$ 3.97	$ 7.94	
6	4	Pounds of Strawberries	$ 2.49	$ 9.96	
7	5	Pounds of Red Grapes	$ 0.99	$ 4.95	
8	5	Pounds of Green Grapes	$ 0.99	$ 4.95	
9	3	Whole Pineapples	$ 2.59	$ 7.77	
10	4	Whole Watermelons	$ 2.99	$ 11.96	
11		Total Shopping List Budget		$ 57.96	
12		Average Fruit Cost		$ 7.25	
13					
14					

Figure 4-15

that specifies that calculated numeric values will automatically be adjusted to a specific fixed number of decimal places of precision based on the cells current formatting. If the fractional digit that is one digit beyond the desired number of displayed digits has a value of 5 or greater, then the final displayed value is rounded-up or increased by one value in the last displayed decimal position. But if the fractional digit that is one digit beyond the desired number of displayed digits has a value of 4 or less, then the remaining decimal digits are simply truncated from the final displayed value.

Figure 4-16

In many instances, numeric rounding is perfectly acceptable and even desirable. As in our example, it is sufficient to allow the rounding to occur to show that the average fresh fruit price is $7.25. This is acceptable because we don't have the ability to work with fractional pennies!

But with that being said, it is very important to remember that the **actual** value that the spreadsheet is holding as the calculated value in the cell is the **non-rounded** value!

What this means is that the actual value that is being calculated in cell C12 is actually **$7.245**. Figure 4-16 shows this actual value. The tool in the ribbon that is highlighted with a red circled is the tool that was used to increase the decimal precision of the selected cell. Increasing and decreasing the decimal precision of numeric cells is a very common technique that is often used when working with numeric calculations. It is critical to remember that **rounding** of numeric calculations is the default behavior of spreadsheets. Additionally, rounded numeric results may or may not be what you want to be displayed for a particular calculation. You must remember that you are in complete control of the effects of rounding within your spreadsheets.

LO 4.8 **Categories of Functions**

Now that you have a basic understanding of the concepts of spreadsheet formulas and functions, you are probably beginning to gain an appreciation for the powerful types of calculations that can be performed within a spreadsheet program. But for some, this can also seem a bit overwhelming! Just how many different kinds of calculations can a spreadsheet perform? And how do you go about discovering all of the functions that might be available to work with?

Spreadsheet programs have been continuously evolving for over 20 years. But some of the most basic functions haven't changed a single bit since the very first spreadsheet programs.

So, would it surprise you to know that there are a minimum of over 400 functions in most contemporary spreadsheet programs?! With this many powerful functions at your fingertips, it may indeed seem overwhelming to think about how you will go about learning all of the nuances of all of these functions.

Fortunately, all of the contemporary spreadsheet programs have provided some ways to help you learn about all of the various functions that are available to you.

The first thing that the spreadsheet programs provide for you is a categorization of all of the functions that are available for you. Each of the functions that you could use has been grouped into a category along with other similarly related functions.

The following table shows a partial list of function categories and descriptions of the functions that are found in each category:

Function Category Name	Description
Most Recently Used or **Last Used**	Shows only the functions that have been used recently on this machine.
All or **Not Filtered**	Shows absolutely all of the functions that are available on this machine.
Financial	Shows all of the mathematical financial functions.
Date & Time	Functions used for inserting, calculating and formatting dates and times.
Math & Trig or **Mathematical**	Shows all of the mathematical and trigonometric functions.
Statistical or **Array**	Shows all of the statistical functions and some functions that work on single- or multi-dimensional arrays of values.
Lookup & Reference or **Spreadsheet**	Shows functions that can be used to seek information within the contents of a spreadsheet and then return related information based on the results.
Database	Shows functions that treat a row of data as a single record.
Text	Shows functions that can be used to manipulate text data.
Logical	Shows functions that return the truthiness or falsity of some comparison.
Information	Shows functions that can determine details about a spreadsheet related to the environment of the spreadsheet itself.
User-Defined or **Add-In**	Shows functions that have been created by the user or added in to the program from an external source.
Engineering and **Cube**	Shows functions related to engineering computations and dataset cube processing.

Please note that if you don't find a function by name in one category in one program, that doesn't necessarily mean that the function isn't available in that particular program. Rather, the spreadsheet program vendors have been known to move these functions around from version to version – so you may have to look around to find a particular function. But don't give up! If you know what kind of calculation you want to accomplish, you can use this information to begin your search to find the correct function name to use in your particular spreadsheet program!

LO 4.9   Using the Insert Function Dialog

The second way that the spreadsheet programs helps you learn about the different functions that are available for your use is a concept called an Insert Function Dialog. The Insert Function Dialog is a series of tools or dialogs that help the user perform a step-by-step approach to automatically build a function and compute the desired results.

Continuing on with our Fresh Fruit Shopping List example, let's suppose that the user wanted to figure out which fresh fruit was going to cost the most and which fresh fruit was going to cost the least. As we look at the previous figures, it is actually very easy to simply "eyeball" the values and see that the watermelons are the most expensive items and the bananas are the least expensive items at $11.96 and $4.45 respectively.

But we must always remember that typical spreadsheets don't only have 10 or less rows of data. More often than not, spreadsheet files may actually have hundreds if not thousands of rows of data! With that in mind, you will not typically be able to simply "eyeball" the data to determine which value is the minimum or maximum value, etc.

So with this in mind, the user wants to use a spreadsheet function to determine what is the value of the most expensive and least expensive items that will be purchased. The user knows that the concepts of *minimums* and *maximums* are statistical measurements, so the user will look for these functions in the Statistical Functions category.

The process of searching for a function begins by using either a menu command or a tool to initiate the Insert Function Dialogs. Figures 4-17, 4-18, and 4-19 show the Insert Function Dialog tools that are used in Microsoft's Excel, LibreOffice's Calc, and Google's Sheets spreadsheet programs respectively.

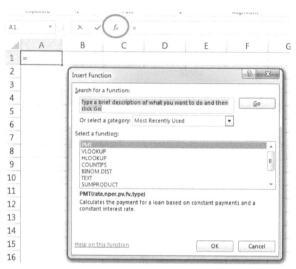

Figure 4-17

In Figure 4-17 and 4-18, you can see by the red highlighted tool that a small symbol *fx* is used as the tool to begin the Insert Function Dialogs.

Clicking on this tool opens up the associated Insert Function Dialog to help the user begin the process of searching for and building the desired function.

As you can see in Figures 4-17 and 4-18, the actual physical layout of these two dialogs are somewhat different, but the intention of these two dialogs are the same.

By using these dialogs, the user can search for a desired function by selecting a category of functions to choose from. Then, after selecting a category, the user can look for the function name that will perform the desired calculation.

Figure 4-18

In Figure 4-19, however, we see that there is not an actual dialog that is shown to the user to help pick out the desired function. Instead, when using the menu command as shown, an online listing of all of the available functions is displayed, which will let the user narrow the search by choosing a category of functions on the online web page.

Although the specific layout and design of how these three different programs allow users to choose desired functions in slightly different ways, it is more important to notice the similarities!

All spreadsheet programs provide a means for you to find and learn how to use their named Functions to perform calculations!

So now, to see how the rest of the Insert Function Dialogs work, we will return to our Fresh Fruit Shopping List example.

The user now decides that she wants to add two additional rows of information at the bottom of the spreadsheet to show the minimum and the maximum costs for the most expensive and least expensive items on the shopping list.

Figure 4-20 shows the labels added to rows 13 and 14, which will represent the most expensive line item value and the least expensive line item value for the shopping list. Also, in cell D13, we can see that the user has begun to use the Insert Function Dialog and has selected the category of **Statistical** functions and has scrolled down and has highlighted the **MAX** function.

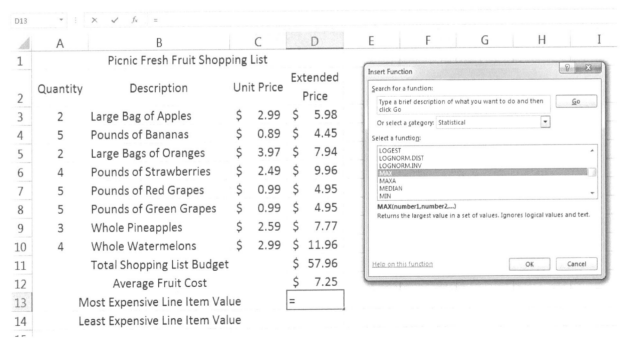

Figure 4-19

Figure 4-20

By simply highlighting the function that you want to use, the dialog begins to show you more detailed information about the function that has been chosen. Below the list of functions, you can see that the syntax of the function is being shown. Syntax is the specific rules about how the function needs to be typed into the spreadsheet program in order for it to work correctly.

We see that the function name is **MAX** and so that function name is highlighted with bold. Although you do not have to adhere to case sensitivity (e.g. all upper case or lower case) you do have to remember that function names ***must be spelled correctly*** or they will return a **#NAME?** error. We will be discussing spreadsheet errors in more detail in the next chapter.

Next we see that there are parenthesis with ***number1, number2,...*** shown in the syntax for the MAX function. These represent the required and/or optional parameters or arguments that are needed for this function to work properly. The fact that these items are bold means that at least one of these is required. The ellipsis (i.e. the three dots in a row) means that there can be any number of these possible arguments but that each one of them must be separated by a comma (,).

The user can also see that there is a description of the function just below the function syntax, which describes how the function works and what value the function will return.

In this example, the function says that it, "*Returns the largest value in a set of values. Ignores logical values and text.*"

This function does appear to be the function that the user wants to calculate, so the user will continue this dialog by clicking on the OK button. Notice how in both the active cell and in the formula bar, the program has begun to build the function by "typing" in the equal sign (=) on behalf of the user!

Once the user clicked on the OK button, a second dialog box appeared. Figure 4-21 shows that this next dialog box is designed to help the user fill in the required and optional parameters or arguments that will be needed to make this function work.

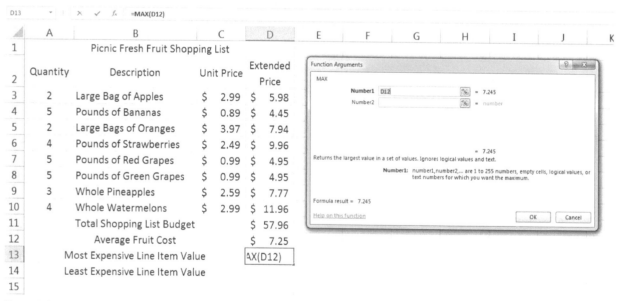

Figure 4-21

Let's look at this dialog box in close detail. In the upper left corner we see that we are working with the MAX function. Next we see a bolded field called *number1*. This field is described below as it says that the numbers are, "number1, number2,... are 1 to 255 numbers, empty cells, logical values, or text number for which you want the maximum." Also, below this description of the first parameter is a current representation of the formula's result.

BUT WAIT! Did you notice what was already filled in at the middle of the dialog? There is a cell reference to cell D12. So how did *that* get in there?

One of the very good things about contemporary spreadsheet programs is that they are currently designed to try to help new users out by *guessing* at what it *thinks* the user is trying to achieve at every step along the way. Sometimes, this means that with just a single click or two, the spreadsheet practically builds itself on behalf of the user! For new users who may be a little intimidated by the power of spreadsheets, this may seem like very good news!

But, alas, now here comes the bad news: Spreadsheet programs don't always *guess* correctly!

In our example, the Insert Function Dialog realized that the user is trying to insert a MAX function and that the MAX function tries to discover the maximum value in a collection of values. So, the program looked around the current cell D13 (where the MAX function is going to reside) and discovered that there was a calculated value immediately above this cell. So that is what the program **guessed** to be the argument for the MAX function . . . just the single cell D12.

But this is certainly **not** what the user wants. What the user wants to know is what value is the largest in the collection of values that begins in cell D3 and ends in cell D10. In other words, the user wants to know the MAX of the values that are within the range D3:D10.

Figure 4-22 shows how the user changed the proposed cell reference in the argument list to be the desired range of cells D3:D10.

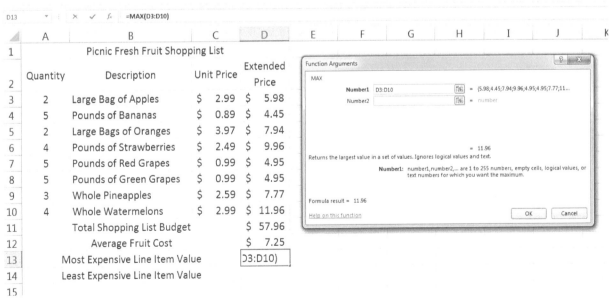

Figure 4-22

Notice that several things happened when the user changed the proposed parameter by manually selecting the actual desired function parameters:

1. The formula bar and the active cell both have been updated to show the changed values for the parameter list.

2. In the middle of the dialog, you see a list of all of the values that will be used by the function to determine the final value to be calculated.

3. The formula result has been updated to show the new (correct) result of this function calculation.

When the user hits the enter key to complete this function, the cell D13 will be updated to have a displayed resulting value of $11.96. But remember, this is just the resulting value that is displayed in the active cell. The actual cell contents will have the correct function =**MAX(D3:D10)**. In Chapter 6 we will revisit these and other limitations with using the Insert Function Dialogs and other tools that may not always deliver precisely what the user wants.

But for now, you can see that by using the Insert Function Dialog, you can quickly build functions that you have never used before and can begin to learn and remember the syntax of the more commonly used functions.

Please do remember that these are only tools to help you learn how to create functions – you don't have to always use these dialogs. In fact, over time, you will begin to master the more common functions and you won't need to use the dialogs at all.

For example, now the user knows that the MAX function is the function that is used to determine the *maximum* value of a collection of values and the syntax for the MAX function is simply =**MAX(*number1, number2...*)**. From this knowledge, she correctly infers that the function for the *minimum* calculation is going to be nearly identical!

Figure 4-23 shows that the user can confidently add the MIN function without using the Insert Function Dialog. In this figure, we see that she proceeds to cell D14 and simply types directly into the cell =**MIN(D3:D10)**.

MAX	▼ : × ✓ fx	=MIN(D3:D10)		
	A	B	C	D	E
1		Picnic Fresh Fruit Shopping List			
2	Quantity	Description	Unit Price	Extended Price	
3	2	Large Bag of Apples	$ 2.99	$ 5.98	
4	5	Pounds of Bananas	$ 0.89	$ 4.45	
5	2	Large Bags of Oranges	$ 3.97	$ 7.94	
6	4	Pounds of Strawberries	$ 2.49	$ 9.96	
7	5	Pounds of Red Grapes	$ 0.99	$ 4.95	
8	5	Pounds of Green Grapes	$ 0.99	$ 4.95	
9	3	Whole Pineapples	$ 2.59	$ 7.77	
10	4	Whole Watermelons	$ 2.99	$ 11.96	
11		Total Shopping List Budget		$ 57.96	
12		Average Fruit Cost		$ 7.25	
13		Most Expensive Line Item Value		$ 11.96	
14		Least Expensive Line Item Value		=MIN(D3:D10)	
15					

Figure 4-23

Using the Insert Function Dialogs is a great way to learn about all of the various functions that are available in the spreadsheet programs that you use. They help you understand what the purpose of each function is and what value each function will return. They help you understand the function syntax including which parameters or arguments are required, which parameters or arguments are optional, and in what order these parameters or arguments must appear in the function syntax. They also help you see the interim results of the functions as they are helping you build the final functions in your spreadsheet.

Overall, the Insert Function Dialogs are possibly the most powerful tools you will use in a spreadsheet program to help you to continue to learn about all that a spreadsheet program can help you accomplish.

Almost all of the desktop versions of spreadsheet programs will have some sort of Insert Function Dialog similar to that which was just outlined here. But please do remember that not all spreadsheet programs will have the exact same layout or look as they help you accomplish your tasks.

This is easily shown if we look at Google sheets, for example, as well as some other online or web-based spreadsheet programs. In Figure 4-24 we see that the Insert Function Dialog may appear as more of an integrated display as opposed to separate, movable dialog boxes.

But the purpose of this functionality is still the same: The program is trying to help the user understand the purpose of the function that is being built, the syntax of the function, and is helping to actually build the function in the final destination cell.

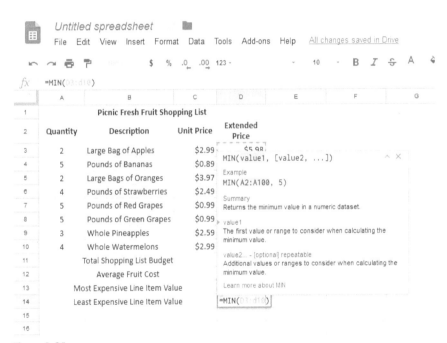

Figure 4-24

Chapter 4 – Assignments and Projects

Directed Assignments

DA 4-1. For this directed assignment, you will be using the student data file named **DA_4-1.xlsx** to complete the required information. This file is in Microsoft Excel 2007 or newer format and should open in any contemporary spreadsheet program.

Required student data file: *DA_4-1.xlsx*

In this workbook, you will find information about a planned shopping list for some canned goods and non-perishable food items. Your team collected canned food and non-perishable items for a food drive in your community, but some people chose to donate cash instead of food items. Now, your team has created a shopping list to get more of the kinds of items that were not donated.

This workbook contains a planned shopping list with the quantities of each item to be purchased, the description of the items, the unit cost of the items, and some other labels added to represent some planned calculations. Your task will be to complete this spreadsheet following the instructions below.

1. Open the student data file named **DA_4-1.xlsx**.

2. Immediately save a copy of this file using the following specifications:

    a. File name: Rename this file using the filename **YourName_DA_4-1**

    b. File location: Place this file in any location you choose, but make a note of the location as you will need it later.

    c. File format: Because this file will be sent in to your professor, you must check with him or her to see what format **he or she** will want this file to be saved in. Don't just assume that the original file format or the default file format for your own computer will be acceptable!

3. Use the skills you learned in the previous chapter to apply basic formatting including:

    a. Format the ranges C3:D13 and D14:D16 to be formatted as currency or money.

    b. Format the range A2:D2 to have its alignment wrapping the text in the cells.

    c. Format the ranges A14:C14 to be merged with the text labels aligned to the right.

    d. Use the format painter tool to repeat the formatting applied in the previous step to the range A15:C15 and then again to the range A16:C16.

    e. Adjust the column widths so that there is no text truncation or inappropriate wrapping.

4. Create a simple formula in cell D3 to calculate the extended cost of the first line item. Extended costs are calculated by multiplying the quantity of an item by the item's unit price. Make sure you use relative cell references in your calculation.

5. Use the fill handle on cell D3 to copy that formula to the range D4:D13.

6. In cell D14, enter the SUM function to calculate the new total of all of the extended prices in the range D3:D13.

7. In cell D16, we want to calculate the balance that will be the difference between how much cash was collected and the total of our shopping list. Enter in cell D16 the simple math formula that subtracts the new total that you calculated in cell D14 *from* the cash donations that were collected and has been entered in cell D15.

8. At this point, you notice that cell D16 is showing a negative balance! Depending on which spreadsheet program you are using and the type of currency or money formatting that you have chosen, this number might look like $(178.57), or $-178.57, or $(178.57) , or $-178.57. Either way, this is showing you that you are trying to spend more money than your donations will allow! To correct this, change the quantity of the number of boxes of cereal that you intend to purchase (cell A11) by lowering it until the balance in your spreadsheet is no longer negative.

9. You now discover that when you will only buy 133 boxes of cereal, and your new balance is $2.38. This means that you can get one more can of **pears** and one more can of **potatoes.** Increase each of these quantities (cells A13 and A6 respectively) by one more can so that you can optimize your shopping list.

10. Merge and center the cell range A1:D1 and add an appropriate label to describe this overall worksheet.

11. Add any additional formatting (color, highlighting, etc.) as you think would be appropriate.

12. Don't forget to name the worksheet an appropriate sheet name and remove any unnecessary sheets.

13. Make any final necessary adjustments to ensure readability and correctness of your work. Then, once you are sure that everything is correct, you should save your work and then submit it in accordance with your class instructions.

	A	B	C	D
1		Food Drive Shopping List		
2	Qty.	Description	Unit Price	Extended Price
3	150	Cans of Soup	$0.79	$ 118.50
4	38	Cans of Corn	$0.99	$ 37.62
5	61	Cans of Beans	$0.99	$ 60.39
6	23	Cans of Potatoes	$0.99	$ 22.77
7	187	Cans of Beets	$0.99	$ 185.13
8	94	Cans of Peas	$0.99	$ 93.06
9	85	Cans of Carrots	$0.99	$ 84.15
10	52	Boxes of Pasta	$2.29	$ 119.08
11	133	Boxes of Cereal	$3.29	$ 437.57
12	160	Cans of Peaches	$1.19	$ 190.40
13	127	Cans of Pears	$1.19	$ 151.13
14			Total:	$1,499.80
15		Cash Donations Collected:		$1,500.00
16			Balance:	$ 0.20

Figure DA_4-1_Completed

At the completion of this directed assignment, your final work should look very similar to Figure DA_4-1_Completed found here.

DA 4-2. For this directed assignment, you will be using the student data file named **DA_4-2.ods** to complete the required information. This file is in LibreOffice Calc 4.2 or newer format and should open in any contemporary spreadsheet program.

Required student data file: *DA_4-2.ods*

In this workbook, you will find information that a radio station recently collected over the last four weeks. This radio station has decided to change its format and is doing some market research to see what type of music is being requested most often by listeners who call in and make requests during the station's four week long "open-format".

This workbook contains the name of the genres of music that the station could play and the number of times each type of music was requested in each of the four weeks. Your task will be to complete this spreadsheet following the instructions below.

1. Open the student data file named **DA_4-2.ods**.

2. Immediately save a copy of this file using the following specifications:

   a. File name: Rename this file using the filename ***YourName_DA_4-2***

   b. File location: Place this file in any location you choose, but make a note of the location as you will need it later.

   c. File format: Because this file will be sent in to your professor, you must check with him or her to see what format **he or she** will want this file to be saved in. Don't just assume that the original file format or the default file format for your own computer will be acceptable!

3. Add labels to cells F2 and A13 called "Totals".

4. Add a simple SUM function in cell B13 to calculate the total of all requested songs that were played in Week 1. Make sure that you use relative cell references.

5. Use the fill handle in cell B13 to copy this formula over to cells in the range C13:E13.

6. Add a simple SUM function in cell F3 to calculate the total number of times Hip-Hop songs were requested over the full four week period. Make sure that you use relative references.

7. Use the fill handle in cell F3 to copy this formula down to cells in the range F4:F13.

8. Apply basic formatting to adjust the column widths so that there is no text truncation or inappropriate wrapping.

9. Add a label in cell G2 called "Percent of Total".

10. Create a simple formula to calculate the relationship between the individual song totals and the overall total of all songs played. This is known as a percentage of a total. To calculate this, in cell G3, you will divide the total number of times that Hip-Hop was requested (cell F3) by the total number of all song types that were requested (cell F13). Note, the reference to cell F3 should be a relative reference and the reference to cell $F$13 should be an absolute reference.

11. Use the fill handle in cell G3 to drag down and copy this formula to the cell range (G4:G12).

12. Change the formatting for the range G3:G12 to format these values as percentages with 2 decimal places of precision.

13. In cell G13, add a simple sum function to add up all of the percentages in the range G3:G12. If you have done the previous steps correctly, this should now add up to 100.00%.

14. Merge and center the cell range A1:G1 and add an appropriate label to describe this overall worksheet.

15. Add formatting to highlight the 4 most popular genres requested based on their percentages.

16. Add any additional formatting (color, highlighting, etc.) as you think would be appropriate.

17. Don't forget to name the worksheet an appropriate sheet name and remove any unnecessary sheets.

18. Make any final necessary adjustments to ensure readability and correctness of your work. Then, once you are sure that everything is correct, you should save your work and then submit it in accordance with your class instructions.

At the completion of this directed assignment, your final work should look very similar to Figure DA_4-2_ Completed found here.

Genre	Week 1	Week 2	Week 3	Week 4	Totals	Percent of Total
			Listener Requested Songs			
Hip-Hop	151	160	134	123	568	16.00%
Rock	108	111	34	168	421	11.86%
Country	80	157	37	118	392	11.04%
Pop	69	142	100	109	420	11.83%
Blues	117	100	49	71	337	9.49%
Easy Listening	48	62	91	111	312	8.79%
Latin	81	30	135	16	262	7.38%
Folk	40	15	10	36	101	2.85%
R&B	68	46	140	35	289	8.14%
Electronic	62	138	158	90	448	12.62%
Totals	824	961	888	877	3550	100.00%

Most Requested Genres

Figure DA_4-2_Completed

DA 4-3. For this directed assignment, you will be using the student data file named **DA_4-3.xlsx** to complete the required information. This file is in MS Excel version 2007 or newer format and should open in any contemporary spreadsheet program.

Required student data file: *DA_4-3.xlsx*

In this workbook, you will find a larger collection of information from a materials processing lab where they have been experimenting with the failure points of different materials based on high and low temperatures.

This workbook contains the 200 rows of temperature data including the Low Temperature when the material failed (broke or cracked), the High Temperature when the material failed (melted, caught on fire, or broke or cracked) and the Average Temperature when the material showed any signs of being adjusted by the temperature.

Your task will be to complete this spreadsheet following the instructions below.

1. Open the student data file named **DA_4-3.xlsx**.
2. Immediately save a copy of this file using the following specifications:
   a. File name: Rename this file using the filename **YourName_DA_4-3**
   b. File location: Place this file in any location you choose, but make a note of the location as you will need it later.
   c. File format: Because this file will be sent in to your professor, you must check with him or her to see what format **he or she** will want this file to be saved in. Don't just assume that the original file format or the default file format for your own computer will be acceptable!
3. The first thing you notice is that all of the material names have been stripped out of this data (to protect the materials from being biased during the review process.) Insert a new column A before these three columns.
4. In cell A1, enter the column label "Materials Tested".
5. In cell A2, enter the label "Material 001" for the first material measurements.
6. Using the fill handle in cell A2, drag this label down to fill the series of material names in the range A3:A201.
7. Use the skills you learned in the previous chapter to apply basic formatting including:
   a. Format the numeric measurement values in the range B2:D201 to have 5 digits of decimal precision.
   b. Automatically adjust the column widths to make sure none of the data is truncated.
   c. Use the format painter tool to repeat the formatting applied in the previous step to the range A15:C15 and then again to the range A16:C16.
8. Merge and center cells F1 and G1 and enter the label "Low Temperature Analysis".
9. Enter the label "Lowest Low" in cell F2.
10. Enter the label "Highest Low" in cell F3.
11. In cell G2, enter the MIN function to calculate the smallest value from the range B2:B201.
12. In cell G3, enter the MAX function to calculate the largest value from the range B2:B201.
13. Adjust the widths of columns F and G so that all of the data can be seen.

14. Merge and center cells F5 and G5 and enter the label "High Temperature Analysis".

15. Enter the label "Lowest High" in cell F6.

16. Enter the label "Highest High" in cell F7.

17. In cell G6, enter the MIN function to calculate the smallest value from the range C2:C201.

18. In cell G7, enter the MAX function to calculate the largest value from the range C2:C201.

19. Merge and center cells F9 and G9 and enter the label "Average Temperature Analysis".

20. Enter the label "Lowest Average" in cell F10.

21. Enter the label "Highest Average" in cell F11.

22. In cell G10, enter the MIN function to calculate the smallest value from the range D2:D201.

23. In cell G11, enter the MAX function to calculate the largest value from the range D2:D201.

24. Insert a heading row at the very top and merge and center the cells in the range A1:G1 and add the label "Analysis of Material Temperature Failure Values".

25. Add highlighting to color the main heading and the three analysis blocks with different colors and cell outlines similar to the sample shown in the Figure DA_4-3_Completed found below.

26. Make any final necessary adjustments to ensure readability and correctness of your work. Then, once you are sure that everything is correct, you should save your work and then submit it in accordance with your class instructions.

As this directed assignment shows, it is often more typical that spreadsheets will work with and process larger and larger collections of data. This is another reason why the effective use of cell ranges in formulas and functions is an important skill to master.

At the completion of this directed assignment, your final work should look very similar to Figure DA_4-3_Completed found here.

Figure DA_4-3_Completed

DA 4-4. For this directed assignment, you will be using the student data file named **DA_4-4.xlsx** to complete the required information. This file is in MS Excel version 2007 or newer format and should open in any contemporary spreadsheet program.

Required student data file: *DA_4-4.xlsx*

In this workbook, you will find a spreadsheet that has been laid out to help you compare loans as you consider buying a new home! This is a very big decision for you and your family so you want to make sure that you are making the best possible decision based upon the best possible information.

In the first three rows, there are places to enter the new home price, the down payment you will be making on the house, and then calculate the loan amount for your new home loan. Then in row 4, you will see that the column labels have been created for you so you will now be entering the data for 6 different possible loans and the appropriate calculations to help you compare these loans.

Your task will be to complete this spreadsheet following the instructions below.

1. Open the student data file named **DA_4-4.xlsx**.
2. Immediately save a copy of this file using the following specifications:
   a. File name: Rename this file using the filename ***YourName_DA_4-4***
   b. File location: Place this file in any location you choose, but make a note of the location as you will need it later.
   c. File format: Because this file will be sent in to your professor, you must check with him or her to see what format ***he or she*** will want this file to be saved in. Don't just assume that the original file format or the default file format for your own computer will be acceptable!
3. You have found the home of your dreams and it has a listing price of $227,000.00. In cell B1 (which is actually a merged cell of cells B1:D1) enter the listing price of the home by entering 227000. Remember to key in the value without any symbols and then simply format this cell as currency or money.
4. At this time, you don't know how much (if any) down payment you will be able to afford, so at this time, just key in a 0 in cell B2 and then format this cell also as currency or money.
5. Calculate the Loan Amount (Principal Value) in cell B3 by subtracting the down payment from the New Home Price.
6. Next, you will enter the known values for the 6 loans that you want to compare. Typical home loans are offered with different annual percentage rates of interest (APRs) based upon the term of the loan (usually specified in 30 years, 20 years, 15 years, or 10 years.) Since this is your first home loan, you are only considering 30- or 20-year loans. But you have found three different lenders who could offer you a loan at either 20- or 30-years.

   For the first loan perform the following data entry of the known data:

   a. In cell A5 enter the lender's name of "First National Bank".
   b. In cell B5 enter 30 as the term in years.
   c. In cell D5 enter the 4.625%. Remember, it is often best to enter percentage values as decimal values and then simply format the cell as a percentage with the appropriate number of decimal places of precision. Make sure that the final value has 3 decimal places of precision.

7. Repeat the steps listed in 6a, 6b, and 6c above to fill in the rest of the known data using the following information:

Lenders (A6:A10)	Term in Years (B6:B10)	APR (D6:D10)
First National Bank	20	4.375%
Metropolis Bank	30	5.252%
Metropolis Bank	20	4.336%
Country Bank	30	4.588%
Country Bank	20	4.250%

8. Although there is only one single transaction to create a home loan, loans are not paid back in just a single lump payment. Also, if the loan is for 20 or 30 years, then these loans also are not typically paid back with only one annual payment each year. No, typically, loans are paid back monthly. Therefore, we need to create calculations to convert everything into monthly terms.

   In cell C5, calculate the term of the first loan in months by multiplying the term in years (B5) by the number of months that are in each year (12).

9. Copy the formula in cell C5 to the other terms in months for the other loans in the range C6:C10.

10. Likewise, the interest rates that the banks quote to you are **Annual Percentage Rates** also known as the APRs. Since this is an annual rate, we need to calculate what this interest rate is when it is expressed as a monthly rate.

    In cell E5, calculate the monthly interest rate for the first loan by dividing the annual percentage rate or APR (D5) by the number of months that are in each year (12). Format this value to be a percentage with 5 decimal places of precision.

11. Copy the formula in cell D5 to the other monthly interest rates for the other loans in the range D6:D10.

12. Next, in cell F5, use the Insert Function Dialogs to create a PMT function to calculate the monthly loan payment for the first loan. Here are some things you will want to remember when you create this function:

    a. The interest rate parameter should be a relative cell reference to this loan's monthly interest rate (E5).

    b. The number of periods parameter (Nper) should be a relative cell reference to this loan's term of loan in months (C5).

    c. The present value parameter (Pv) should be an **absolute cell reference** to the Loan Amount ($B$3).

    When you complete this function, your resulting value should show you a payment amount of ($1,167.10). Yes, this is the correct answer. This number appears negative because you borrowed a positive amount of money from the bank and now, with the payments, there will be a negative amount of money coming out of your pockets . . . it's an accounting thing!

13. Because people don't typically think about monthly loan payments as being "negative amounts" we typically will change the sign of the loan payment calculation to be a positive number. To do this, edit the PMT formula in cell F5 to insert a minus sign (-) in front of the PMT function. This will effectively change the negative number into a positive number.

14. Copy the function from cell F5 to the range F6:F10 to calculate the other loan payments.

15. Next, we want to see how much total money will be paid back over the life of each loan. In cell G5 enter a simple formula to calculate the monthly payment (F5) multiplied by the total number of payments for the loan (C5) . . . Wow! That's a big number!

16. Copy the formula from cell G5 to the range G6:G10 to calculate the totals for the other loans.

17. Next, let's figure out how much total interest would be paid to each lender for each loan. In cell H5 we will enter a simple formula to subtract the original loan amount *as an absolute reference* ($B$3) from the first loan's total repayment amount (G5).

18. Copy this function from cell H5 to the range H6:H10 to calculate the total interest that would be paid for the other loans.

19. Locate the loan that has the smallest monthly payment and highlight that payment amount with some shade of green.

20. Locate the loan that has the smallest amount of total interest being paid over the life of the loan and highlight that total interest amount with the same shade of green.

21. Make any final necessary adjustments to ensure readability and correctness of your work. Then, once you are sure that everything is correct, you should save your work and then submit it in accordance with your class instructions.

At the completion of this directed assignment, your final work should look very similar to Figure DA_4-4_Completed found here. Notice how the lowest APR doesn't always mean the best loan! Also notice that if you can afford a higher monthly payment, then you can end up paying less in total over the life of the loan. Also, you can experiment with making minor changes to the down payment amount or the sale price of the house to get some other ideas of what other possible loans might look like.

	A	B	C	D	E	F	G	H
1	New Home Price:	$		227,000.00				
2	Down Payment:	$		-				
3	Loan Amount (Principal Value):	$		227,000.00				
4	Lender Name	Term of Loan (In Years)	Term of Loan (In Months)	Annual Percentage Rate (APR)	Monthly Interest Rate	Monthly Loan Payment	Total Amount Paid Over Entire Loan	Total Interest Paid Over Entire Loan
5	First National Bank	30	360	4.625%	0.38542%	$1,167.10	$420,154.81	$193,154.81
6	First National Bank	20	240	4.375%	0.36458%	$1,420.84	$341,002.26	$114,002.26
7	Metropolis Bank	30	360	5.252%	0.43767%	$1,253.78	$451,362.10	$224,362.10
8	Metropolis Bank	20	240	4.336%	0.36133%	$1,416.10	$339,863.20	$112,863.20
9	Country Bank	30	360	4.588%	0.38233%	$1,162.08	$418,347.12	$191,347.12
10	Country Bank	20	240	4.250%	0.35417%	$1,405.66	$337,358.94	$110,358.94
11								

Loan Comparisons   +

Figure DA_4-4_Completed

DA 4-5. For this directed assignment, you will be using the student data file named **DA_4-5.ods** to complete the required information. This file is in LibreOffice Calc version 4.2 or newer format and should open in any contemporary spreadsheet program.

Required student data file: *DA_4-5.ods*

In this workbook, you are creating a spreadsheet to encourage your parents to help contribute to your personal savings account. You received $500 for your graduation and you want to save that money and try to grow the balance up to $1000 in just one year. You want to save this extra money for any unexpected college expenses. By completing this spreadsheet you will be able to show them how you will be saving some money each month and how, if they would just give you some small monthly percentage of your savings balance, you can begin to save up to pay for any unplanned expenses.

Your task will be to complete this spreadsheet following the instructions below.

1. Open the student data file named **DA_4-5.ods**.

2. Immediately save a copy of this file using the following specifications:

   a. File name: Rename this file using the filename ***YourName_DA_4-5***

   b. File location: Place this file in any location you choose, but make a note of the location as you will need it later.

   c. File format: Because this file will be sent in to your professor, you must check with him or her to see what format ***he or she*** will want this file to be saved in. Don't just assume that the original file format or the default file format for your own computer will be acceptable!

3. In cell B1, enter your opening balance by entering the $500 that you received for graduation. Make sure you format this cell as money or currency.

4. In cell D1, enter the amount of money you will save each week. Let's be conservative and start small – just enter $1 for now. We'll adjust this later.

5. In cell F1, enter the interest rate that you will ask your parents to contribute. Let's start with 5%. Make sure this cell is formatted as a percentage with two decimal places.

6. In cell B3, set the original beginning balance to be a simple, relative reference to the opening balance in cell B1.

7. In cell C3, set this cell equal to an absolute reference to cell $D$1.

8. In cell D3, enter the simple formula to calculate the new subtotal before interest is added.

9. In cell E3, enter the calculation to determine how much interest your parents will contribute to your account. This will be a simple formula to multiply the new subtotal before interest ***as a relative reference*** by the generous monthly interest % ***as an absolute reference***.

10. In cell F3, enter the simple formula to add this month's interest onto the new subtotal before interest to create the new ending monthly balance. We have now completed the formulas for the first month's savings.

11. For the next month of savings, we will need to set the beginning balance equal to a relative reference to the ending balance from the previous month. Select cell B4 and set it equal to a relative reference to cell F3.

12. For cells C4:F4, you can simply copy down the corresponding cells from row 3. This will complete the formulas for the second month's savings.

13. Now, you can select the range B4:F4 and use the fill handle to fill all of the cells down to row 14.

14. Next you want to calculate some totals to see how much you are saving with your own contributions and how much your parents are helping you through their interest contributions. In cells C15 and E15, enter SUM functions to total up the cell ranges C3:C14 and E3:E14 respectively.

15. With all of these calculations completed, you notice three things that concern you:

    a. Cell C15 shows that you are only contributing an extra $12 in savings over the course of the year.

    b. Cell E15 shows that you would be asking your parents to contribute *over $400* in interest to your savings account.

    c. The final ending balance in cell F14 shows that you haven't met your goal of $1000 in savings.

    To correct these issues you decide to make the following adjustments to your spreadsheet:

    a. Adjust your monthly contribution amount (cell D1) to be $20.

    b. Adjust your parents' generous monthly interest % down to 3.00%.

16. You now notice that both you and your parents are contributing a nearly equal amount and you have surpassed your goal of $1000 by the end of the year.

17. Add a new row at the top of the spreadsheet and merge the new cells A1:F1 and enter the label "Personal Savings With Parental Support".

18. Adjust cells A2, C2, and E2 to be aligned to the right, and adjust cells B2, D2, and F2 to be aligned in the center of the cells. Make all of the cells in row 2 be centered vertically in the row.

19. Add appropriate coloring to your spreadsheet to help make the critical information appear highlighted.

20. Make any final necessary adjustments to ensure readability and correctness of your work. Then, once you are sure that everything is correct, you should save your work and then submit it in accordance with your class instructions.

At the completion of this directed assignment, your final work should look very similar to Figure DA_4-5_Completed found here.

	A	B	C	D	E	F
1			**Personal Savings With Parental Support**			
2		Opening Balance	$500.00	Monthly Contribution	$20.00	Generous Monthly Interest %	3.00%
3			Beginning Balance	My Monthly Savings	New Subtotal Before Interest	This Month's Interest	Ending Monthly Balance
4	January		$500.00	$20.00	$520.00	$15.60	$535.60
5	February		$535.60	$20.00	$555.60	$16.67	$572.27
6	March		$572.27	$20.00	$592.27	$17.77	$610.04
7	April		$610.04	$20.00	$630.04	$18.90	$648.94
8	May		$648.94	$20.00	$668.94	$20.07	$689.01
9	June		$689.01	$20.00	$709.01	$21.27	$730.28
10	July		$730.28	$20.00	$750.28	$22.51	$772.78
11	August		$772.78	$20.00	$792.78	$23.78	$816.57
12	September		$816.57	$20.00	$836.57	$25.10	$861.66
13	October		$861.66	$20.00	$881.66	$26.45	$908.11
14	November		$908.11	$20.00	$928.11	$27.84	$955.96
15	December		$955.96	$20.00	$975.96	$29.28	$1,005.24
16	Totals			$240.00		$265.24	
17							

Personal Savings

Sheet 1 / 1   Default   Sum=0

Figure DA_4-5_Completed

Creative Projects

CP 4-1. For this creative project, you will be creating a simple spreadsheet to calculate what type of pizzas are most popular among the members of your class or in your family or among a group of your friends, etc. This exercise is a very typical example of the way that simple ranking surveys are set up and calculated.

Required student data file: None: Start with a new, blank workbook file and name the file *YourName_CP_4-1*.

To set up your spreadsheet, create a listing across the top of 5 or more different pizza toppings. Some examples might be cheese, sausage, pepperoni, hamburger, veggies, meat lovers, etc. Then, in the first column, create a list of at least 15 people or more. Some examples might be classmates, family, friends, etc. Then, you will ask each person to rate each pizza type on a scale from 0 to 10 where 0 represents a pizza topping that they like the ***least*** and would probably never order or eat and where 10 represents the pizza topping that they like the ***most*** and would probably order most often. Each person should choose some rating for each pizza type.

After you have collected all of the known data, you will then add functions at the bottom of the data to calculate the average ratings for each pizza type.

Finally, you should highlight the pizza type that is most popular by average with a green highlight and highlight the pizza type that is the least popular by average with a red highlight.

Make sure that all of the columns have meaningful text labels. Also, make sure that there is an overall label for the entire contents of the worksheet and that the worksheet tab itself has been properly named. Once you have completed setting up the worksheet, apply appropriate basic formatting to the entire sheet and don't forget to give the worksheet itself an appropriate sheet name.

Remember to check your final work for spelling, grammar, and overall correctness and then submit your file in the manner prescribed for your class.

CP 4-2. For this creative project, you have been hired as an intern at the local parks department to help oversee a new pilot project to employ up to 10 summer employees to work as "park promoters" for eight weeks over the summer. These employees will basically get "paid to play" in the parks and to interact with other park patrons to try to improve the overall image of outdoor fun in the parks. Your task is to create a spreadsheet to track the payroll for each of these employees for the 8 weeks.

Required student data file: None: Start with a new, blank workbook file and name the file *YourName_CP_4-2*.

To set up your spreadsheet, your supervisor has no time to help you out so you are completely on your own to set up the layout, enter the known data, and create the calculations to determine the unknown data.

The supervisor has told you that there will not be more than 10 total people (including yourself) in the program. So you can add your own name in the sheet and then some placeholders like "Employee 2" through "Employee 9" in the first column. Also, you know that your own hourly rate will be $15.25 per hour, but the rate for the other employees has not been set yet. However, you have been told that all of the other employees will have the same pay rate. Therefore, you can have a single field on the sheet somewhere for the other employees' rate. This way, you can then use an absolute reference whenever you need to reference the other employees' pay rate.

For each of the eight weeks, the employees will work not more than 20 hours each week, so you will need a column for each of the 8 weeks to record the employees' hours as well as a column for each of the 8 weeks' payroll for each employee.

The spreadsheet should then perform the following calculations:

✦ Calculate your own weekly wages for each week using your own weekly hours and a reference to your own employee pay rate.

✦ Calculate the weekly wages for each of the other employees for each week using their weekly hours and an **absolute reference** to the employees' pay rate.

✦ Create a column at the end of the data to sum up the total of all 8 weeks of payroll for every employee including yourself.

✦ Create a row at the bottom of the data to sum up each week's payroll as well as the overall payroll for the entire 8 weeks.

✦ Create some fictitious sample hours for the first three weeks to prove that your calculations are performing correctly but leave the other 5 weeks of hours blank.

Make sure that all of the columns have meaningful text labels. Also, make sure that there is an overall label for the entire contents of the worksheet and that the worksheet tab itself has been properly named.

Remember to check your final work for spelling, grammar, and overall correctness and then submit your file in the manner prescribed for your class.

CP 4-3. For this creative project, you are considering doing a Study Abroad class in London over next summer's break and you are trying to determine if you will be able to afford the trip. You have learned that some of the expenses can be covered by the university, but that others will have to be paid for out-of-pocket so you need to see if the trip will be financially feasible for you.

Required student data file: None: Start with a new, blank workbook file and name the file *YourName_CP_4-3*.

To set up your spreadsheet, you will begin by creating a list of all of the planned expenses that will be associated with the trip. Several of the known expenses are as follows:

Mostly Known Expenses	Minimum Cost	Maximum Cost
Roundtrip airfare from your hometown to London	Lookup online	Lookup online
Hotels around campus (per night)	$100	$421
Weekly grocery bill (including food, laundry, and toiletries)	£80	£100
Average pub meal	£8	£12
Average restaurant meal	£15	£25

(Continued)

Pint of beer		£3	£3.50
Mostly Known Expenses	**Minimum Cost**		**Maximum Cost**
Weekly Ground Transportation	£32.10		£60.20
Tuition and Fees (per credit hour)	£750		£750

Additionally, there is some known assistance that your home university will provide to help you for your trip:

Some Known Calculations	Rate or Quantity
Your University will pay for as much as 90% of your tuition and fee costs	90%
Your University will reimburse you for up to 75% of your lodging fees	75%
Your University has a Travel Abroad Scholarship for $1500 that you are eligible to use	1 @ $1500
You would be needing lodging for a fixed number of days	14 days
You would probably buy one week's worth of groceries	1 week
You would probably eat out with friends for the other week's meals	7 days
You will choose either one 3-credit hour course or one 4-credit hour course . . . but you haven't decided yet.	3 or 4 hours
There is a known exchange rate between US Dollars ($) and British Pounds (£)	Lookup online

Using the known data and the known calculations, layout a spreadsheet that performs the following calculations:

+ Create a column for the various expense categories
+ Create a cell somewhere on the worksheet that will hold the current exchange rate. This rate will be used as an absolute reference to convert all of the values that are in British Pounds to US Dollars.
+ Create two columns, one each for the minimum and maximum possible expenses using their original (native) currency values.
+ Create two more columns, one each for the minimum and maximum possible expenses using US Dollars currency values.
+ Wherever necessary, for all British Pounds values, use the exchange rate to calculate the US Dollar equivalent.
+ Create a column for any variable data named something like "Quantity". For some of these items, like the round trip airfare, the quantity will be 1. But for some of these items, like the lodging, the quantity will be 14.

✦ Create two more columns to calculate the Extended Min. Cost and the Extended Max. Cost by multiplying each of the quantities by the Min. Cost in US Dollars and then the Max. Cost in US Dollars

✦ Calculate a Subtotal of Expenses for all of the Extended expenses.

✦ Beneath this subtotal, create a list of the three University-paid credits that you will be able to use. List each credit in the same column as the expense categories. These items would be "University-Paid Tuition and Fees", "University-Paid Lodging Assistance", "Travel Abroad Scholarship".

✦ Create calculations that show the amount of US Dollars that the University will contribute to your trip for each University-Paid contribution.

✦ Calculate a Subtotal of University Credits for these three credits.

✦ Create a final Total of Out-of-Pocket Costs, which subtracts the Subtotal of University Credits from the Subtotal Expenses to determine your possible final costs.

Figure CP_4-3_Sample shows a *possible* version of the completed project. Your own project will vary with different rates, quantities, and other values, etc.

Remember to check your final work for spelling, grammar, and overall correctness and then submit your file in the manner prescribed for your class.

	A	B	C	D	E	F	G	H	I
1	Budget Planning Sheet for Two Week Study Abroad in London					$ to £ Exchange Rate		1.32	
2	Expense	Native Min Cost	Native Max Cost	Min Cost in USD	Max Cost in USD	Quantity	Min Ext. Cost	Max Ext. Cost	
3	Roundtrip airfare from St. Louis to London	$2,700.00	$ 3,400.00	$2,700.00	$3,400.00	1	$ 2,700.00	$ 3,400.00	
4	Hotels around campus (per night)	$ 100.00	$ 421.00	$ 100.00	$ 421.00	14	$ 1,400.00	$ 5,894.00	
5	Weekly grocery bill (including food, laundry & toiletries)	£ 80.00	£ 100.00	$ 105.60	$ 132.00	1	$ 105.60	$ 132.00	
6	Average pub meal	£ 8.00	£ 12.00	$ 10.56	$ 15.84	5	$ 52.80	$ 79.20	
7	Average restaurant meal	£ 15.00	£ 25.00	$ 19.80	$ 33.00	2	$ 39.60	$ 66.00	
8	Pint of beer	£ 3.00	£ 3.50	$ 3.96	$ 4.62	10	$ 39.60	$ 46.20	
9	Weekly Ground Transportation	£ 32.10	£ 60.20	$ 42.37	$ 79.46	1	$ 42.37	$ 79.46	
10	Tuition and Fees (per credit hour)	£ 750.00	£ 750.00	$ 990.00	$ 990.00	3	$ 2,970.00	$ 2,970.00	
11	Subtotal of Expenses						$ 7,349.97	$ 12,666.86	
12	University-Paid Tuition and Fees			$ 891.00	$ 891.00	3	$ 2,673.00	$ 2,673.00	
13	University-Paid Lodging Assistance			$ 75.00	$ 315.75	14	$ 1,050.00	$ 4,420.50	
14	Travel Abroad Scholarship			$1,500.00	$1,500.00	1	$ 1,500.00	$ 1,500.00	
15	Subtotal of University Credits						$ 5,223.00	$ 8,593.50	
16	Total Out-Of-Pocket Costs						$ 2,126.97	$ 4,073.36	
17									
18									

Study Abroad in London (+)

Figure CP_4-3_Sample

Source: Shutterstock, Inc.

Chapter 5

Regular and Conditional Formatting, and Creating Charts

Why do we format spreadsheets with regular and conditional formatting and then also create charts?

As we have learned in the previous chapters, the primary purpose for creating a spreadsheet document is so that the spreadsheet program can perform calculations on known data to derive previously unknown information from that known data. Quite frankly, the spreadsheet program is all about the calculations!

Then why should we concern ourselves with extra formatting of spreadsheet information? Isn't that just a lot of "window-dressing" or just an individual's personal preferences on the look and feel and aesthetics of the final document?

As we will discover in this chapter, the answer is, "No – formatting a spreadsheet is not simply about the look-and-feel or the aesthetics of the spreadsheet document. Rather, formatting a

Key Terms

- area chart
- axes label
- axis range
- bar chart
- basic numeric formatting
- basic text formatting
- basic universal formatting
- bubble chart
- chart area
- chart axes (x-, y-, and z-)
- chart background
- chart part formatting
- chart part sizing & positioning
- chart parts or elements
- chart positioning
- chart title
- chart types
- chart wall
- column chart
- combo chart
- conditional formatting
- conditional formatting rules
- data labels
- data points
- data points background
- data series
- format painter
- formatting shortcuts
- legend
- line chart
- pie chart
- radar or net chart
- scatter plot chart (xy)
- stacked area chart
- stacked bar chart
- stacked column chart
- stock chart
- surface chart

spreadsheet, which includes regular and conditional formatting, and creating meaningful charts are ways in which a spreadsheet author makes the information visually accessible to the intended audience."

You've probably heard the old saying that "a picture paints a thousand words." This is the fundamental idea behind using formatting and charts in a spreadsheet program. By "painting a picture" of the data by using formatting and charts, you can help the intended audience actually "see" the critical information that the calculations in the spreadsheet are trying to convey. Creating charts can turn a huge amount of detailed data into a concise, easy-to-digest representation of what the data *means* to the reviewer.

Additionally, regular formatting and conditional formatting help to make large amounts of detailed data and calculations easily readable as well as quickly draw attention to critical pieces of information – even if the information is frequently changing!

LO 5.1 Regular Formatting of Labels, Known Data, and Calculated Data

In the previous chapters we looked very briefly at the concepts of formatting the data that you type into a spreadsheet program. We said at that time that you only wanted to perform the minimal formatting necessary to avoid text truncation or overflow and to avoid having numbers show up as a bunch of octothorpes (###) in your spreadsheet.

Now it is time to look at the regular formatting of labels, known data, and calculated data once you have this information keyed into your spreadsheet.

First let's look at some basic universal formatting. Basic Universal Formatting involves the formatting that originated in word processing programs and is fully incorporated into spreadsheet programs. As we have discussed previously, each new blank spreadsheet will have all of the cells in the sheet set up with what is commonly known as *general* formatting. What this means is that, by default, when you type information into a cell, that information will be formatted with a specific default font face, a specific default font size, specific default alignment of data (e.g. text on the left, numbers on the right as we discussed previously), specific font color (e.g. black), specific cell background color (e.g. white), specific border style, color and weight (e.g. typically none), etc. You didn't have to set any of this formatting up when you started a new, blank worksheet. Rather, all of this basic universal formatting is already preset for you.

But, let's face it – the basic universal formatting is, well, pretty boring! I mean, if you like simple black text on a white background with only minimal alignment variation . . . then that's OK too . . . But for most people, adjusting the basic formatting of a spreadsheet beyond the original basic universal formatting is typically more desirable.

So let's look at some other basic formatting that we can easily apply to our spreadsheet data.

First, let's consider some additional basic text formatting that can be accomplished. To think about this concept, it is helpful to simply think about your favorite word processing program. What kind of formatting can you accomplish with text in a word processor? Also, how do you go about changing the formatting of text in a word processor? Once you answer those two questions, you have basically stated how to accomplish the same task in a spreadsheet program.

So let's look at some visual examples of how basic text formatting is accomplished in a spreadsheet program.

Figures 5-1 and 5-2 show the ribbon and toolbars for two popular spreadsheet programs.

In these two figures several colored annotations have been made to highlight certain basic formatting tools that you are mostly probably familiar with. Also, highlighted are several spreadsheet-specific

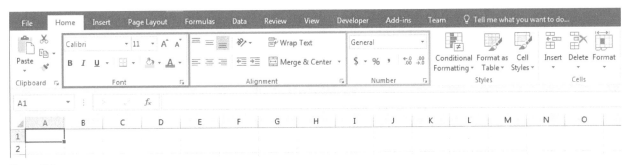

Figure 5-1

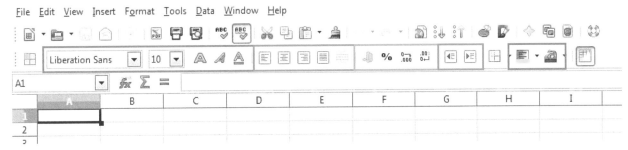

Figure 5-2

formatting tools. Please use the following table as a reference key to compare the tools for each of these spreadsheet programs:

Highlighting Symbol	Formatting Tools	Outcome of Using These Formatting Tools
Red Rectangle	Basic Text Formatting Tools	Change the typeface of the font, the font size, the font color, the background color, the weight of the font, turn on and off italics, turn on and off underlining.
Green Rectangle	Basic Alignment Formatting Tools	Change the alignment of the contents of a cell. Alignment includes left alignment, right alignment, centered alignment, justified alignment, merged alignment, top alignment, middle alignment, bottom alignment, indented and outdented alignment, and text wrapping.
Blue Rectangle	Spreadsheet Basic Numeric Formatting Tools	Change the formatting of any numeric data to be formatted as currency, percentages, comma style, increasing or decreasing decimal precision (with rounding as previously discussed).

By using these simplest of formatting tools, you can very quickly dress up your spreadsheet so that it accurately and professionally represents that information you want to convey.

Here are some tips that you will want to consider before using the various formatting tools.

✦ You don't have to apply formatting individually, to one cell at a time! In fact, it is more efficient to select all cells that are going to be formatted the same way and format them all together, as a single selection of cells.

✦ Once you have changed the format of a cell, that cell format will be used for any new data that is entered into cells directly below this cell.

✦ There are several formatting shortcuts that can help you with this task. Formatting Shortcuts are predefined mechanisms to help you quickly adjust the formatting of the selected cells. For example, there are many keyboard shortcuts that are attached to some of the more common formatting tasks. For example, just like in a word processor, the Ctrl+B keystroke combination will format a cell to be **bold.** Additionally, there are predefined formatting **styles** as well as user-defined styles that you can create and name and then easily use whenever you need.

✦ If you have already formatted a cell a particular way, and then you want to apply that very same formatting to other cells very easily, then you are in luck! There is a special tool called a format painter designed specifically for that purpose. The Format Painter is a tool that copies the formatting of a particular cell and allows you to *paint* that formatting onto any other cells that you select.

✦ Changing the format of a cell may affect the overall size of the resulting values of the columns. As a result, the issues of text truncation, numeric overflow octothorpes (###), and rounding effects may all be introduced after you change the format of the cells. You must remember to double-check to make sure that the formatting of the cells did not introduce any display problems for your spreadsheet.

✦ It is often more efficient to simply do all of the data entry (labels and known data values) first before applying any formatting. That way, you aren't "hopping around" between data entry and formatting tasks.

✦ Likewise, calculations that you enter (formulas and functions) will pick up and use the formatting of the cells that are referenced within the formulas and functions to determine the final format of the resulting value of the new cell. If the cell formatting that is *guessed* for you by your spreadsheet program is not the correct format that you need, you can simply change it to the format that you want it to be.

By using these simple tips, you will be able to quickly plan, lay out, enter, compute, and format any spreadsheet in no time!

LO 5.2   Conditional Formatting

For this next discussion, we will use an example of middle school child who is selling cookies as a fund raiser for their little league team. Figure 5-3 shows this sample spreadsheet after the labels, known data, and unknown calculations have been entered and basic formatting was applied. The steps that follow the figure show the step-by-step actions that were taken to create this example file. If you want, you can repeat the steps that are listed below to build your own version of this sample spreadsheet.

1. Enter the label "Little League Cookie Sales" in cell A1 and then merge-and-center this cell across cells A1:D1. Format this new single cell to be bold with a font size of 14 pts.

2. Enter the column labels in row 2 as shown and then format those cells to be bold, centered, and with text wrapping within the cells.

3. Enter the labels in cells A3:A9 and the known values in cells B3:C9.

4. Enter simple formulas in cells D3:D9 to compute the extended prices. This will be the quantity (column B) multiplied by the unit price (column C). Format all of the numbers in column D as currency or money.

5. Select the entire worksheet and auto-fit the selected columns to spread out the data.

6. Create the Totals line in row 10 and create a SUM function in cell B10 and D10 to compute the totals for those two columns.

7. In row 11, this is a single label in cell A11 and a single known value in cell D11. Make sure that cell D11 is formatted like currency or money.

8. In row 12, this is a single label in cell A12, and a simple formula in cell D12 to compute the remaining balance by subtracting the total sales (cell D10) from the team goal (cell D11).

Little League Cookie Sales			
Cookie Type	Quantity	Unit Price	Extended Price
Chocolate Chip Cookies	144	$1.99	$286.56
Peanut Butter Cookies	103	$1.99	$204.97
Chocolate Mint Cookies	51	$2.49	$126.99
Lemon Cookies	111	$1.99	$220.89
Sugar Cookies	125	$1.49	$186.25
Ginger Cookies	87	$2.29	$199.23
Shortbread Cookies	87	$1.49	$129.63
Totals	708		$1,354.52
Team Sales Goal ($1,500)			$1,500.00
Balance Remaining			$145.48
Average Cookie Price		$1.96	
Minimum Cookie Price		$1.49	
Maximum Cookie Price		$2.49	
Number Left to Sell (at average price)	74		
Number Left to Sell (at minimum price)	98		
Number Left to Sell (at maximum price)	58		

Figure 5-3

9. In rows 13, 14, and 15, the first column contains simple labels and then column C contains an AVERAGE, MIN, and MAX function respectively. Each of these functions is using the range C3:C9 for the function parameter or argument.

10. In rows 16, 17, and 18, the first column contains simple labels and then column B contains simple formulas that divide the balance remaining (cell D12) by the average price (cell C13), the minimum price (cell C14), and the maximum price (cell 15) respectively. These values should be formatted with general number formatting and rounded up with zero decimal places of precision.

11. In rows 10 through 18 – these should all be made bold.

12. Format all of the numeric values in columns C and D to be currency or money.

13. Format all of the numeric values in column B to be centered.

14. Perform various levels of text indenting for the text labels in column A to provide a visual indention for these items.

As we can quickly see, in just 14 steps or so, a simple spreadsheet can be created and minimally formatted to easily show some pertinent information about the ongoing sales efforts of the little league team!

But what if we now wanted to know which cookies have brought in the most money? Maybe we are interested in knowing which cookies have brought in more than $200. We could manually look through the totals in column D and then manually highlight or color the best-selling cookies with some special highlighting (like maybe green for money!) But as we discussed previously, most spreadsheets aren't working with such a small amount of data, so the task of simply "eyeballing" the data doesn't work in most cases. Additionally, if the data changes, than any manual highlighting of special cells will have to be manually reviewed and possibly changed as there may be newer or different cells that would then need to be highlighted.

Fortunately, spreadsheet programs provide a means where you can conditionally format cells based upon some criteria. Conditional formatting is the act of specifying some type of cell formatting that will be used only if certain criteria are met. In our example, we want to highlight any cell in the range D3:D9 *but only if the condition is true that the value is greater than $200*. If this condition is true, then we will want to highlight the cell with a green background color.

To accomplish this task, we will set up a conditional formatting rule. A Conditional Formatting Rule is the condition that is used to test to see if some conditional formatting should be applied to a cell. Cells can be given multiple different conditional formatting rules so that very specific formatting can be applied under the right conditions.

A key point to remember is that although the specific steps required to set up and apply conditional formatting may vary across the different spreadsheet programs, the key concepts remain the same:

1. For the first step, you will select all of the cells that you want to have tested to see if the conditional formatting should be applied to them.

2. Next, you will set the condition or rule that will be used to test the cells to see if the specific formatting should be applied. There are many, many possible conditions; some examples of conditional rules are:

   a. If the cells are greater than some value . . .

   b. If the cells are less than some value . . .

   c. If the cells are between some values . . .

   d. If the cells are in the top or bottom 10% . . .

3. Finally, you will decide the specific formatting that you will want to apply to the cells that match your chosen conditions. In some programs, you will just specify all of the formatting properties that you want to apply. In other programs, you may also choose from some predefined or named styles to apply.

Figure 5-4 shows the first two steps described above being applied to our cookie sales spreadsheet.

The highlighted cells show how step 1 was completed by selecting the cell range D3:39. Then, using the menus, the Conditional Formatting Dialog was initiated to complete step 2. Here we see that the first Conditional Formatting Rule is being established where the cell values are being compared to the literal value 200 and, if the condition is true, then the formatting will be applied. If there was a previously named style available, then it could simply be selected at this time.

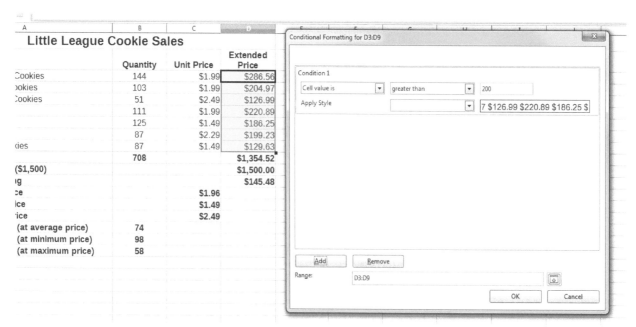

Figure 5-4

In Figure 5-5, we see that the specific formatting is being set for all cells that meet the specified condition.

Looking at this dialog, we can see that we have complete control over all of the formatting aspects for the cells that meet our criteria. Number format, font, alignment, borders, and background colors – every bit of cell formatting – can be conditionally controlled.

Between using standard basic formatting and conditional formatting, you can very easily control every bit of the final visual appearance of your spreadsheet data!

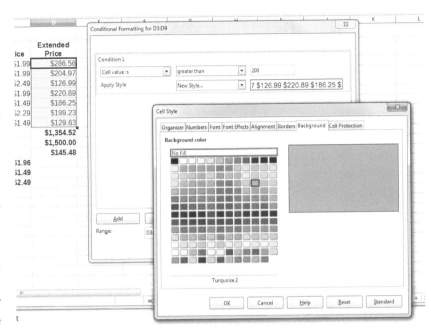

Figure 5-5

But remember, although our examples show only a very few number of rows and columns, the "real-world" spreadsheets typically have very, very, many rows and columns of data. Sometimes, just applying basic formatting and even conditional formatting may not be enough to help the reviewer of a spreadsheet understand the critical pieces of information that you may want them to know. This is where charts come into play.

In the next five learning objectives, we will be looking at charting information in spreadsheets. The concepts of charts works independently of any basic of conditional formatting that may already be applied in a spreadsheet. Very often, these concepts are used together to produce multiple ways of looking at and thinking about the information that is contained within a spreadsheet.

LO 5.3   Things to Do before Creating Any Charts

In the next several sections, we will see just how easy it has become to create visually appealing charts from the data within a spreadsheet. It is so easy, in fact, that often we are tempted to just "jump right in and make a chart" before we address some very critical steps first.

There are several things that you should always do *before* creating any charts in your spreadsheet program.

1. Before attempting to create any charts in spreadsheet programs, the most important thing you should do first is **double-check the accuracy of all of your work.** You have just completed creating a spreadsheet that has very many labels, a lot of data-entry of known values, and a lot of formulas and functions to calculate unknown data. Now before you attempt to use this data to create a chart, you should *always* double-check your work to make sure you don't have any mistakes.

    For example – do you have any typos in your column or row labels? If so, those same typos will show up in the chart! What about the data entry of the known values? Did you make sure that all of the numbers that you entered were correct? If any of those numbers are incorrect . . . guess what . . . that's what will show up in the chart!

And how about those calculations – all of the formulas and functions that you added to calculate the unknown data? Are all of those functions pointing to the correct cell ranges and cell references? If not, you will still see an answer, but it would be the **wrong** answer. And any chart that is based on that data will also show the wrong information.

This step is the most critical step and must be completed first before you begin to think about creating a chart!

2. Next, you should ask yourself, "Who is the intended audience for this chart and what do they want or need to see?" In our cookie sales example, if the chart is being made for all of the team members and you want to show how each team member is doing compared to each other, then this audience will want to see some detail in the chart that will help them understand where they fit in and how they compare to their other teammates.

But if you are creating the chart for the cookie manufacturer and they just need to see the total number of boxes of each cookie type that need to be shipped, well then that is a totally different audience who has a completely different need.

The same spreadsheet of data will be used for both of these kinds of charts, but the actual chart that would be built would be completely different for each of these types of audiences.

3. Next, you should ask yourself which type of chart will best convey the information that the intended audience wants to see? In the next learning objective (LO 5.4) we will be exploring the different types of charts and discovering how certain charts are better suited for specific purposes and specific sets of data.

4. And finally, you should ask yourself how will your target audience be reviewing your chart? If your intent will be to simply produce the chart and then use a picture of that chart in some presentation file, then you have no more worries. But if you intend to actually share this file with your intended audience and want them to open up the file and view your chart there, well then, we might run into some problems.

You see all of the information that we have covered in the first four chapters hasn't really changed that much at all since the earliest versions of spreadsheet programs. From the earliest days of spreadsheets, entering labels hasn't changed; entering known data values hasn't changed; performing basic calculations with formulas and functions hasn't changed; performing basic layout and formatting of the data hasn't changed.

But with advances in graphics technology over the years, many of the new features that were added in more recent versions of spreadsheet programs were all improvements in graphic representations of data, also known as advance charts. Because of this, a number of advanced charts have been created in each new version of various spreadsheet programs and, as such, these newer charts **may not** actually be viewable in any other spreadsheet program other than the one it was created within.

The good news is that there are very many basic, common, or standard charts that will show up just fine across versions of spreadsheet programs. But there are an equal number of charts that are going to be only available in the program in which they were created. Therefore, it is very important that you think about **how** the intended audience is going to see your chart before you choose which chart to create and how you create that chart.

Answering these questions and, if necessary, correcting any errors in the original spreadsheet, are some of the most important things you should do **before** you begin to create your desired charts.

LO 5.4   Different Chart Types and Purposes and Selecting the Best Chart

Charts are visual representations of data. They exist to help an audience quickly see patterns and comparisons of data without necessarily needing to see all of the detail that went in to making up those eventual comparisons and patterns.

When we start to think about charts and graphs, it is helpful to know that charts can be typically grouped into categories that reflect the primary purpose of the charts.

The following table shows several different categories of charts, some of the more common Chart Types, also known as chart names that are members of each category, and the general information that can be shown by using charts of each category. The focus of the examples provided in this table are the

Chart Category	Chart Name	Chart Sample	Chart Description
Charts Commonly Used for Comparing Values to Each Other	Column Chart		Column charts are used to compare values across a few categories.
	Line Chart		Line charts are to show trends over time.
	Area Chart		Similar to a line chart, an area chart show data values as they change over time with a cumulative aspect.
	Bar Chart		Bar charts are similar to column charts and compare values across a few categories.
Charts Commonly Used to Show the Composition of a Group	Pie Chart		Pie charts are used to show all of the proportional components that make up a whole value.
	Stacked Column Chart		Stacked column charts group values over each category to show cumulative totals.

(continued)

Chart Category	Chart Name	Chart Sample	Chart Description
	Stacked Line Chart		Stacked line charts group values over each category to show cumulative totals over time.
	Stacked Bar Chart		Stacked bar charts group values over each category to show cumulative totals.
	Stacked Area Chart		Stacked area charts show parts as they relate to the whole and change over time or over categories.
Charts Commonly Used to Show the Distribution of Data	**Scatter Plot Chart (XY)**		A scatter plot chart, also known as an XY chart, shows the relationship between two sets of data. Scatter charts are often used to visually show trends and positive and negative correlations between data sets.
	Radar or Net Chart		A radar or net chart compares the values as points connected by some lines, in a grid net that resembles a spider web or a radar display.
	Surface Chart		A surface chart is like a topographical map, which show peaks and troughs corresponding to data combinations.
	Bubble Chart		Similar to a scatter chart, bubble charts show bubble sizes using one value and bubble position using a different value.

(continued)

Specialized Charts	**Stock Chart**		Stock charts show data points associated with the opening value, low value, high value, and closing value of a traded asset with coloring to represent the overall increase or decrease in value.
	Combo Chart	(Various)	This type of chart combines at least two other chart types into a single representation.
	Various Other Charts	There are very many other specialized charts that have been created in each spreadsheet program. The easiest way to discover these is to work directly in each program.	

most common types of charts that are used most often and are most commonly found in all contemporary spreadsheet programs.

This table is by no means a complete list of all charts that are available to you. Rather, it is meant to give you a general idea of the vast variety of charts and graphs that are available to you and the ways in which these different chart types can be used to tell a particular story about your information.

Selecting the correct chart to properly represent your data is an important task that gets easier over time. But you should also know that it is highly expected that newer versions of spreadsheet programs will continue to introduce new and even more exotic charts and graphs to visually represent data and these new charts may or may not be compatible with other spreadsheet programs.

LO 5.5 How to Create a Chart

Once you have prepared your spreadsheet and have chosen the desired chart type, the next thing to do is to actually create the chart. Compared to early versions of spreadsheet programs, creating charts is now a relatively very simple task consisting of three basic steps:

1. Select **all** of the data that you want to show up in the chart including column labels, row labels, known data, and optionally calculated data.

2. Insert a chart from the list of available chart types. This list may automatically change based on the data that you have selected.

3. Make adjustments to the chart elements as desired and place the chart wherever you want it to reside.

If this sounds pretty simple, you won't be surprised when you do it yourself! It is, in fact, pretty simple to create charts.

But with that being said, there are some things that you will want to remember that can help keep you out of trouble when you create your charts. Let's explore in some detail what can go right and what can go wrong when you are creating your charts.

First, let's continue to work with our cookie sales example and let's consider creating a chart for the cookie distributor to show how many boxes of cookies that will need to be shipped to us.

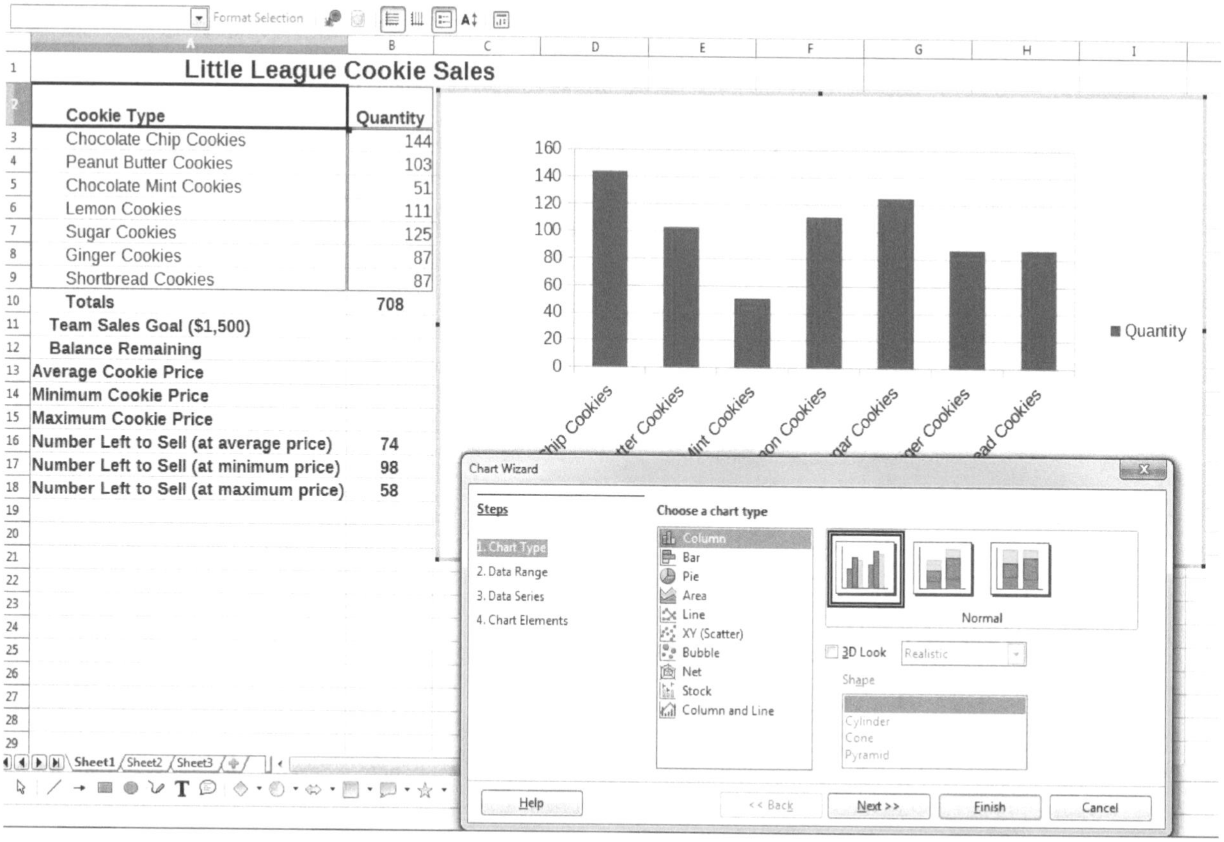

Figure 5-6

Figure 5-6 shows our example spreadsheet after performing steps 1 and 2 listed above. First, we selected the labels and known data in the cell range A2:B9. Since we selected both the labels and the known data values, when we click on the tool to start the creation of the chart, the program automatically attempts to interpret the details of the selected data and then makes a recommendation of an appropriate chart type based on the selected data. You can also see that the program has created an initial version of the chart and placed the chart directly on top of the other information in the spreadsheet. This will have to be moved to a new location later on.

Next, we see that the program has created a chart dialog to help us in the process of building the chart. Here, we could easily choose a different chart type and the chart will automatically be updated!

Simply completing the remaining steps of the chart creation dialogs, you can quickly change many of the options that are available to you to get your chart to look just the way you want it to appear.

After working through the first two steps listed above, we successfully have a chart created and placed in the spreadsheet. But to be prepared to complete the third step, we will need to more fully explore a number of the different parts or elements of the chart so we can make the desired adjustments to our final chart.

LO 5.6 Identifying and Working with Different Parts of a Chart

As we discovered in the last section, spreadsheet charts come in many different shapes and sizes and can be used in many different ways to help visually describe many different kinds of data. With this much diversity and power, it is important to understand the various parts or elements that are included with charts. Chart Parts or Elements are the various components that make up the visual representation of a completed chart object. Some of the parts or elements are universally available to all chart types while others are more unique and may only be available to specific charts.

Figure 5-7 shows our sample chart after some minor modifications have been made. The first modification that was made was the addition of a chart title (circled in orange.) A Chart Title is a text area, usually at the top of a chart that describes the overall contents of the chart.

A second modification was the addition of data labels (circled in green.) Data

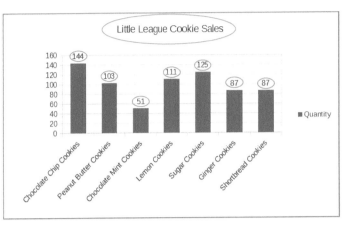

Figure 5-7

Labels are values that are applied next to the graphical objects in a chart to show the specific details about the graphical item. Data labels could be values, percentages, categories, series values, or other items depending on the chart type.

Besides those two chart elements that were added, there were a number of basic chart elements that are automatically included with every chart.

The first common chart element to consider is the chart area. The Chart Area is the overall container area that contains all of the other chart elements. The red solid rectangular border that surrounds the chart itself was added to show the entire chart area. The Chart Background is the overall *canvas* which is where all of the other chart elements or parts are placed. The chart background can be colored or transparent or could be given a picture as a background. The chart background can have an outline drawn (as we did in this example) and can also have special effects like shadows and rounded corners and other advanced graphical features.

It should be noted that almost all chart elements will allow you to change their styling with all of the previously mentioned effects, so we won't repeat them for every chart element that we discuss going forward. This concept is known as chart part formatting. Chart Part Formatting is a concept that states that if you can specifically *select* a chart element, than you can typically update its styling to include things like color fills, transparent fills, picture fills, color borders, border styling, border weight, shadowing, 3-D effects, and many, many more graphic features. The specific chart part formatting will depend on the chart element that you have selected, but many of these concepts are universal for all chart elements.

The next chart elements we will discuss are the axes. Many chart types have two or three axes: these are collectively called the chart axes. The Chart Axes (X-, Y-, and Z-) represent the horizontal scale of the chart, the vertical scale of the chart and, for 3-D charts, the depth scale of a chart respectively. In our Figure 5-7, the cookie name labels became the X-axis values to represent the labels for this main series of data. This was automatically determined simply by including these labels during the initial selection process before creating the chart.

For the Y-axis, we see that the chart created a scale in the range of 0 through 160. This is known as the axis range. The Axis Range is a dynamically adjusting scale that is automatically generated to reflect the minimum and the maximum of the values of the data that is being charted. If the values of the data series change (either smaller or larger) then the axis range is automatically readjusted to reflect the new range of values.

Since this chart was not a 3-D chart type, there was no Z-axis included for this chart.

The Chart Wall is seen in our Figure 5-7 example as the light gray lines that represent a grid for the chart data to be displayed upon. When you select the chart wall, you can change all of the details as previously described, but you can also change things like whether or not the grid lines will show up within the chart area as well as the style, color, weight, and other aspects of the lines themselves. This can help to clarify the data values or, when removed, their absences can also help to unclutter a chart that may be particularly overfilled with data.

The next chart element we will look at is the actual blue columns themselves. These items are called the data points. Data Points are the specific values of data that are depicted graphically within a chart. For column and bar charts (like our example), the data points are represented by the actual columns or bars. For line charts, the data points are represented by the vertices of the line segment intersections. For area charts, the data points are represented by the peaks and valleys or troughs. For pie charts, the data points are represented by the proportional pie slices. As you can imagine, the data points will take on many different graphical aspects based upon the type of chart being displayed.

An interesting concept related to the data points themselves is that the data points can be individually formatted in most spreadsheet programs. For example the Data Points Background can be changed to use more than just simple colors and shading. Data points backgrounds could also be pictures or symbols. So if you had columns representing increasing sales, you could specify that the data points backgrounds are pictures of stacks of money that fill in the data points. Graphically speaking, there are very many creative ways in which charts can be visually represented.

Also related to the data points are the chart elements known as the data series. In charts, the Data Series is simply the group of rows and columns of related data that will allow the charts to compare one collection of the data to another. When charting multiple data series in a single chart, each data series must contain the same number of elements to be properly charted.

Bar charts, column charts, line charts, and area charts must have a minimum of one data series, but may also use more than one data series at a time. Some other charts, however, are designed specifically to work with one and only one data series at a time. Take the ubiquitous pie chart for example. This type of chart is designed to only represent a single data series and to compare how each element of that data series compares to each other and help to comprise the whole of the data series.

The final, nearly universal chart element we will discuss is the legend. The Legend is a text box that typically describes the color coding of the data points and/or data series in a chart. In our example, the legend is the label "Quantity" and is shown with a blue square representing the blue data points. Like all of the other chart elements previously discussed, the legend can be fully formatted in pretty much any way imaginable. Likewise, the legend can be turned on or off and can be placed anywhere within the chart area.

And speaking of legend positioning, it should be noted that all of the chart elements can be independently sized (stretched or shrunk) and independently positioned (moved) to any part of the chart area. This is called the chart part sizing and positioning. In charts and graphs, Chart Part Sizing & Positioning is the concept that you can manually size and move the various chart elements to different locations within the chart area. This is particularly helpful when some elements (like the axes labels, data labels, or the legend etc.) become too filled with data and begin to overlap the other elements of the chart. By manually adjusting the chart part positioning, you can insure that all of the critical elements of the chart remain visible to your intended audience.

Finally, once you have completed your chart and all of the desired elements have been added, formatted, and positioned **within** the chart itself, the last step is to position the overall chart into a meaningful and nondisruptive position within the spreadsheet file itself. This is called chart positioning. Chart Positioning is the placement of a chart object in an appropriate location on a worksheet within a workbook such that it does not obscure any other data and so that it is not distracting of confusing with the other data as well.

In Figure 5-8, we see our final chart has been positioned to the right of the data itself. But once again, you should always consider who the target audience is for each chart that you create. If this chart

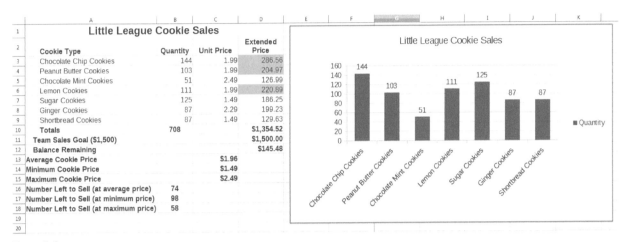

Figure 5-8

was being created for the cookie manufacturer so that they would know how many boxes of cookies to ship to the team, then that person may not need to know any of the other data like the pricing or the other calculations that were created in rows 10 through 18.

Therefore, as is often the case, it is very common to create the chart first and then ***cut it*** from its original location and then paste it onto its own worksheet within the workbook file. By doing so, the chart will still reference the data from the original sheet. However, by being on its own sheet, you will have more room to stretch out the chart object and to make sure that all of the information is easily readable for the intended audience.

LO 5.7   Common Mistakes when Creating Charts

There are several mistakes that can happen when you first begin to create charts. Unfortunately, the most common mistake is the one that happens when you forget to double-check your spreadsheet work ***before*** you create a chart. As we discussed in LO 5.3, you must always double-check your work (e.g. labels are all spelled correctly, known data has no data-entry errors, the formulas and functions are properly created and are referencing the correct cells) ***before*** creating any charts!

But even if all of the data is correct when you begin to create your charts, there are still several things that can go "wrong" when creating charts. Let's take a look at some of the more common problems that can arise.

First, problems will arise if you select the wrong data (e.g. either too much data or not enough data) before attempting to create a chart. Figure 5-9 shows an example of selecting too little data before creating the chart.

In this example, we see that the only cells that were selected at the time the chart was created were the known data values in the cell range B3:B9. As a result, when the chart was created, look at what is now shown in the X-axis labels. Since the cookie names were not selected (A3:A9), the program does not know what this series is all about. So instead, it just substitutes the numbers 1 through 7 to represent the seven data points that were selected.

Additionally, we see that the legend says simply "Column B," which has no real meaning for the intended audience. This occurred because we did not select the column label in cell B2, which would have told the program that these data points represent "Quantities."

By not selecting all of the desired labels, we can see that the chart that was created is woefully lacking much of the desired information to make this chart useful to the intended audience.

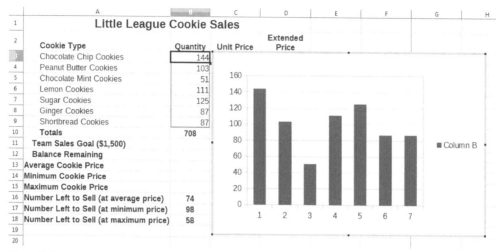

Figure 5-9

And just as selecting too little data can be problematic, selecting too much data can also be a problem when creating charts. Figure 5-10 shows a chart that was created when too much data was selected at the same time. In this example we see that the Totals row (row 10) was also included in the chart. When you include total rows or columns (or other aggregate rows or columns like averages and counts, etc.) in a single chart, you end up comparing the individual data values at the same time as the overall totals for those values. Let's observe what happened to the Y-axis range. As a result of including the total along with the individual data points, the Y-axis range had to be expanded to include the whole total value. This shows that the last column, the total, is towering over the other data points. Additionally, the other data points are all shown as very small and hard to compare graphic values. It becomes very hard to tell whether the Chocolate Chip Cookies or the Sugar Cookies are selling better than the other. By including the totals along with the individual data items, the overall chart becomes distorted in its scale and its visual representation. Instead of making the data easier to visually imagine, this chart actually makes it harder to interpret.

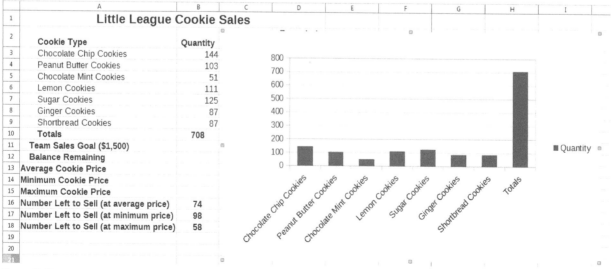

Figure 5-10

We can see this effect also happens with looking at other chart types as well. Let's consider the simple pie chart. In Figure 5-11, we see what happens if we attempt to create a pie chart but then select the total row at the same time as the individual data rows. Here we see what looks like a very large pie piece that is light green. In fact, this pie piece looks to be about ½ of the total pie! This would appear to be a very big selling cookie, that is, if it was actually an individual cookie being sold.

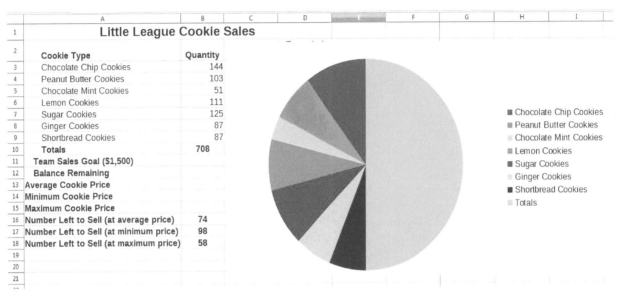

Figure 5-11

But by looking at the legend that was created, we can see that the light green pie piece actually represent the totals and, therefore, is ***not a valid piece of this pie***. This pie chart that was created was actually *double* the size it was supposed to be. All of the colored pieces on the left side of the pie are the only valid pieces for this pie chart.

Another way that this can happen is when you need to select the labels from one column and then select the data values from a non-adjacent column to create the desired chart. This technique is called selecting disjointed cells and was defined briefly in chapter 2.

When selecting disjointed cells, you must select the first group of cells which are typically the data labels for the data series. Let's suppose, for example, that there were 10 rows of data labels that you selected initially.

Then, the next step would be to hold down the control-key (on Windows and Linux machines) or the command-key (on Mac machines) and then select the corresponding data values in the non-adjacent cell range. The key here is that ***you must select precisely the same number of cells in the second selection as the number of cells that you selected in the first selection.*** If you do not select the precise number of cells with each selection, then the program will not know how to properly match up the data labels with the data values that you are trying to chart. The end result will be a broken and nonsensical chart that will need to be deleted and then recreated.

Now, Figure 5-12 here shows a corrected version of the pie chart that properly omits the total value from row 10. In this example, we can see that the individual cookies now represent their individual pie pieces, which, together, make up the total value that is calculated in cell B10.

Making sure that you have selected just the right cells before creating a chart is a critical step that becomes easier with practice.

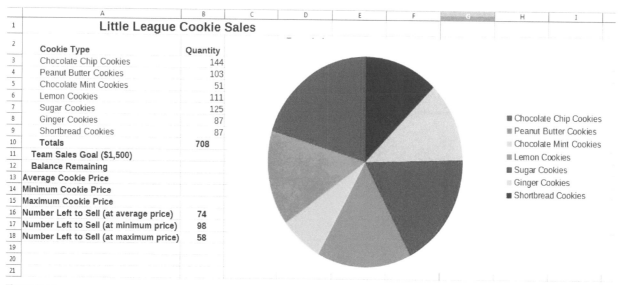

Figure 5-12

One more problem that can occur is if you do not properly control the positioning and placement of the chart elements and of the chart itself. For example, in Figure 5-12, while the chart itself does seem to have all of its chart elements fully visible, the chart itself is placed directly over the additional data that exists in columns C and D. This is not acceptable.

Generally speaking, ***charts should not*** be allowed to obscure other data that is behind the chart object.

More examples of chart errors can be found by observing Figure 5-13. In this example, we see that a Chart Title *element* has been added to the chart but the actual chart title has not been updated. Leaving elements with their default, nondescriptive values is not considered *best practices* and should be avoided.

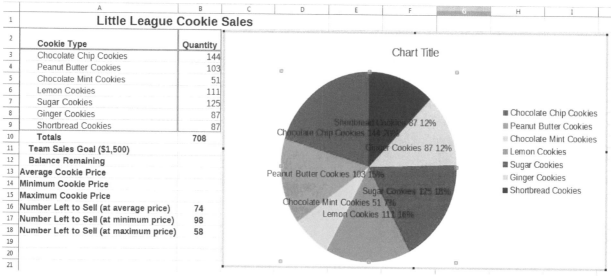

Figure 5-13

Additionally, in this example we see that data labels were added to include the legend label, the data point values, as well as the percentage calculation for each data point. While this is all useful and meaningful information, by including all of the information together, it now becomes nearly impossible to tell which data labels go with which data points.

Here again, the act of adding additional information doesn't help to clarify the chart data but rather causes confusion by the undesirable cluttering effect. The good lesson to remember here is, "just because you *can* do a thing, doesn't necessarily mean that you *should* do that thing!"

LO 5.8   Differences Between Spreadsheet Programs Regarding Charts

As mentioned in Learning Objective 5.4 (LO 5.4) one of the major differences between different versions of spreadsheet programs can be found when comparing the different kinds of charts that each program creates and supports. Many of the basic charts that have been discussed in this chapter will be found in any contemporary spreadsheet program. And likewise, each of these more common kinds of charts will be compatible across the different spreadsheet program vendors and versions.

What this means is that if you create a simple bar, column, line, pie, or area chart in one spreadsheet program, it is very likely that a different spreadsheet program will be able to open and possibly update these basic chart types as well.

But the newer and more advanced charts are becoming more complex to build and render and, as such, may become more isolated with regard to their compatibility. In fact, some of the more contemporary spreadsheet program versions *from the same single vendor* are now creating charts that are wholly incompatible with other contemporary versions from the same vendor! Examples of this include that some online versions of a spreadsheet program cannot open and view charts made from the desktop version by the same vendor and vice versa.

The software vendors obviously have their own reasons for creating these incompatibilities, though I am certain that none of those reasons are in the best interests of you and me, the end consumers.

But with that being said, it is critical to understand that this is merely a fact to be contended with and is likely to continue on into the foreseeable future.

The lessons learned in Learning Objective 5.3 (LO 5.3) will help guide you to make good decisions when it comes to creating spreadsheet charts: If you first consider who the target audience is for your chart and what software *they* will be using to view the chart, this will help you make sure that you are not using an incompatible chart type that will not be easily seen by your intended audience.

Chapter 5 – Assignments and Projects

Directed Assignments

DA 5-1. For this directed assignment, you will be using the student data file named **DA_5-1.xlsx** to complete the required information. This file is in Microsoft Excel 2007 or newer format and should open in any contemporary spreadsheet program.

Required student data file: *DA_5-1.xlsx*

In this workbook, you will find a rather interesting collection of data. This spreadsheet shows some *random* sales dollar amounts for 10 departments for the first six months of the year. Because the actual functions in the cell range B3:G12 includes the RAND function, every time you make any little change to this spreadsheet (or intentionally press the function key F9 on the keyboard), the random numbers are all re-generated This means that the data is constantly changing! We will be going over the RAND function in more detail in the next chapter. But for now, we want the numbers to keep changing so we can experiment with conditional formatting.

Your task will be to complete this spreadsheet following the instructions below.

1. Open the student data file named **DA_5-1.xlsx**.

2. Immediately save a copy of this file using the following specifications:

   a. File name: Rename this file using the filename **YourName_DA_5-1**

   b. File location: Place this file in any location you choose, but make a note of the location as you will need it later.

   c. File format: Because this file will be sent in to your professor, you must check with him or her to see what format **he or she** will want this file to be saved in. Don't just assume that the original file format or the default file format for your own computer will be acceptable!

3. In cell A13, add the label "Totals" and in the cell range B13:G13 add SUM functions to calculate the totals for each month.

4. In cell H2, add the label "Totals" and in the cell range H3:H13 add SUM functions to calculate the totals for each department and for the grand total in cell H13.

5. In cell A14, add the label "Averages" and in the cell range B14:H14 add AVERAGE functions to calculate the average sales for each month and the average of all of the first 6 months' totals. Make sure you **do not** include the monthly totals from row 13 in the average calculations!

6. In cell I2, add the label "Averages" and in the cell range I3:I14 add AVERAGE functions to calculate the average sales for each month as well as the average of the monthly totals and also a final overall average in cell I14. Make sure you **do not** include the total values found in column H in the average calculations!

7. Next, you will add some calculations to show the MIN and the MAX of the random sales data. As mentioned before, these values will constantly change whenever we make any changes to the spreadsheet. To complete this requirement, perform the following steps:

   a. Merge and center cell A16 and B16 and enter the label "Minimum Sales".

   b. Merge and center cell A17 and B17 and enter the label "Maximum Sales".

   c. Enter the MIN function in cell C16 using the range B3:G12 as the function argument.

   d. Enter the MAX function in cell C17 using the range B3:G12 as the function argument.

8. Next, we will apply conditional formatting to highlight the specific cells in our data range of B3:G12 that match our MIN and MAX values. To accomplish this, complete the following steps:

   a. Select the desired range of B3:G12.

   b. Initiate the Conditional Formatting Dialogs to enter the desired rules and formatting.

   c. Create the first rule to highlight any cell that is exactly equal to the minimum sales (=$C$16) with a red background, bold font, and a solid black cell outline.

   d. Create the second rule to highlight any cell that is exactly equal to the maximum sales (=$C$17) with a green background, bold font, and a solid black cell outline.

9. Next, we will apply conditional formatting to highlight the specific averages that are greater than the overall average. To accomplish this, complete the following steps:

   a. Select two desired ranges of non-adjacent cells. First select the monthly averages that are found in the range B14:G14. Then, holding down either the control key (for Windows or Linux machines) or the command key (for Mac machines), select the department averages that are found in the range (I3:I12).

   b. Initiate the Conditional Formatting Dialogs to enter the desired rule and formatting.

   c. Create a rule to highlight any of the select cells that are greater than or equal to the overall average (>=$C$16) with a light yellow background, bold font, and a solid black cell outline.

10. Perform some final basic formatting cleanup including the following:

    a. Extend the merged cell in A1 to include the cells H1 and I1 so that the heading will be overall **all** of the columns including the two new columns that were added.

    b. Increase the font size in cell A1 to 14 points and make it bold with a tan background color.

    c. Use the format painter tool to copy the formatting of the cell that is currently showing the highlighted minimum value and "paint'" that formatting onto the cell C16.

    d. Use the format painter tool to copy the formatting of the cell that is currently showing the highlighted maximum value and 'paint' that formatting onto the cell C17.

11. Make any final necessary adjustments to ensure readability and correctness of your work. Then, once you are sure that everything is correct, you should save your work and then submit it in accordance with your class instructions.

At the completion of this directed assignment, your final work will look similar in structure and layout to the Figure DA_5-1_Completed found here. However, it is important to remember that this spreadsheet is constantly generating random numbers for the sales data, so your *specific* file **will not** look identical to this figure.

	A	B	C	D	E	F	G	H	I
1				Random Sale Amounts For 10 Departments					
2		January	February	March	April	May	June	Totals	Averages
3	Dept. 1	$ 618.69	$ 470.75	$ 3,794.28	$ 1,717.56	$ 2,791.08	$ 1,824.70	$ 11,217.06	$ 1,869.51
4	Dept. 2	$ 650.90	$ 2,170.73	$ 29.49	$ 1,681.58	$ 216.63	$ 2,542.95	$ 7,292.28	$ 1,215.38
5	Dept. 3	$ 995.97	$ 1,752.19	$ 1,010.11	$ 1,454.67	$ 2,997.49	$ 3,482.36	$ 11,692.79	$ 1,948.80
6	Dept. 4	$ 130.72	$ 2,195.55	$ 471.47	$ 4,425.17	$ 1,294.98	$ 2,402.70	$ 10,920.59	$ 1,820.10
7	Dept. 5	$ 1,058.59	$ 2,566.28	$ 3,964.31	$ 2,469.45	$ 3,221.79	$ 3,205.27	$ 16,485.69	$ 2,747.62
8	Dept. 6	$ 1,192.63	$ 1,091.49	$ 1,361.65	$ 974.02	$ 3,203.85	$ 3,813.68	$ 11,637.32	$ 1,939.55
9	Dept. 7	$ 4,362.72	$ 3,381.22	$ 3,272.21	$ 3,534.46	$ 2,473.99	$ 1,286.25	$ 18,310.85	$ 3,051.81
10	Dept. 8	$ 4,917.97	$ 2,240.48	$ 1,703.02	$ 4,083.89	$ 2,642.26	$ 3,976.34	$ 19,563.96	$ 3,260.66
11	Dept. 9	$ 1,593.10	$ 4,046.90	$ 4,281.40	$ 4,427.49	$ 3,728.59	$ 486.19	$ 18,563.67	$ 3,093.95
12	Dept. 10	$ 2,797.52	$ 1,549.74	$ 2,157.51	$ 4,375.16	$ 1,083.74	$ 2,888.01	$ 14,851.68	$ 2,475.28
13	Totals	$ 18,318.81	$ 21,465.33	$ 22,045.45	$ 29,143.45	$ 23,654.40	$ 25,908.45	$ 140,535.89	$ 23,422.65
14	Averages	$ 1,831.88	$ 2,146.53	$ 2,204.55	$ 2,914.35	$ 2,365.44	$ 2,590.85	$ 14,053.59	$ 2,342.26
15									
16	Minimum Sales		$ 29.49						
17	Maximum Sales		$ 4,917.97						
18									
19									

First 6 Months

Figure DA_5-1_Completed

DA 5-2. For this directed assignment, you will be using the student data file named **DA_5-2.ods** to complete the required information. This file is in LibreOffice Calc version 4.2 or newer format and should open in any contemporary spreadsheet program.

Required student data file: *DA_5-2.ods*

In this workbook, you are working with a spreadsheet that has data about the total number of calls handled by the New-Tech Enterprises Customer Service Centers. This company has a call center in each one of the territories in the US. The spreadsheet has already been laid out and the known data has been entered. Your boss wants you to complete the spreadsheet and then create two charts about the data.

Your task will be to complete this spreadsheet following the instructions below.

1. Open the student data file named **DA_5-2.ods**.
2. Immediately save a copy of this file using the following specifications:
   a. File name: Rename this file using the filename *YourName_DA_5-2*
   b. File location: Place this file in any location you choose, but make a note of the location as you will need it later.
   c. File format: Because this file will be sent in to your professor, you must check with him or her to see what format *he or she* will want this file to be saved in. Don't just assume that the original file format or the default file format for your own computer will be acceptable!
3. Enter the SUM function in cell B8 to calculate the total for all territories in the first quarter.
4. Use the fill handle to copy this function from cell B8 to the range C8:E8.
5. Enter the AVERAGE function in cell B9 to calculate the average for all territories in the first quarter. Make sure that you **do not** include the total in cell B8. Set this cell to have two decimal places of precision.
6. Use the fill handle to copy this function from cell B9 to the range C9:E9.
7. Enter the SUM function in cell F3 to calculate the total for the North territory for all quarters.
8. Use the fill handle to copy this function from cell F3 to the range F4:F8.
9. Enter the AVERAGE function in cell G3 to calculate the average for all quarters for the North territory. Make sure that you **do not** include the total in cell F3. Set this cell to have two decimal places of precision.
10. Use the fill handle to copy this function from cell G3 to the range G4:G7.
11. Now, as you review the data and your formulas and functions to make sure you have entered all of the data and calculations correctly, you discover that there are three corrections that need to be made:
   a. In cell A7, you remember that the company renamed the Central territory to the "Midwest" territory last year. Make that correction.
   b. You also remember that last year the company also split out Alaska and Hawaii from the West territory and created a new territory called the "Pacific" territory . . . and that territory is completely missing! Insert a row between rows 5 and 6 and enter the following known values:

Pacific	1989	2124	3133	2821

   c. Copy the contents of the range F5:G5 to the range F6:G6.

12. Now that the data is correct, you are ready to create the two charts that the boss wanted. The first chart is supposed to compare all of the territories to each other for each quarter as well as comparing the average for each territory at the same time. You decide that a clustered column chart makes the most sense for this chart. Complete the following steps to create this chart:

   a. Select the cell range A2:E8. Then, hold either the control key (for Windows and Linux) or the command key (for Mac) and then select the non-adjacent cell range of G2:G8.

   b. With the correct cells selected, use the tool in your spreadsheet program to initiate the chart creation dialogs.

   c. Select a column chart (preferably 3-D) to show the quarters and the averages as columns for each of the selected territories.

   d. Step through the chart dialogs and make any necessary changes to make sure that the chart has an appropriate chart title, correct X-Axis and Y-Axis labels, and a legend.

   e. When the chart is completed, cut this chart from the main sheet and place it on its own separate sheet named "Quarterly and Average Chart".

13. The next chart your boss wants you to create is a chart that shows each territory and their total call volume for the year as a simple pie chart. Complete the following steps to create this chart:

   a. Select the cell range A2:A8 to select the appropriate labels. Then, hold either the control key (for Windows and Linux) or the command key (for Mac) and then select the non-adjacent cell range of F2:F8 to select the total call volume for each territory.

   b. With the correct cells selected, use the tool in your spreadsheet program to initiate the chart creation dialogs.

   c. Select a pie chart (preferably 3-D) to show the territories' total call volumes for the year.

   d. Step through the chart dialogs and make any necessary changes to make sure that the chart has an appropriate chart title, data labels on the outside of the pie pieces that show the percentage of each pie piece, and a legend.

14. When the chart is completed, cut this chart from the main sheet and place it on its own separate sheet named "Total Call Volume Chart".

15. Below are three Figures that you can use to compare your own work. Figure DA_5-2_Completed_Data is the first sheet with the labels, known data, and unknown data calculations completed. Figure DA_5-2_Completed_Chart-1 is the first column chart completed. Figure DA_5-2_Completed_Chart-2 is the second pie chart completed.

	A	B	C	D	E	F	G	H
1		New-Tech Enterprises Customer Service Calls By Territory						
2		Qtr. 1	Qtr. 2	Qtr. 3	Qtr. 4	Totals	Average	
3	North	3954	6085	5184	3868	19091	4772.75	
4	South	3728	5557	5322	4574	19181	4795.25	
5	East	5981	3936	5046	5647	20610	5152.50	
6	Pacific	1989	2124	3133	2821	10067	2516.75	
7	West	4902	2916	5252	4388	17458	4364.50	
8	Midwest	3166	4381	3482	5804	16833	4208.25	
9	Totals	23720	24999	27419	27102	103240		
10	Average	3953.33	4166.50	4569.83	4517.00			
11								
12								
13								
14								
15								
16								
17								
18								
19								

2018 Call Volume / Quarterly and Average Chart / Total Call Volume Chart

Sheet 1 / 3   Default   Sum=0   100%

Figure DA_5-2_Completed_Data

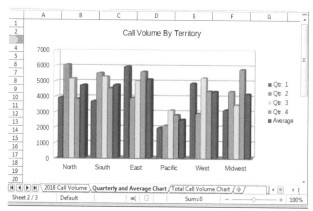

Figure DA_5-2_Completed_Chart-1

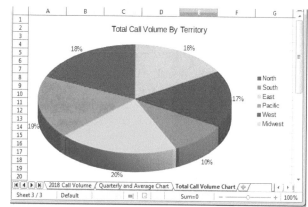

Figure DA_5-2_Completed_Chart-1

16. Make any final necessary adjustments to ensure readability and correctness of your work. Then, once you are sure that everything is correct, you should save your work and then submit it in accordance with your class instructions.

At the completion of this directed assignment, your final work should look very similar to the Figures shown here.

DA 5-3. For this directed assignment, you will be using the student data file named **DA_5-3.xlsx** to complete the required information. This file is in MS Excel version 2007 or newer format and should open in any contemporary spreadsheet program.

Required student data files: *DA_5-3.xlsx and Tomatoes.jpg*

In this workbook, you are working with a spreadsheet that has been used to collect data about the number of tomato blossoms that have been counted on each of three plants. One plant was watered only 1 time per day. The second plant was watered 2 times per day. And the third plant was watered 3 times per day. The spreadsheet has already been laid out and the known data has been entered. You have been asked to create a chart to show the changes in the plants over time.

Your task will be to complete this spreadsheet following the instructions below.

1. Open the student data file named **DA_5-3.xlsx**.

2. Immediately save a copy of this file using the following specifications:
   a. File name: Rename this file using the filename ***YourName_DA_5-3***
   b. File location: Place this file in any location you choose, but make a note of the location as you will need it later.
   c. File format: Because this file will be sent in to your professor, you must check with him or her to see what format ***he or she*** will want this file to be saved in. Don't just assume that the original file format or the default file format for your own computer will be acceptable!

3. Before you begin to create the charts, you inspect the current data and discover that there are two day's data values that are missing. When you check with your colleagues you discover that the missing values were the exact same as the previous day in each case. Update cells B21:D21 to have the same values as B20:D20. Also update cells B28:D28 to have the same values as cells B27:D27.

4. Now that the data has been corrected, you are thinking about which type of chart might represent this data best. You know that there are two different kinds of charts that are similar to each other

but which may make the data appear slightly different. The first chart that you decide to create is a simple line chart, which shows all of the data being charted and compared to each other. You will complete this chart by performing the following steps:

    a. Select the cell range A2:D32 to include the labels as well as the data.

    b. With the correct cells selected, use the tool in your spreadsheet program to initiate the chart creation dialogs.

    c. Select a line chart with markers to show the number of tomato blossoms on each plant as the plants grew over time.

    d. Step through the chart dialogs and make any necessary changes to make sure that the chart has an appropriate chart title, correct X-Axis and Y-Axis labels, and a legend.

    e. Adjust the X-Axis labels to be angled (–70°) so that all of the day names will fit on the chart.

    f. When the chart is completed, cut this chart from the main sheet and place it on its own separate sheet named "Tomato Line Chart".

5. For the second chart, you are thinking that a scatter chart with smooth lines might be a better representation. You will complete this chart by performing the following steps:

    a. Select the cell range A2:D32 to include the labels as well as the data.

    b. With the correct cells selected, use the tool in your spreadsheet program to initiate the chart creation dialogs.

    c. Select a scatter chart with smooth lines to show the number of tomato blossoms on each plant as the plants grew with the days represented simply as unlabeled intervals.

    d. Step through the chart dialogs and make any necessary changes to make sure that the chart has an appropriate chart title, correct X-Axis and Y-Axis labels, and a legend.

    e. When the chart is completed, cut this chart from the main sheet and place it on its own separate sheet named "Tomato Scatter Chart".

6. After you have completed both charts, you decide that you want to "dress up" both of the charts a little bit. You decide you will add a graphic background to each chart. For the first chart, select the chart area and set the background to be "filled" with the picture file from the student data files name "*Tomatoes.jpg*". This will create a background for the entire chart.

7. For the second chart, you decide to use the same picture file but this time, you only want the picture to show up in the "Plot Area".

8. Below are two figures that you can use to compare your own work. The figure named Figure DA_5-3_Completed_Chart-1 is the first line chart that was completed. The figure named Figure DA_5-3_Completed_Chart-2 is the second scatter chart that was completed.

9. Make any final necessary adjustments to ensure readability and correctness of your work. Then, once you are sure that everything is correct, you should save your work and then submit it in accordance with your class instructions.

At the completion of this directed assignment, your final work should look very similar to the figures shown here.

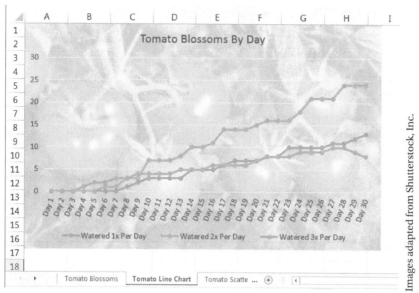

Figure DA_5-3_Completed_Chart-1

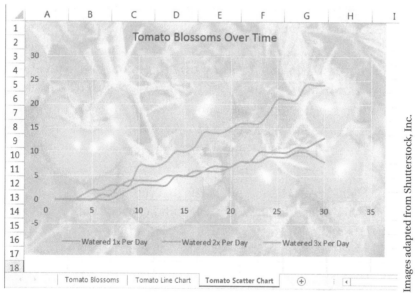

Figure DA_5-3_Completed_Chart-2

DA 5-4. For this directed assignment, you will be using the student data file named **DA_5-4.xlsx** to complete the required information. This file is in MS Excel version 2007 or newer format and should open in any contemporary spreadsheet program.

Required student data files: *DA_5-4.xlsx*

In this workbook, you are working with a spreadsheet that has been created to track your company departments who have agreed to participate in a charity fund raising campaign for the first six months of the year. Each department had an individual departmental goal of trying to raise $2000 over the six months. This spreadsheet has been laid out and has all of the known data filled in and most of the required calculations already created.

Your task will be to complete this spreadsheet following the instructions below.

1. Open the student data file named **DA_5-4.xlsx**.

2. Immediately save a copy of this file using the following specifications:

    a. File name: Rename this file using the filename ***YourName_DA_5-4***

    b. File location: Place this file in any location you choose, but make a note of the location as you will need it later.

    c. File format: Because this file will be sent in to your professor, you must check with him or her to see what format ***he or she*** will want this file to be saved in. Don't just assume that the original file format or the default file format for your own computer will be acceptable!

3. The first thing you notice is that there is a missing calculation. In cell J1 add a label that says "% of Goal".

4. In cell J2 enter a formula that shows that the goal itself is already at 100% by entering the formula that divides cell H1 as ***relative reference*** by cell H1 again, but this time as ***an absolute reference.*** This may seem a little strange at first but it will make sense in the next step.

5. Use the fill handle in cell J2 to copy this formula to the range J3:J10. This effectively computes the percentage that each department has progressed toward raising the full $2000 goal.

6. Now that the calculations are completed, you decide that the first chart you would like to create is a stacked column chart. This chart will show all of the donations collected so far, the fact that the June numbers are still yet to be collected, and also the calculated column of what's left to go. You will complete this chart by performing the following steps:

    a. Select the cell range A2:G10 to include the labels as well as the majority of the data. Then, hold either the control key (for Windows and Linux) or the command key (for Mac) and then select the non-adjacent cell range of I2:I10 to select the amount of money that is still left to be raised for each department.

    b. With the correct cells selected, use the tool in your spreadsheet program to initiate the chart creation dialogs.

    c. Select a stacked column chart (preferably 3-D) to show the cumulative donations collected by each department plus the remaining funds to be raised.

    d. Step through the chart dialogs and make any necessary changes to make sure that the chart has an appropriate chart title, correct X-Axis and Y-Axis labels, and a legend.

    e. Select the topmost series (e.g. the "Left To Go" series) and add a data label to this series. Format this data label so that it is showing the value for the data points as black text on a white background with a black border around the labels to help it stand out visually.

    f. When the chart is completed, cut this chart from the main sheet and place it on its own separate sheet named "Chart of What's Left".

7. Now you decide there is one final chart that would also help show how the departments are comparing to each other with regards to how much they have left to raise. You decide to create a 3-D bar chart that shows each department's progress toward their 100% goal. You will complete this chart by performing the following steps:

    a. Select the cell range A2:A10 to begin with the labels. Then, hold either the control key (for Windows and Linux) or the command key (for Mac) and then select the non-adjacent cell range of J2:J10 to select the amount of money that is still left to be raised for each department.

    b. With the correct cells selected, use the tool in your spreadsheet program to initiate the chart creation dialogs.

c. Select a bar chart (preferably 3-D) to show the progress of each department toward the end goal of 100%.

d. Step through the chart dialogs and make any necessary changes to make sure that the chart has an appropriate chart title, correct X-Axis and Y-Axis labels, and a legend.

e. Change each of the data series to have a cylinder column shape and make sure that each data point gets its own color. Also, make sure that the legend colors stay "in sync" with the colors you choose for each data point.

f. When the chart is completed, cut this chart from the main sheet and place it on its own separate sheet named "Progress Towards Goal".

8. Below are two figures that you can use to compare your own work. The figure named Figure DA_5-4_Completed_Chart-1 is the first stacked column chart that was completed. The figure named Figure DA_5-4_Completed_Chart-2 is the second bar chart that was completed.

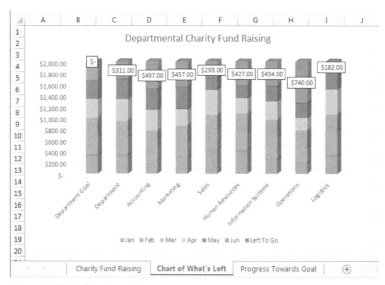

Figure DA_5-4_Completed_Chart-1

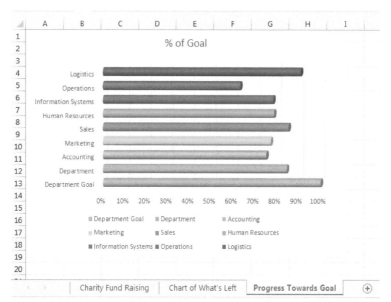

Figure DA_5-4_Completed_Chart-2

9. Make any final necessary adjustments to ensure readability and correctness of your work. Then, once you are sure that everything is correct, you should save your work and then submit it in accordance with your class instructions.

At the completion of this directed assignment, your final work should look very similar to the figures shown here.

DA 5-5. For this directed assignment, you will be using the student data file named **DA_5-5.xlsx** to complete the required information. This file is in MS Excel version 2007 or newer format and should open in any contemporary spreadsheet program.

Required student data files: *DA_5-5.xlsx,* **and 5 graphic files named** *bushes.jpg, flowers.jpg, tools. jpg, trees.jpg, and vegetables.jpg.*

In this workbook, you are working with a spreadsheet that has been created to show the total sales dollars for 5 categories of items sold at the nursery where you work. A summer worker started this spreadsheet but never completed the work. You are being asked to complete the work and create some charts to show some interesting information from the data.

Your task will be to complete this spreadsheet following the instructions below.

1. Open the student data file named **DA_5-5.xlsx**.
2. Immediately save a copy of this file using the following specifications:
   a. File name: Rename this file using the filename *YourName_DA_5-5*
   b. File location: Place this file in any location you choose, but make a note of the location as you will need it later.
   c. File format: Because this file will be sent in to your professor, you must check with him or her to see what format *he or she* will want this file to be saved in. Don't just assume that the original file format or the default file format for your own computer will be acceptable!
3. The first thing you notice is that there are no calculations yet and the data has not been formatted. Select the entered, known sales data in the range B2:F6 and format the values as currency or money.
4. Next add labels for totals in column G (cell G1) and row 7 (cell A7).
5. Create SUM functions to total up the monthly sales and place these calculations in the range (B7:F7).
6. Create SUM functions to total up the sales by type of Nursery Item and place these calculations in the range (G2:G7).
7. Create a SUM function in cell G8 to calculate a grand total.
8. For the first chart you decide you want to show the total sales for each kind of nursery item. Create this chart by completing the following steps:
   a. Select the labels by selecting the range A1:A6. Make sure you **do not** include the Totals label in cell A7.
   b. Next, hold either the control key (for Windows and Linux) or the command key (for Mac) and then select the non-adjacent cell range of G1:G6 to select the totals of each category.
   c. With the correct cells selected, use the tool in your spreadsheet program to initiate the chart creation dialogs.

d. Select a 3-D column chart to show the total sales for each category.

e. You decide that this chart looks a little "plain" so you decide you want to "spruce" it up a bit. (*Pardon the shrubbery pun!*) To do this, you decide to change the actual look of each column so that it will be a round cylinder instead of a box shape. You also decide that you will use a graphic image for each one of the categories. To accomplish this, complete the following steps:

    i. Select all of the data points and change the entire series options so that the column shape is a cylinder instead of a box.

    ii. Next, select the "Trees" column to isolate that data point from the rest of the series. Make sure you have ***only*** the "trees" data point selected.

    iii. Format the data point to change the "fill" so that it uses a picture or texture fill. Next, you can insert the picture by using the student data file named "trees.jpg".

    iv. Set the picture so that it will stack multiple copies of the picture instead of stretching a single picture over the length of the whole column.

    v. Repeat steps 8.e.ii through 8.e.iv for each one of the other data points so that each column shows its own appropriate pictures of bushes.jpg, flowers.jpg, vegetables.jpg, and tools.jpg.

f. Update the chart title of this chart so it says, "Total Sales from May – July".

9. Now, as you look over your chart, you see that it very creatively shows the total sales from each category. But now you are beginning to think that your boss might want to know some more details about the sales in each category. So you decide to create a second chart that will be similar to the first chart but will also show some more detail. You decide that a stacked column chart would be effective. Create this chart by completing the following steps:

a. Select all of the labels and the known data from the range A1:F6. This time, **do not** include any of the totals.

b. With the correct cells selected, use the tool in your spreadsheet program to initiate the chart creation dialogs.

c. Select a 3-D stacked column chart to show the total sales for each category. When you first create this chart, you may need to switch the row and column data so that the categories are shown on the X-Axis. Each program has its own way for you to easily switch rows and columns when creating charts.

d. Update this chart title so it says "Total Sales By Month".

10. Place these two charts so that they are side-by-side and beneath the raw data in the main worksheet.

11. Below are two figures that you can use to compare your own work. The figure named Figure DA_5-5_Completed_Chart-1 is the first cylindrical column chart with graphics. The Figure named Figure DA_5-5_Completed_Chart-2 is the second stacked column chart that was completed.

12. Make any final necessary adjustments to ensure readability and correctness of your work. Then, once you are sure that everything is correct, you should save your work and then submit it in accordance with your class instructions.

At the completion of this directed assignment, your final work should look very similar to the figures shown here.

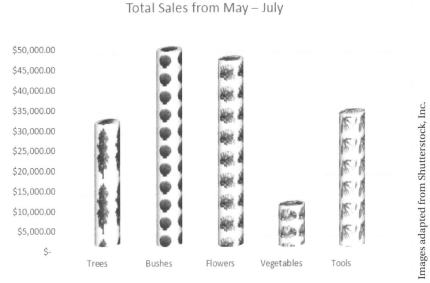

Figure DA_5-5_Completed_Chart-1

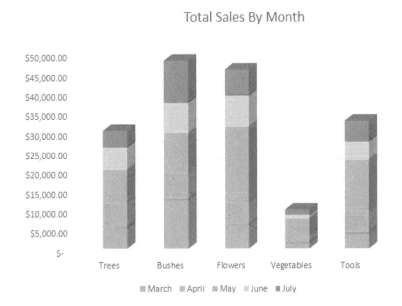

Figure DA_5-5_Completed_Chart-2

Creative Projects

CP 5-1. You may have heard it said that most people today don't know how to look directly at each other and talk directly to each other anymore. You may have heard it said that most people have their heads buried in their phones all the time. For this creative project, you have decided to do a little analysis and reflection on your own personal use of your electronic devices. You've decided to use a spreadsheet to create a daily log to help you track the number of times you "check your phone" or other electronic devices and what are the specific tasks you are doing with the phone.

Required student data file: None: Start with a new, blank workbook file and name the file *YourName_CP_5-1.*

Here is some of the information that you would like to capture:

✦ The name of the task that you use your phone or other electronic device to complete. Make sure that this list represents your own personal use. Some examples *might* include:
   - Make or receive a phone call
   - Make or receive a video call
   - Check email
   - Send or receive text messages
   - Send or receive photos
   - Browse the internet
   - Use maps or GPS
   - Play a game or use an app
   - Others – make this realistic for your own use

✦ Make a column for each day of the week and then enter the approximate number of times that you do each of the tasks that you have identified on each day of the week.

✦ Create a total row that adds up the total number of times you "checked your phone" for each day of the week. Also create a total column that adds up the total number of times you performed each task for all days in the week.

✦ Once you have completed setting up the worksheet, apply appropriate basic formatting to the entire sheet.

✦ Now, you've decided to create three charts.
   - The first chart will chart all of the data (except the totals) to show how all of the tasks compare to each other for all of the days of the week. Choose an appropriate chart that helps to compare these values.
   - For the second chart, you will inspect your own data and see which day of the week had the largest total number of times "checking your phone". For that particular day only, create a chart that shows that single data series only. Choose an appropriate chart that helps to compare these values.
   - For the third chart, you will use only the day labels and the task totals column to create a chart with the same chart type as the second chart. This way, you can have a side-by-side comparison to show how the overall totals compare.

✦ After the charts have been created, make adjustments to the charts to make sure that they have appropriate chart titles, legends, and if necessary, appropriate X- or Y-axis labels.

✦ For the second and third charts only, add data labels to show either the values, or the percentages, or both. Make sure that the data labels are easily readable.

✦ Choose appropriate coloring and styling to make your chart visually appealing.

Remember to check your final work for spelling, grammar, and overall correctness and then submit your file in the manner prescribed for your class.

CP 5-2. For this creative project, you will be creating a simple spreadsheet to calculate what types of pizzas are most popular among the members of your class or in your family or among a group of your friends, etc. This exercise is a very typical example of the way that simple ranking surveys are set up and calculated. And if this creative project description seems like "déjà vu", to you . . . well, you would not be mistaken! This is the same exercise that we used in CP 4-1!

So, the good news is if you already created that file that was required for Creative Project 4-1, you can use that file here as your starting point for this assignment! (Just make sure you make a copy of your original file and rename the copy to *YourName_CP_5-2* so that you don't lose your original work!) The bad news is if you haven't already created the file from CP 4-1, then you'll need to create that file now . . . go ahead . . . we'll wait.

Required student data file: Either the file you completed from CP 4-1 *or* You will need to start with a new, blank workbook file and complete the exercise CP 4-1 to create a starting point for this project. Make sure that you name *this* file *YourName_CP_5-2*.

To refresh your memory if you are using a copy of the file from CP 4-1, this spreadsheet now contains a list of 15 or more classmates, family, or friends etc. and their own personal ratings of several (at least 5 or so) pizza toppings. In other words, you should be working with a spreadsheet that is helping you analyze pizza topping popularity.

So now it is time to use this data to create some charts that will help visualize the popularity of the different types of pizza. For the first chart, select the pizza topping labels, the people names, and the raw data values to create a stacked column chart. Make sure that the pizza toppings are along the X-axis. To accomplish this task, you may need to use the tool to adjust the data source for the chart to switch the rows and columns for the chart. This will show which topping had the overall popularity as well as each topping's popularity as compared to each other.

The second chart is going to be a little bit too obvious. For this chart, you will create . . . wait for it . . . a *pie* chart! For this pie chart, you will select the topping labels and then select the disjointed cells representing the averages. Next, you will create a pie chart showing the averages as individual pie pieces reflecting each topping's popularity. Update this chart to have data labels for each pie piece. The data labels should show the category name and the percentage only – not the value. Make sure that the data labels are completely readable.

After both charts have been completed, make any necessary changes to make sure that the chart has an appropriate chart title, correct X-Axis and Y-Axis labels (if appropriate), and a legend. Also make sure all parts of the chart are readable and the charts are placed appropriately within the worksheet or on their own properly named worksheets.

Remember to check your final work for spelling, grammar, and overall correctness and then submit your file in the manner prescribed for your class.

CP 5-3. For this creative project, you will be using either the original student data file named **DA_4-3.xlsx** or if you have already completed the assignment DA_4-3, then you will use **your own completed file named *YourName_DA_4-3*** to complete this assignment. This file has a large collection of information from a materials processing lab where they have been experimenting with the failure points of different materials based on high and low temperatures. This exercise uses the same spreadsheet data that was used in DA 4-3!

So, the good news is if you already created that file that was required for Directed Assignment 4-3, you can use that file here now as your starting point for this assignment! (Just make sure you make a copy of your original file and rename the copy to ***YourName_CP_5-3*** so that you don't lose your original work!) The bad news is if you haven't already created the file from DA 4-3, then you'll need to create that file now . . . go ahead . . . we'll wait.

Required student data file: Either the file you completed from DA 4-3 *or* you will need to start with a new, blank workbook file and complete the exercise DA 4-3 to create a starting point for this project. Make sure that you name *this* file YourName_CP_5-3.

To refresh your memory if you are using a copy of the file from DA 4-3, this spreadsheet now contains a list of 200 materials and some temperature measurements when the material fails.

So now it is time to use this data to create a chart for this data. First, you will need to select the headings in row 2 and *all* of the data values all the way down to row 202. When you initiate the Insert Chart Dialogs with all of this data, you will quickly discover that most of the charts would result in just one large blob of unreadable information . . . and you know that would defeat the purpose of creating a chart. Remember, you are trying to make a visual representation of the selected data so that the viewer can understand some important information about the related data. If the chart that is created is just a big blob, then we will have failed in the task!

The chart type that will help make sense for this large amount of data and this type of data is a scatter chart. Create a scatter chart that shows the Low Temp., the High Temp., and the Avg. Temp. as the legend and the scattered data points. Make any additional necessary adjustments to ensure readability and correctness of your work. Place this chart on its own sheet named "Scatter Chart of Failure Points".

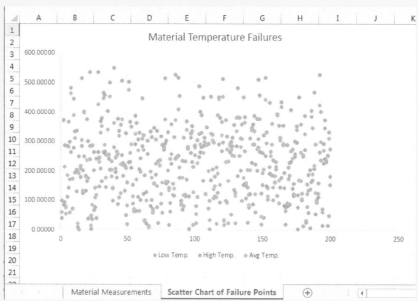

The Figure CP_5-3_Completed_ Chart below represents how

Figure CP_5-3_Completed_Chart

this chart should look when completed.

Remember to check your final work for spelling, grammar, and overall correctness and then submit your file in the manner prescribed for your class.

CP 5-4. For this creative project, you've decided to help your young neighbor create a lemonade stand and you want to create a spreadsheet to help her understand what all is involved. But you know that she may not understand the numbers of the spreadsheet, so you want to create a chart that will help her understand "revenues and expenses" without overwhelming her.

Required student data file: None: Start with a new, blank workbook file and name the file *YourName_CP_5-4.*

Here is the type of information that the friend would like to see tracked:

✦ Before you can create the charts for your neighbor, you will need to first create a spreadsheet with the basic data for a lemonade stand. A sample of the basic spreadsheet is shown in Figure CP_5-4_SampleSpreadsheet below. Remember to include both consumable expenses as well as fixed expenses. Also remember to show her wages as an expense to help her understand that she will get paid for her efforts each week. And finally, remember to use all of your other spreadsheet skills and create formulas and functions wherever appropriate and don't just key in literal values where formulas or functions belong.

✦ Make sure that all of the columns have meaningful text labels. Also, make sure that there is an overall label for the entire contents of the worksheet and that the worksheet tab itself has been properly named. Also make sure that the calculations in the worksheet are correct so that if you or your neighbor makes changes to the data that the entire spreadsheet properly updates and the chart updates as well. Some changes that the neighbor might want to make include changes to the prices, changes to the quantity, changes to the wages, or other changes like if the table and chairs could be borrowed instead of purchased, etc. Make sure that you have also applied appropriate basic formatting to the entire sheet.

✦ Once you have created the spreadsheet with the labels, known data, and calculations of unknown data for this lemonade stand, you are now ready to create a chart to show your friend the revenue and expenses and how they relate to each other. You decide that a combination chart of stacked columns for the expenses with a line chart for the revenue might work nicely. The default settings for this kind of chart will most probably not be what you want the chart to look like in the end, so you will definitely need to make adjustments to the various chart components to get the chart to look just the way you want it to look. An example of a final combo chart is shown in Figure CP_5-4_Completed_Chart below.

	A	B	C	D	E	F	G	H	I	J
1	Neighborhood Lemonade Stand									
2	**Expenses**	**Week 1**	**Week 2**	**Week 3**	**Week 4**	**Week 5**	**Week 6**	**Week 7**	**Week 8**	**Totals**
3	Lemons	$ 15.00	$ 20.00	$ 20.00	$ 20.00	$ 20.00	$ 20.00	$ 20.00	$ 20.00	$ 155.00
4	Sweetener	$ 5.00	$ -	$ 5.00	$ -	$ 5.00	$ -	$ 5.00	$ -	$ 20.00
5	Cups	$ 15.00	$ -	$ -	$ 10.00	$ -	$ 10.00	$ -	$ 10.00	$ 45.00
6	Pitchers and Spoons	$ 20.00	$ -	$ -	$ -	$ 10.00	$ -	$ -	$ -	$ 30.00
7	Table, Chairs, Cashbox	$ 40.00	$ -	$ -	$ -	$ -	$ -	$ -	$ -	$ 40.00
8	Wages	$ 20.00	$ 25.00	$ 25.00	$ 25.00	$ 25.00	$ 25.00	$ 25.00	$ 25.00	$ 195.00
9	**Expenses Total**	$ 115.00	$ 45.00	$ 50.00	$ 55.00	$ 60.00	$ 55.00	$ 50.00	$ 55.00	$ 485.00
10	**Revenue**	Week 1	Week 2	Week 3	Week 4	Week 5	Week 6	Week 7	Week 8	Totals
11	Sales Price	$ 1.00	$ 1.00	$ 1.00	$ 1.00	$ 1.00	$ 1.00	$ 1.00	$ 1.00	
12	Quantity Sold	50	55	60	65	65	65	65	60	
13	**Revenue Total**	$ 50.00	$ 55.00	$ 60.00	$ 65.00	$ 65.00	$ 65.00	$ 65.00	$ 60.00	$ 485.00
14									Balance	$ -

Figure CP_5-4_SampleSpreadsheet

✦ Remember to make sure that the X-Axis properly shows the 8 weeks that the stand is going to be open and that the two Y-Axes (Primary and Secondary) show the appropriate two different scales. The first scale is the dollar amounts for the cumulative expenses shown in the stacked columns of the chart. The second scale is the dollar amounts for the revenues each week as shown by the line part of the chart.

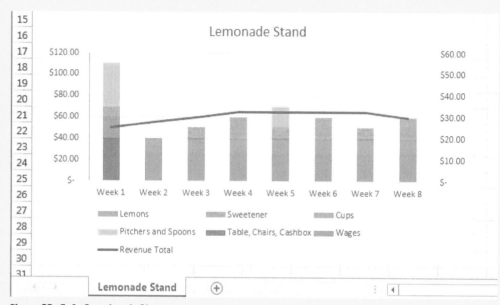

Figure CP_5-4_Completed_Chart

✦ Also make sure that all of the other chart components are properly entered and formatted such as the Chart Title and the Legend, etc.

✦ Place this chart directly beneath the spreadsheet data so that you can show your neighbor friend how the chart changes whenever you make a change to the spreadsheet numbers. That way she can start to understand how changing one thing affects the rest of her efforts.

Remember to check your final work for spelling, grammar, and overall correctness and then submit your file in the manner prescribed for your class.

Chapter 6

More Functions, Tool Limitations, and Nesting Functions

Source: Shutterstock, Inc.

So, you might already know about a "shortcut" called the "AutoSum" tool and maybe you even use it all the time ... So why would you need to know how to create functions "the long way" instead of using these special function tools?

If you have not yet heard of the AutoSum tool, no worries! We will be covering this tool in detail in this chapter. But for some of you, not only have you heard of the AutoSum tool, but perhaps you have been using it all along. You may have even used this tool as you have worked through the assignments and projects of the previous chapters ... and that's OK!

But in this chapter, we are going to see that there are several limitations to the AutoSum tool and several of the other special function tools that are available in most spreadsheet programs. If you are not aware of these limitations, you may create

Key Terms

- autosum, auto-average, auto-min, auto-max, and auto-count
- clean, proper, concatenate
- count, counta, countblank, countif
- date and time parts, now, today
- financial functions, PMT
- function syntax
- if, and, or, iferror
- isnumber, iserror
- hlookup, vlookup, index
- left, right, mid, len, trim
- most common functions
- nesting functions
- parameter or argument count
- parameter or argument sequence
- rand, randbetween
- round, rounddown, roundup
- sum, average, sumif, averageif

incorrect information and functions in your spreadsheets and then, in the end, you will have *the **wrong** answers to your questions!*

Also in this chapter, we will be looking at a number of the more commonly used functions in more detail so that you will have some direct experience with each of these functions.

And finally, we will work through the topic of *nesting* functions and some of the issues that can arise with nested functions.

LO 6.1   Reviewing Basic Functions and Function Syntax

In the previous chapters, we have explored some basic functions that are available in spreadsheet programs to perform consistent calculations on large sets of data with very minimal effort. Some of the basic and Most Common Functions we have already used are the SUM, AVERAGE, MIN and MAX, and others. Table 4-1 in Chapter 4 listed just a few of the more common functions including the function name, the syntax for the function, a description of the parameters or arguments that are used in the function and the purpose and results of the function. To review, a function in a spreadsheet is a uniquely named, predefined calculation that will return a specific value when it is given its appropriate required and/or optional parameters or arguments.

Every function has a specific syntax or rules that specify how the function must be keyed in and the order in which information must be placed in the function. The Function Syntax is the formal specification and format that each function requires in order for it to be able to perform its calculation. For every spreadsheet, the basic syntax of a function follows the format:

=FUNCTION_NAME(*argument_list***)**

As we learned in Chapter 4, all functions, like all formulas, start out with an equal sign. The function name which is unique for each specific calculation must be entered immediately after the equal sign and must have exact spelling. Functions are not case sensitive, so =SUM(A1:A15) is the same as =sum(a1:a15).

After the function name, there will always be a minimum of one set of parentheses () that surrounds the argument list or parameter list for the function. As we learned in Chapter 4, some functions take no parameters or arguments so those functions have a simple open parenthesis followed immediately with a close parenthesis. An example of the syntax of a function with no arguments would be the TODAY function, which would look like this: =**TODAY()**

But many functions have one or more parameters or arguments that make the function work properly. Some of these parameters or arguments may be required while others may be optional. If there are more than one argument or parameter supplied to a function, these references or values must be separated by commas.

If a parameter is required for a function, then that parameter will be shown in **bold** to let you know that you must provide a cell reference or a value for this parameter to make the function work properly. If a parameter or argument is optional, then it will be typically shown in plain font weight and may also be surrounded in square brackets [].

Additionally, some functions allow for many additional parameters or arguments beyond the first one that is required. Additional arguments that you may or may not choose to use are shown in the syntax with an ellipsis (. . .). An example of the syntax of a function that allows for multiple additional arguments would be the SUM function, which would look like this: =**SUM(*argument1*,** *argument2* . . .)

In this example, we see that ***argument1*** is required, but argument 2 or any additional arguments are all optional. The comma after argument1 is only required if there is, in fact, a second argument supplied.

When working with functions, especially for the first time or two, it will be helpful to pay attention to the parameter or argument count and parameter or argument sequence for the function.

The Parameter or Argument Count is the notion that every function will have a count of required parameters or arguments that are necessary to make the function work as well as a number of optional parameters or arguments that may be optionally supplied as well. Some functions will have a required parameter count of 0 while others may have as many as 5 or more required parameters.

The Parameter or Argument Sequence is the concept that for functions that have required parameters or arguments, these parameters must be entered in the proper sequence in order for the function to work properly. Each function's syntax will specify the required order for each of its parameters or arguments. The more you work with functions, the more comfortable you will become with getting the right cell references and values to serve as function parameters in the correct sequence for each function.

LO 6.2 Special Function Tools and Their Limitations

At the opening of this chapter, we introduced the concept of a special function tool called the AutoSum tool. Most of today's contemporary spreadsheet programs have added this special function tool into the programs and, quite bluntly it is both a blessing and a curse for the new user of spreadsheet programs.

Let's explore these tools in more detail including the pros to using these tools as well as the cons that arise as a part of their limitations.

First let's look at what the AutoSum tool is and how it works. The **AutoSum** tool is found in most contemporary spreadsheet programs and is usually represented with the Greek letter sigma Σ. Figure 6-1 shows the AutoSum tool in three popular spreadsheet programs.

Microsoft Excel   LibreOffice Calc   Google Sheets

Figure 6-1

These tools were designed to be efficiency tools to help users very quickly enter the most commonly used functions in spreadsheet. Some of the common functions that have been connected to this tool in some programs include the AutoSum, Auto-Average, Auto-Min, Auto-Max, and Auto-Count functions. So how do these special function tools actually work?

For this discussion, let's consider a sample spreadsheet that has been started and currently only contains the data labels as row and column headings and some known data. Figure 6-2 is the sample worksheet that we will be using for this discussion. We will be using a Microsoft Excel program for this

	A	B	C	D	E	F
1	Sorority Semester Event Planning					
2	Event Description:	Welcome 'home' party at the sorority house	Homecoming Booth for 1/2 day only	Mid-Term party at the house to help people recover from mid-term exams	Last Big Fling at Banquet Center with Awards for Seniors	
3	Event Costs	Welcome Event	Homecoming Event	Mid-Term Recovery Event	End of Semester Formal	Total Expenses By Type of Expense
4	Entertainment	$ 150.00	$ 50.00	$ 150.00	$ 350.00	
5	Food and/or Snacks	$ 75.00	$ 50.00	$ 100.00	$ 250.00	
6	Drinks	$ 200.00	$ 100.00	$ 300.00	$ 250.00	
7	Location Costs		$ 75.00		$ 600.00	
8	Advertising Costs	$ 25.00	$ 25.00	$ 25.00	$ 25.00	
9	Party Swag / Awards	$ 50.00	$ 50.00		$ 150.00	
10	Total Event Costs					

Figure 6-2

discussion, but it should be noted that the following described behaviors are generally consistent in any contemporary spreadsheet program.

This spreadsheet shows a sorority's event planning sheet for a school semester for tracking anticipated expenses for each event. As you can see in this figure, the labels and the known values have already been entered and now it is time to perform the calculations to derive the unknown data by using formulas or functions appropriately.

By this time, you already know that we will want to have SUM functions in the cell ranges of F4:F9 to show the totals for each type of expense. Also, we will want to have SUM functions in the total row 10 in the range B10:F10 so we can see what each event will cost as well as the total expenses for all events over the semester.

To start off, we already know that we could simply select cell F4 and then type the desired SUM function, but this is where the AutoSum tool was designed to come into play. To use this tool, simply select the cell where you want the sum (or other auto-function) to end up, and then click the tool!

Figure 6-3 below shows the effect of clicking on this tool. By using this tool, the program automatically looks *around the destination cell* to see if there are any numeric values nearby that could be used as the arguments to the SUM function.

	A	B	C	D	E	F
1				Sorority Semester Event Planning		
2	Event Description:	Welcome 'home' party at the sorority house	Homecoming Booth for 1/2 day only	Mid-Term party at the house to help people recover from mid-term exams	Last Big Fling at Banquet Center with Awards for Seniors	
3	Event Costs	Welcome Event	Homecoming Event	Mid-Term Recovery Event	End of Semester Formal	Total Expenses By Type of Expense
4	Entertainment	$ 150.00	$ 50.00	$ 150.00	$ 350.00	=SUM(B4:E4)
5	Food and/or Snacks	$ 75.00	$ 50.00	$ 100.00	$ 250.00	SUM(number1, [number2]
6	Drinks	$ 200.00	$ 100.00	$ 300.00	$ 250.00	
7	Location Costs		$ 75.00		$ 600.00	
8	Advertising Costs	$ 25.00	$ 25.00	$ 25.00	$ 25.00	
9	Party Swag / Awards	$ 50.00	$ 50.00		$ 150.00	
10	Total Event Costs					
11						

Figure 6-3

First, the AutoSum function looks **up** to see if there are any numeric values on top of the active cell. In our example, the cell directly above cell F4 does not have any numbers but rather has text. So, if the AutoSum function does not find any numeric values *above* the destination cell, then it tries again by looking to the left of the destination cell. In our example, this means it looks into cell E4 and this time it does, in fact, find numeric values. So the tool then keeps expanding the range of cells as long as it keeps finding numeric values. As you can see from the example, the tool keeps looking left until it finds all of the numeric values starting at cell E4 and working backwards to cell B4. But then, when it inspects cell A4, it discovers that cell A4 does not have a numeric value so it stops looking at that point.

The end result is that by just a single click of the AutoSum tool, the program has built a ***proposed SUM function including correctly* guessing *the desired arguments*** simply by looking at all of the data around the current, active cell! I think you will agree that this is a pretty powerful tool!

At this point in our example, this tool has done exactly what we might want it to do! All we have to do is hit the enter key to accept the proposed results!

Now, let's say that we want to repeat this activity in the next row. So once again, we can select cell F5 and repeat the process. This time, however, the cell directly above cell F5 actually **does** have a numeric value. So what will get summed up this time? Will the single value in cell F4 be "summed up" all by itself or will the desired range of B5:E5 be supplied as the *guess* for the range?

As we can see in Figure 6-4, the AutoSum tool in the program did actually make the right guess! So how did this happen? Well, first the AutoSum function looked up and this time it did actually find a numeric value. But it also recognized that it was a SUM function, just like the one you are trying to create now. So it infers that you are trying to perform a similar calculation as the one above this cell and so it likewise looks to the left and finds the desired cells. So as you can see, this tool sure does seem to have some pretty powerful observation skills!

	A	B	C	D	E	F	G
1				Sorority Semester Event Planning			
2	Event Description:	Welcome 'home' party at the sorority house	Homecoming Booth for 1/2 day only	Mid-Term party at the house to help people recover from mid-term exams	Last Big Fling at Banquet Center with Awards for Seniors		
3	Event Costs	Welcome Event	Homecoming Event	Mid-Term Recovery Event	End of Semester Formal	Total Expenses By Type of Expense	
4	Entertainment	$ 150.00	$ 50.00	$ 150.00	$ 350.00	$ 700.00	
5	Food and/or Snacks	$ 75.00	$ 50.00	$ 100.00	$ 250.00	=SUM(B5:E5)	
6	Drinks	$ 200.00	$ 100.00	$ 300.00	$ 250.00	SUM(number1, [number2], ...)	
7	Location Costs		$ 75.00		$ 600.00		
8	Advertising Costs	$ 25.00	$ 25.00	$ 25.00	$ 25.00		
9	Party Swag / Awards	$ 50.00	$ 50.00		$ 150.00		
10	Total Event Costs						
11							

Figure 6-4

So, let's try it one more time. If we select cell F6 as the active cell and then we click the AutoSum tool, this time we get a very different and possibly surprising proposed SUM function. Figure 6-5 shows the proposed SUM function after clicking the AutoSum tool from cell F6. As we can see in this figure, the proposed range of cells that the program chose as its *guess* turns out to be wrong! In this cell, we do not want the total of just the first two rows (F4:F5), but rather, we want the sum of the Drinks category (B6:E6). What we are seeing here is the major limitation of the AutoSum tools: *The AutoSum and other*

	A	B	C	D	E	F	G
1				Sorority Semester Event Planning			
2	Event Description:	Welcome 'home' party at the sorority house	Homecoming Booth for 1/2 day only	Mid-Term party at the house to help people recover from mid-term exams	Last Big Fling at Banquet Center with Awards for Seniors		
3	Event Costs	Welcome Event	Homecoming Event	Mid-Term Recovery Event	End of Semester Formal	Total Expenses By Type of Expense	
4	Entertainment	$ 150.00	$ 50.00	$ 150.00	$ 350.00	$ 700.00	
5	Food and/or Snacks	$ 75.00	$ 50.00	$ 100.00	$ 250.00	$ 475.00	
6	Drinks	$ 200.00	$ 100.00	$ 300.00	$ 250.00	=SUM(F4:F5)	
7	Location Costs		$ 75.00		$ 600.00	SUM(number1, [number2], ...)	
8	Advertising Costs	$ 25.00	$ 25.00	$ 25.00	$ 25.00		
9	Party Swag / Awards	$ 50.00	$ 50.00		$ 150.00		
10	Total Event Costs						

Figure 6-5

***Auto- tools attempt to guess** the required parameters for the function you are using but, sometimes, the* **guess** *that the program comes up with is WRONG!*

If you hit enter at this point, you **will** get an answer, because the function has been built and it is syntactically correct! But the resulting value you get is ***not*** the answer you wanted to appear in that cell!

To correct this situation, when using the AutoSum tools, you must remember that you, yourself (not the program) is responsible to verify that the actual cell references are correct. If the guessed or proposed cell references are *not correct,* you must change those cell references to the correct references before hitting the enter key. So, in our example, the range needs to be changed from F4:F5 to be B6:E6.

Do you see how easily someone who doesn't know about this limitation might get tripped up?!

Some good news is that we remember that we can use the fill handle or the copy-and-paste functions to properly copy cells once we have the first formula correct. So that is what we'll do from the range F7:F9.

Next, let's look at another limitation that can happen when using the AutoSum tools.

Let's use the AutoSum tool to calculate the totals in row 10 for each of the individual events in each column. First, we will select cell B10 and then use the AutoSum tool. Figure 6-6 shows the proposed SUM function that the program creates for us. Do you see the problem here? The guessed cell range for the SUM function is, once again, incorrect.

	A	B	C	D	E	F
1			Sorority Semester Event Planning			
2	Event Description:	Welcome 'home' party at the sorority house	Homecoming Booth for 1/2 day only	Mid-Term party at the house to help people recover from mid-term exams	Last Big Fling at Banquet Center with Awards for Seniors	
3	Event Costs	Welcome Event	Homecoming Event	Mid-Term Recovery Event	End of Semester Formal	Total Expenses By Type of Expense
4	Entertainment	$ 150.00	$ 50.00	$ 150.00	$ 350.00	$ 700.00
5	Food and/or Snacks	$ 75.00	$ 50.00	$ 100.00	$ 250.00	$ 475.00
6	Drinks	$ 200.00	$ 100.00	$ 300.00	$ 250.00	$ 850.00
7	Location Costs		$ 75.00		$ 600.00	$ 675.00
8	Advertising Costs	$ 25.00	$ 25.00	$ 25.00	$ 25.00	$ 100.00
9	Party Swag / Awards	$ 50.00	$ 50.00		$ 150.00	$ 250.00
10	Total Event Costs	=SUM(B8:B9)				
11		SUM(**number1**, [number2], ...)				

Figure 6-6

What we are seeing here is that the AutoSum function looks up and does, in fact, see a numeric value so it begins to build the guess of the cell range by looking up for more numeric values. It finds just one more and then it hits a completely blank cell in cell B7.

You and I are looking at the whole sheet and we can *physically see* that there are still some more cells to be included in this range of cells, but the program found a blank cell and stops looking! If we were to hit enter at this point, we would have an answer, but once again, it would be the ***wrong answer!*** To fix this limitation, just like before, we must adjust the cell range to include the entire range B4:B9. Another way to fix this would be to make sure that all of the blank cells are not left blank, but rather have a zero entered into the cells as the values. If those blank cells had been zeros, then the AutoSum function wouldn't have stopped prematurely!

As you can see, these special function tools like the AutoSum tool are actually very powerful tools and can be huge time savers! But at the same time, these tools aren't perfect in their guesses. As a result, if you use these tools, you must always remember that ***you are the one ultimately responsible for the correctness of your spreadsheets.*** Your boss won't ever want to hear, "the program got it wrong . . . " because the program doesn't do all of the work for you. You are still responsible to make sure that the program's guesses are correct and, if they aren't correct, you must fix them!

The latest versions of several of the contemporary spreadsheet programs have added more of these kinds of "helper tools" to make it easier for people to create and use spreadsheet functions. Most of these helper tools are merely extensions of the basic functions that haven't changed at all since the earliest spreadsheet versions. But be very cautious: Many of these helper tools have similar limitations as those discussed here with the AutoSum tool! Make sure you understand the limitations of the various tools you might choose to use.

LO 6.3   Some Math Functions and Statistical Functions

We have already been using some of the basic math and statistical functions as these are the functions that are used most commonly in all spreadsheets. In this and the following sections, you will find a table of some select functions in each of these function categories. **Function Categories** are explored in detail in LO 4.8 in chapter 4.

To start out, let's look at some familiar functions and a couple of new math and statistical functions by looking at Table 6-1.

Function Name	Function Syntax	Function Parameters or Arguments	Purpose and Results of Function
SUM	=SUM(***arg1***, *arg2* . . .)	At least one required argument must be supplied.	This function will perform addition on all of the values, references, or ranges that are included in the comma-separated argument list and will return a numeric value
AVERAGE	=AVERAGE(***arg1***, *arg2* . . .)	At least one required argument must be supplied.	This function will calculate the average of the values, references, or ranges that are included in the comma-separated argument list and will return a numeric value.
SUMIF	=SUMIF(**range, criteria,** *sum_range*)	Two required parameters must be supplied.	This function adds the cells specified in the optional parameter *sum_range* (if it is supplied) or the **range** parameter if the values in **range** parameter match the **criteria** specified.

Table 6-1

Function Name	Function Syntax	Function Parameters or Arguments	Purpose and Results of Function
AVERAGEIF	=AVERAGEIF(range, criteria, *average_ range*)	Two required parameters must be supplied.	This function calculates the arithmetic mean of the cells specified in the optional parameter *average_range* (if it is supplied) or the **range** parameter if the values in **range** match the **criteria** specified.
RAND	=RAND()	This function takes no arguments.	This function returns a random number greater than or equal to 0 and less than 1, evenly distributed.
RANDBETWEEN	=RANDBETWEEN (bottom, top)	This function takes two required numeric arguments that don't have to be integers but the resulting value will always be an integer.	This function returns a random integer (whole number) between the bottom and top parameter numbers you supply.
ROUND	=ROUND(number, num_digits)	This function takes two required numeric arguments.	This function rounds the first argument supplied to the number of digits supplied by the second argument.
ROUNDDOWN	=ROUNDDOWN (number, num_digits)	This function takes two required numeric arguments.	This function rounds the first argument supplied **down** to zero using the number of digits supplied by the second argument.
ROUNDUP	=ROUNDUP (number, num_digits)	This function takes two required numeric arguments.	This function rounds the first argument supplied **up** away from zero using the number of digits supplied by the second argument.

Table 6-1 (Continued)

Function Name	Function Syntax	Function Parameters or Arguments	Purpose and Results of Function
COUNT	=COUNT(*arg1*, *arg2 . . .*)	At least one required argument must be supplied.	This function will count the number of cells in all of the arguments that contain **numbers.** Only numbers are counted.
COUNTA	=COUNTA(*arg1*, *arg2 . . .*)	At least one required argument must be supplied.	This function will count the number of cells in all of the arguments that **are not empty.** All non-empty cells are counted.
COUNTBLANK	=COUNTBLANK (*arg1*, arg2 . . .)	At least one required argument must be supplied.	This function will count the number of cells in all of the arguments that **are empty.** Only empty cells are counted.
COUNTIF	=COUNTIF(range, criteria)	Two required parameters must be supplied.	This function counts the cells specified in the **range** that match the **criteria** specified.

Table 6-1 (Continued)

Remember that if you have not used these functions before, you can (and probably should) use the Insert Function Dialogs to help you enter the functions until you become familiar with the way each function works.

LO 6.4   Some Date/Time and Financial Functions

When we think of working with dates and times, we should consider that in spreadsheet programs, dates and times are actually stored as numbers for the most part, not text. This may be a strange concept for you, because when you see a date like "Thursday, May 31, 2018" you might say that you can certainly see *some* numbers in this date, but it mostly looks like text, doesn't it? This format is typically called "Long Date" format. That same date may also be seen in this "Short Date" format: 5/31/2018 or "International Date" format: 31-May-18, or several other formats.

And what if we are concerned with the *time* of day as well? Then, consider a specific moment in time. This entry might look something like "5/31/2018 7:03:09 PM"! So, how can we think of dates and times as simply numbers when we work with spreadsheets. To help understand this topic, let's key in some significant dates into a spreadsheet and then look at this same spreadsheet in several different spreadsheet programs. Figures 6-7, 6-8, and 6-9 show the same spreadsheet in the programs Microsoft Excel, LibreOffice Calc, and Google Sheets respectively.

	A	B	C	D	E
1			Date Formats		General Number
2	Historical Events	Short Date	Long Date	YYYY-mm-dd	Format
3	US Independence Day	7/4/1776 7/4/1776		7/4/1776	7/4/1776
4	Neil Armstrong walks on the moon	7/20/1969	Sunday, July 20, 1969	1969-07-20	25404
5	First Spreadsheet Program VisiCalc Sold Commercially	11/1/1979	Thursday, November 01, 1979	1979-11-01	29160
6	Some really nice guy was born	10/29/1963	Tuesday, October 29, 1963	1963-10-29	23313
7	The 'magic' starting date in Excel	1/1/1900	Sunday, January 01, 1900	1900-01-01	1

Figure 6-7 – MS Excel Dates

	A	B	C	D	E
1			Date Formats		General Number
2	Historical Events	Short Date	Long Date	Y-M-D	Format
3	US Independence Day	7/4/1776	Thursday, July 4, 1776	1776-07-04	-45103
4	Neil Armstrong walks on the moon	7/20/1969	Sunday, July 20, 1969	1969-07-20	25404
5	First Spreadsheet Program VisiCalc Sold Commercially	11/1/1979	Thursday, November 1, 1979	1979-11-01	29160
6	Some really nice guy was born	10/29/1963	Tuesday, October 29, 1963	1963-10-29	23313
7	The 'magic' starting date in LibreOffice	12/31/1899	Sunday, December 31, 1899	1899-12-31	1

Figure 6-8 – LibreOffice Calc Dates

	A	B	C	D	E
1			Date Formats		General Number
2	Historical Events	Short Date	Long Date	YYYY-mm-dd	Format
3	US Independence Day	7/4/1776	Thursday, July 4, 1776	1776-07-04	-45,103
4	Neil Armstrong walks on the moon	7/20/1969	Sunday, July 20, 1969	1969-07-20	25,404
5	First Spreadsheet Program VisiCalc Sold Commercially	11/1/1979	Thursday, November 1, 1979	1979-11-01	29,160
6	Some really nice guy was born	10/29/1963	Tuesday, October 29, 1963	1963-10-29	23,313
7	The 'magic' starting date in Google Sheets	12/31/1899	Sunday, December 31, 1899	1899-12-31	1

Figure 6-9 – Google Sheets Dates

As you can see from these three Figures, all spreadsheet programs seem to handle dates and times, but *how* they represent the dates internally is slightly different between spreadsheet programs.

In the simplest terms, you should know that dates beginning *around* 1/1/1900 are all stored internally in spreadsheet programs as *serial date numbers*. This is sort of a "magic" starting point in each program. As you can see in row 7 of each figure, the number 1 translates to a "magic" starting date in each program. You might notice that the Excel starting date is different than the other two. This is due to a computer program bug that was introduced by a very early but popular spreadsheet program called **Lotus 1-2-3**. In that program, the date functions incorrectly thought that they year 1900 was a leap year and, therefore, incorrectly included a date of Feb. 29, 1900. Because this program had the error,

Microsoft chose to keep the incorrect date in its program and has kept it ever since. So, while this difference does exist, the important thing to know is that dates are typically stored as serial data numbers.

Now, since you know that dates are basically just numbers, what can we do with number? Well, we can count and add and . . . well you get the idea!

So looking back at the day that Neil Armstrong walked on the moon, the history books tell us this was Sunday, July 20, 1969. But now we see that in a spreadsheet program, this date is the *date serial number of* **25,404.**

From here, you can start thinking about concepts of "date math." Since dates are stored as numbers in spreadsheets, you can have one cell that contains a date. Then, with a simple formula, you could have another cell that calculates the date that would be 21 days from the first date by simply referencing the first date and adding 21.

The same concept applies for representing *time* in spreadsheets. Just as dates are stored as whole numbers in a spreadsheet, times are stored as the fractional parts of the date serial number. This fractional part of the number represents the number of milliseconds since midnight on a particular day. To see how this works, please consider Figure 6-10.

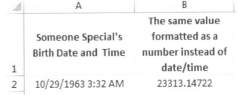

Figure 6-10

Here we can see in cell A2 that someone very special was born on 10/29/1963 at 3:32 in the morning. Cell B2 has a simple reference formula that says =**A2**. So, effectively the cells A2 and B2 have the exact same value! But cell B2 has been formatted to be a number with **General Number** formatting. As a result, we can see that the date serial number of this special person's birth date and time is 23313.14722.

So just like with "date math," we can also do "time math" in spreadsheet programs!

With this background information in how spreadsheets handle and work with dates and times, now let's look at some date and time functions by looking at Table 6-2.

Function Name	Function Syntax	Function Parameters or Arguments	Purpose and Results of Function
NOW	**=NOW()**	No arguments.	This function takes no parameters or arguments but returns the current computer system date and time and stores the information as a date serial number.
TODAY	**=TODAY()**	No arguments.	This function takes no parameters or arguments but returns the current computer system date.
Date and Time parts functions	**DAY, MONTH, YEAR, HOUR, MINUTE, SECOND**	One parameter that is a date serial number	These functions return the specific part of a date or time as a numeric value.

Table 6-2

Remember that not all spreadsheet programs handle old dates (dates before the specific "magic" starting date of each program) the same. Some programs treat old dates as negative serial date values. Others treat old dates simply as text. This is a minor difference that you will need to discover about your own particular spreadsheet program.

Financial Functions

In Chapter 4, the Directed Assignment DA 4-4 introduced you to the PMT Financial function. If you don't recall that particular assignment, let's refresh your memory. In that assignment, you will find a spreadsheet that has been laid out to help you compare loans as you consider buying a new home! Buying a home and taking on a home loan is very big decision that you and your family will make so you want to make sure that you are making the best possible decision based upon the best possible information. If you haven't already worked through that particular assignment, you really should consider doing so. The reason will become clear in just a moment.

It is important to know that all contemporary spreadsheet programs have a large selection of Financial Functions to perform all types of financial calculations. Now, not everyone will be heading down a career path in Finance, like Corporate Finance, or Hedge Funds, or Investment Banking, etc. So not everyone needs to know all of the functions that can be found in the Financial Functions category in a spreadsheet. Take, for instance, the **OPT_PROB_INMONEY** financial function. In Figure 6-11 you can see this function as described in the LibreOffice Calc program.

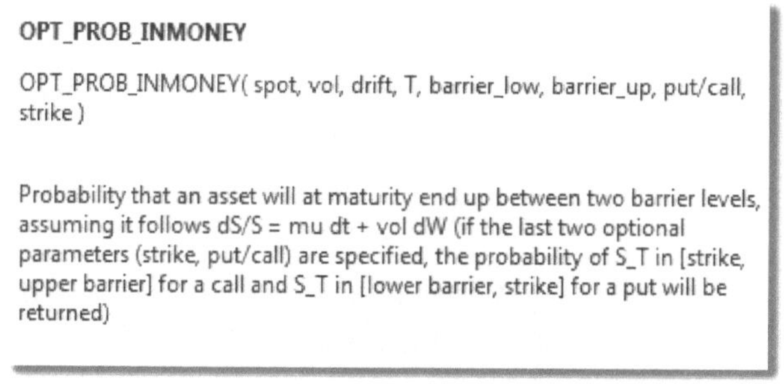

Now, unless you are working directly in the finance arena, chances are that you may never, *ever* need to use this function. Just looking at the names of the parameters and the description, one can infer that this function will be helpful when making a decision about buying or selling assets like stocks or possibly other types of assets, but the reality is, unless you are working in this area, you probably won't need to use these types of advance financial functions.

But that doesn't mean that you should just completely ignore the whole category of Financial

OPT_PROB_INMONEY

OPT_PROB_INMONEY(spot, vol, drift, T, barrier_low, barrier_up, put/call, strike)

Probability that an asset will at maturity end up between two barrier levels, assuming it follows dS/S = mu dt + vol dW (if the last two optional parameters (strike, put/call) are specified, the probability of S_T in [strike, upper barrier] for a call and S_T in [lower barrier, strike] for a put will be returned)

Figure 6-11

functions in your spreadsheet program. As we discussed at the start of this section, the **PMT** function is used to calculate the payment for a loan. And who *won't* be dealing with a loan at some point in time? You might already have experience with loans – maybe you already have a car loan. Or maybe you already have a home loan. Or maybe you have taken out student loans.

Even if you haven't worked with loans just yet, there is a *very high probability* that you will, at some time in the future, be involved with a loan – either in your personal life or in your professional life. Loans are probably one of the most common types of long-term financial transactions that most people will experience in their lives.

Therefore, if you never work with any other financial functions, you should at least be familiar with how the PMT function works in a spreadsheet. Table 6-3 shows the structure of the PMT function.

Function Name	Function Syntax	Function Parameters or Arguments	Purpose and Results of Function
PMT	=PMT(*periodic_interest_rate, total_loan_periods, present_value*, *future_value, payment_type*)	Three required arguments or parameters and two optional parameters.	This function takes a periodic interest rate, the total number of payments for a loan, and the original value of the loan and calculates a loan payment based on those three values and returns a *negative* value representing the payment amount to be paid back during each periodic payment.

Table 6-3

Please also remember when working with the PMT function that the resulting value from the calculation is typically a negative number. To help you visualize why this is correct, think about the "flow of money" in each of the related transactions. When you first receive a loan from a lender, the "flow of money" of the initial loan is that you received *a positive amount of money flowing* <u>into</u> *your wallet*. So now, you have your loan and you have this big wad of money in your wallet! Yay!

Now you go and buy that thing that you needed the loan for . . . maybe it was a loan for a new car, or maybe it was a loan for new equipment for your music studio . . . No matter what the money was for, once you use the money, you now are indebted to the lender and need to make your monthly payments back to the lender to pay off your loan.

So, by using the PMT financial function in a spreadsheet, you can calculate exactly what your monthly payment will be. But when you use the PMT function, you see that it returns a *negative value*! If you think about your monthly payment transactions, then the "flow of money" is *a negative amount of money flowing* <u>out</u> *of your wallet*. And from an accounting perspective, the money *coming in* from one transaction needs to be offset by some other transaction *going out* on the other side of the balance sheet.

As was described in the Directed Assignment 4 in Chapter 4 (DA 4-4), people don't typically think about monthly loan payments as being "negative amounts" so we typically will change the sign of the loan payment calculation to be a positive number. To accomplish this, there are several approaches you could take:

✦ First, you could adjust the PMT formula to insert a minus sign (–) in front of the PMT function. This will effectively change the final resulting number from being a negative number into a being a positive number.

✦ Another way this can be accomplished is by putting a minus sign before the reference for the Present Value (PV) argument in the PMT function. This will also result in a positive payment value.

✦ Another way is to *nest* the PMT function inside of an ABS function, which calculates the absolute value of calculation. We will be looking at *nesting functions* later on in this chapter.

The ability to properly use a spreadsheet program to set up and compare loans is a very important skill that can help you in both your personal and business affairs.

LO 6.5   Some Logical Functions and Information Functions

So far, most of the functions that we have been using in the spreadsheet programs have been numeric-based functions. We have looked at simple Math functions like the SUM(), ROUND() and RAND() functions. We have also looked at some Financial functions like PMT() and some Date and Time functions like TODAY() and NOW().

Next we're going to look at a category of functions that are intended to enable your spreadsheet to help you make decisions by answering some common questions that you will have. One of the most common ways that we make any decision is we first ask ourselves a question about the decision to be made. If the answer to our question is **true**, then we will take one action. But if the answer to our question is **false**, then we will take some other action.

This concept is the simple IF-THEN-ELSE construct that we use every day as we go about our business. Consider these situations that are outlined in Table 6-4:

IF ... *some condition is true* ...	THEN ... *what happens if the condition is TRUE?*	ELSE ... *what happens if the condition is FALSE?*
IF ... I am hungry ...	**THEN** ... stop now and eat something ...	**ELSE** ... keep doing whatever it is I'm doing.
IF ... my car's gas gauge is very close to "E" ...	**THEN** ... find a gas station and fill up the car ...	**ELSE** ... keep on driving.
IF ... the dog is barking by the back door. . .	**THEN** ... let the dog outside to do his business ...	**ELSE** ... be prepared to clean up a mess on the kitchen floor!

Table 6-4

We use the concept of the IF-THEN-ELSE countless times each day. So, it only makes sense that the spreadsheet programs implemented a way for us to do these same kinds of calculations in a spreadsheet. The basic syntax of the **IF** function, along with several other logical and informational functions, can be found in Table 6-5.

Function Name	Function Syntax	Function Parameters or Arguments	Purpose and Results of Function
IF	=IF(conditional_test, value_if_true, value_if_false)	Three required arguments or parameters.	This function takes a first parameter that is a conditional test that can be evaluated as either being **TRUE** or **FALSE**. Then, the second parameter is the value that will be returned if the condition is true. The third and final parameter is the value that will be returned if the condition is false.

Table 6-5

Function Name	Function Syntax	Function Parameters or Arguments	Purpose and Results of Function
AND	=AND(conditional_ test1, *conditional_ test2, . . .*)	One required argument or parameter and zero to many additional optional parameters.	This function looks at all of the conditional tests that are supplied as arguments and returns **TRUE** if *all* of the conditions are true and returns **FALSE** if at least one conditions is false.
OR	=OR(conditional_ test1, *conditional_ test2, . . .*)	One required argument or parameter and zero to many additional optional parameters.	This function looks at all of the conditional tests that are supplied as arguments and returns **TRUE** if *at least one* of the conditions are true and returns **FALSE** if all of the conditions are false.
IFERROR	=IFERROR(value, value_if_error)	Two required parameters.	This function returns the second value_if_error parameter if the first parameter value evaluates to be an error and returns the first parameter value if there is no error. This function is often used as part of a nested function when there is a risk that the inner function might have invalid or missing data. We will cover nested functions in more detail later on in this chapter.
ISNUMBER	=ISNUMBER(value)	One required parameter.	This function checks whether a value is a number and then returns **TRUE** or **FALSE** accordingly.
ISERROR	=ISERROR(value)	One required parameter.	This function checks whether a values contains a spreadsheet error such as #VALUE!, #REF!, #DIV/0!, #NUM!, #NAME?, or #NULL!. If the value parameter results in one of these errors, then this function returns **TRUE** or **FALSE** accordingly.

Table 6-5 (Continued)

These logical and informational functions can be used by themselves but are often used as components of **nested functions**. We will be looking at nested functions in detail in Learning Objective LO 6.7.

LO 6.6   Some Text Functions and Lookup Functions

Just as we have seen that there are functions for working with numbers as well as there are functions for working with logical conditions, now we are about to discover that there are also functions specifically designed to work with text-based data.

To help you think about text functions, it might be helpful to first think about text as being nothing more than a string of characters. Take, for example, the phrase **"This is some text."** What are some of the things that we can notice about that phrase? How many characters (including spaces and other punctuation) are in that string of characters? What is the capitalization involved? If we wanted to look at just the left-most 4 characters of this string, what would we see? If we wanted to look at the middle characters in this string that start in position 9 and continues on for a length of 4 characters, what would we see in this situation?

When we investigate text functions what we discover is that there are very many different functions that allow us to inspect, parse, and otherwise manipulate any kind of text-based data. Table 6-6 shows a number of common Text functions.

Function Name	Function Syntax	Function Parameters or Arguments	Purpose and Results of Function
LEFT	=LEFT(**Text,** num_chars)	One required parameter and one optional parameter.	This function returns the specified number of characters from the start of a text string. If no num_chars parameter is given, the number 1 is used instead.
RIGHT	=RIGHT(**Text,** num_chars)	One required parameter and one optional parameter.	This function returns the specified number of characters from the end of a text string. If no num_chars parameter is given, the number 1 is used instead.
LEN	=LEN(**Text**)	One required parameter.	This function returns the number of characters (including spaces and punctuation **and nonprinting characters**) in a text string. We will be exploring nonprinting characters when we discuss cleaning data and importing data in Chapter 8.

Table 6-6

Function Name	Function Syntax	Function Parameters or Arguments	Purpose and Results of Function
TRIM	=TRIM(Text)	One required parameter.	This function removes all leading and trailing spaces and redundant spaces from the text string except for single spaces between words.
MID	=MID(Text, Start_num, Num_chars)	Three required parameters.	This function returns the characters from the middle of a text string, given a starting position and length of characters to be returned.
CLEAN	=CLEAN(Text)	One required parameter.	This function removes all nonprintable characters from text. This function becomes extremely useful when working with external data (e.g. from a website). We will be covering this activity in detail in Chapter 8.
PROPER	=PROPER(Text)	One required parameter.	This function converts a text string to proper case which means that the first letter in each word is forced to uppercase and all of the other letters in each word are forced to lowercase. From here, you can probably infer the results of the **UPPER** and **LOWER** functions as well!
CONCATENATE	=CONCATENATE (Text1, *text2 . . .*)	One required parameter and any number of optional additional parameters.	Joins several text strings into one single text string. This is the function equivalent to the & operator, which is the concatenation operator. Sometimes, it is easier to use the function and sometimes, it is easier to use the operator.

Table 6-6 (Continued)

Text functions are often used when you need to "clean up" some data that was supplied to you from some other source. Sometimes, this data has extraneous and/or nonprintable characters contained within the data. Other times, the data you receive is, generally speaking, "jumbled up."

Before you can begin to add any of your own desired calculations to make meaningful information out of the data, you will need to clean up the data. These text functions are often used to help with that preliminary "clean up" processing. Then, after the data is cleaned up, then you can start adding in the other types of functions you need to analyze the data. All of this will be discussed in detail in Chapter 8.

But for now, the last types of functions that we will be looking at are the Lookup type of functions.

Lookup Functions

Frequently when creating spreadsheets, you may discover that you need to use one piece of information in one cell to *look up* or locate a related piece of information from some other part of the spreadsheet. Fortunately, the spreadsheet programs have a number of functions that were created specifically for these kinds of tasks. Table 6-7 shows a number of these common lookup functions.

Function Name	Function Syntax	Function Parameters or Arguments	Purpose and Results of Function
VLOOKUP	=VLOOKUP(Lookup_value, Table_array, Col_index_num, Range_lookup)	Three required parameters and one optional parameter.	This function looks for the Lookup_value parameter in the leftmost column of the Table_array (range), and then returns the value from the column specified in the Col_index_num parameter. Optionally, if the Range_lookup parameter is **true** then the function will return the *nearest* match but not necessarily an exact match. If that parameter is **false** then the function will return an *exact* match only. In order for this function to work properly, the range represented by Table_array must be **sorted** in ascending order. We will be exploring sorting in detail in the next chapter.
HLOOKUP	=HLOOKUP(Lookup_value, Table_array, Row_index_num, Range_lookup)	Three required parameters and one optional parameter.	This function looks for the Lookup_value parameter in the top row of the Table_array (range), and then returns the value from the column specified in the Row_index_num parameter. Optionally, if the Range_lookup parameter is **true** then the function will return the *nearest* match but not necessarily an exact match. If that parameter is **false** then the function will return an *exact* match only. In order for this function to work properly, the range represented by Table_array must be **sorted** across in ascending order. We will be exploring sorting in detail in the next chapter.

Table 6-7

Function Name	Function Syntax	Function Parameters or Arguments	Purpose and Results of Function
INDEX	=INDEX(Array, Row_num, Column_num)	For this form of the function, two required parameters and one optional parameter. There is another form of this function not covered here.	This function returns a value from the cell at the intersection of the Row_num parameter and the Column_num parameter (if given) from the range that is specified in the Array parameter. This is the most common use of the INDEX function, however, there is another form of this function not covered here.

Table 6-7 (Continued)

These functions are very often used as a part of some larger, nested function. We will be looking into nested functions right now, in the next section.

LO 6.7   Nesting Functions

Several different times in the previous chapters, we have mentioned the concept of *nested functions*. By now, you may have some idea of what these are all about, but let's make sure that we're all on the same page.

First, let's just think about the general concept of a *nest* and do a quick question-and-answer session about *nests*.

Q: When you hear the word "nest," what comes to mind?
A: If you are like most people, the first thing you thought of was a bird's nest. So let's start there.

Q: Where might you typically find a bird's nest?
A: *Within* the branches of a tree. The keyword here is going to be *within*.

Q: How many bird's nests might you find *within* that particular tree?
A: *Within* a single tree you might find from zero to many bird's nests.

Q: And what might you find *within* any single particular bird's nest that is *within* the tree?
A: *Within* a single bird's nest, you might find from zero to many eggs.

Q: And what might you find *within* a single egg that is *within* the single bird nest that is *within* the tree?
A: *Within* a single egg, you will probably find a developing baby bird!

Within this analogy, is the concept that *nesting* involves having some things *within* other things and all of it all working well together. Nesting functions in spreadsheets is precisely the same.

In all spreadsheet programs, the concept of Nesting Functions is when you have one or more functions that are completely contained *within* a different function and are serving as one or more of the parameters of the *outer function*. So, for example, if FunctionA is a function that has two required parameters, and FunctionB is a function that takes no parameters, then FunctionB could be nested within FunctionA as such:
    =FUNCTIONA(*parameter1*,FUNCTIONB())

In this example, we see that FunctionB is wholly contained within FunctionA and is serving as the second required parameter for FunctionA. This is the essence of nested functions.

You may recall that in several of the assignments and projects in the previous chapters, we used nested functions as a part of the overall assignments. For example, let's review the screenshot shown in Figure 6-12.

In an earlier section, we learned that the RAND() function will return a random number between 0 (inclusive) and 1 (exclusive). Cell A3 in Figure 6-12 shows the results of the RAND function.

So, whenever we use the RAND function, we end up with some decimal number with a lot of random decimal digits. If we multiply the RAND() function by some larger number, we end up with a random number between 0 (inclusive) and that larger number (exclusive). Cell B3 in Figure 6-12 shows the results of multiplying the RAND function by 5000.

◢	A	B	C
1	RAND Function Alone	RAND Function * 5000	RAND Function * 5000 *Nested Inside* the ROUND Function
2	=RAND()	=RAND()*5000	=ROUND(RAND()*5000,2)
3	0.738097539	1953.830473	2761.25
4	Remember that each one of the functions in Row 3 are using their *own* RAND functions... so that is why they all have different values.		

Figure 6-12

So, consider what happens if we want to use this answer as a money value. As you see in cell B3, we would end up with "fractional pennies." So to get rid of the extra digits that we don't want, we can take that *entire function* and nest it inside of the ROUND function. Cell C3 in Figure 6-12 shows the results of nesting the RAND function and calculation on the inside of the ROUND function and then rounding the results to two decimal places.

Also, please remember when you review Figure 6-12 that there is a note in cell A4 that reminds you that each one of the functions in Row 3 are using their own RAND functions, so that is why they all have different values.

In contemporary spreadsheet programs it is possible to nest *many levels* of functions within functions. In some programs, the limit is as many as 64 functions nested within each other! Now, as we have said several times before, when working with spreadsheets – just like when working at life – just because you **can** do something doesn't necessarily mean that you **should** do that particular thing! Nesting 64 functions inside of each other would be a prime example of something you absolutely **should not do!**

Once you get too many functions nested within each other, the functions become nearly impossibly complicated and too difficult to check, or validate or maintain if something needs to change.

Nesting one, or two, or *several* functions together is just fine – in fact, it is typical! But you must always consider the complexity that is being introduced when you start nesting functions with too many levels of depth.

The better practice would be to break those complex calculations into multiple, intermediary calculations. Then, the final functions can simply reference the results of the intermediary calculations. Everything will stay a lot "cleaner" and easier to maintain.

In the next chapter, we will start looking at how you will work with large collections of data that need to be sorted, filtered, and summarized. While all of the basic tools you have learned already will come into play once again, we will discover new tools and techniques that will significantly help us when working with larger spreadsheet files.

Chapter 6 – Assignments and Projects

Directed Assignments

DA 6-1. For this directed assignment, you will be using the student data file named **DA_6-1.ods** to complete the required information. This file is in LibreOffice Calc version 4.2 or newer format and should open in any contemporary spreadsheet program.

Required student data file: *DA_6-1.ods*

In this workbook you are completing a spreadsheet that was begun by a colleague of yours. The purpose of this spreadsheet is to calculate the totals and averages for different kinds of pies that 25 anonymous participants have reported that they have purchased this year.

Your task will be to complete this spreadsheet following the instructions below.

1. Open the student data file named **DA_6-1.ods**.
2. Immediately save a copy of this file using the following specifications:
    a. File name: Rename this file using the filename *YourName_DA_6-1*
    b. File location: Place this file in any location you choose, but make a note of the location as you will need it later.
    c. File format: Because this file will be sent in to your professor, you must check with him or her to see what format *he or she* will want this file to be saved in. Don't just assume that the original file format or the default file format for your own computer will be acceptable!
3. In row 28, you are going to create ***incorrect totals!*** This exercise is to help reinforce what can go wrong by using the AutoSum tool and not making the necessary corrections when the program provides the wrong "*guess*" for the SUM range. To create these wrong calculations complete the following steps:
    a. Select cell B28, then click the AutoSum function and press the enter key *without making any corrections or adjustments to the cell range.*
    b. Repeat step 3.a above four more times for each of the cells C28, D28, E28, and then F28. Make sure you do each cell one-at-a-time to see the different ways that the AutoSum tool might "get it wrong"!
4. Now, in row 29, we will calculate the accurate desired totals for this spreadsheet. First select cell B29 and use the AutoSum tool. Notice that the proposed "guess" of the cell range is not correct! The correct cell range should be B3:B27. Correct the "guess" so that the correct cell range is being used.
5. Repeat step 4 for all of the remaining cells in row 29. Remember to use the AutoSum tool each time in each cell but then correct the cell range from the wrong "guess" to the correct desired range.
6. Make any final necessary adjustments to ensure readability and correctness of your work. Then, once you are sure that everything is correct (**except for the *intentionally* incorrect entries in row 28**), you should save your work and then submit it in accordance with your class instructions.

At the completion of this directed assignment, your final work should look very similar to Figure DA_6-1_Completed found here.

Please observe how both rows 28 and rows 29 have numeric values being displayed. None of these are showing **#ERROR!** or anything like that. In fact, the cells are actually showing legitimate spreadsheet calculations.

The issue is that the functions were allowed to use the *wrong cell references.* Therefore, in your calculations, the bottom line is that there are absolutely right answers and there are absolutely wrong answers . . . and it is up to **you** to make sure that your spreadsheets have the right answers!

	A	B	C	D	E	F
1			Participant Counts of Pies Purchased This Year			
2		Apple Pie	Cherry Pie	Peach Pie	Chocolate Pie	Pumpkin Pie
3	Participant 1	4	3	7	5	6
4	Participant 2	3	7	6	0	2
5	Participant 3	1	0	3	2	4
6	Participant 4	0	3	2	6	6
7	Participant 5	4		0	5	3
8	Participant 6	4	3	2	1	1
9	Participant 7	1	6	5		5
10	Participant 8		5		4	6
11	Participant 9	6	1	0	1	4
12	Participant 10	1	4	4	5	0
13	Participant 11	1	3	6	3	4
14	Participant 12	0	3		3	
15	Participant 13	3	2	7	4	0
16	Participant 14	5	0	1	2	7
17	Participant 15	4	1	4	4	4
18	Participant 16	4	2	4	4	4
19	Participant 17	4	1		0	2
20	Participant 18		1	2	7	6
21	Participant 19	2	5	6	4	5
22	Participant 20	1	5	0	2	1
23	Participant 21	4	0	0	0	6
24	Participant 22	5	6	0	4	7
25	Participant 23	7	1	1	3	3
26	Participant 24	3	1	0	4	0
27	Participant 25	7	2	7		1
28	Incorrect Totals using AutoSum without corrections	29	52	16	97	46
29	Actual Correct Totals	74	65	67	73	87
30						

Figure DA_6-1_Completed

DA 6-2. For this directed assignment, you will be using the student data file named **DA_6-2.xlsx** to complete the required information. This file is in Microsoft Excel version 2007 or newer format and should open in any contemporary spreadsheet program.

Required student data file: *DA_6-2.xlsx*

In this workbook you are completing a spreadsheet that has only a little beginning information. As the boss, you are considering giving all of your employees a small mid-year raise for all of their hard work on last year's huge remodeling project. You have asked the managers of all three shifts to give you their complete bi-weekly payroll total for all employees on each shift. You want to calculate a spreadsheet that contains a cumulative or running total of your full payroll as it is paid out every two weeks. Then, in the first pay period in July, you want to see what a 2% pay raise across the board will look like by the end of the year.

Your task will be to complete this spreadsheet following the instructions below.

1. Open the student data file named **DA_6-2.xlsx**.

2. Immediately save a copy of this file using the following specifications:

    a. File name: Rename this file using the filename *YourName_DA_6-2*

    b. File location: Place this file in any location you choose, but make a note of the location as you will need it later.

    c. File format: Because this file will be sent in to your professor, you must check with him or her to see what format *he or she* will want this file to be saved in. Don't just assume that the original file format or the default file format for your own computer will be acceptable!

3. The first thing you decide to do is update the spreadsheet to include all of the pay dates for this year. First, you know that the first pay date for this year was the second Friday of the year. Lookup that date and enter it in short date format in cell A4.

4. In cell A5, enter the simple formula to calculate the next pay date, which is 2 weeks from the previous pay date. In other words, enter a formula in cell A5 to add 14 days to the relative reference of cell A4.

5. Next, use the fill handle to drag cell A5 down until you fill in all of the pay dates for the rest of this year only. Do not include the first pay date of next year.

6. Now that you have all of the pay dates filled in, the next item you are interested in is calculating the cumulative payroll for the first pay date. In cell E4, this will be a simple SUM function using the range B4:D4.

7. Next, you want to set the payroll amounts for the first 6 months. Each of these pay dates up until the first pay date in July will be equal to the previous pay date. So, starting in cell B5, enter the simple relative cell reference to cell B4.

8. Now, using the fill handle in cell B5, drag this cell over to cells C5:D5.

9. Now that you have the second pay date amounts filled in, you can use these three cells to fill in the rest of the first 6 months. To do this, simply select the cell range (B5:D5) and then use the fill handle for all three cells to copy all three cells down for all of the pay dates that are before July. Here you should see that all of the payroll amounts for the first 6 months are all the same.

10. Next, you want to continue to calculate the cumulative payroll. In cell E5, enter the formula that adds the previous cumulative total (E4) plus the SUM of this pay date's payroll. Make sure that all of the cell references are relative cell references. The correct resulting value for this calculation in $72,378.80.

11. Now, you can use the fill handle in cell E5 and drag this formula down to all of the payroll for the first half of the year.

12. You are now ready to start working up the calculations for the proposed mid-year pay raise. You don't know yet how much of a raise you can afford, so you want to start by seeing if a 2% raise will be possible. In cell G3 enter 2%. Make sure this cell is formatted as a percentage with 1 decimal place of precision.

13. Next, you want to give the raise in the first pay date in July. Locate this cell in column B for the Day Shift for the first pay date in July. Now, to calculate a percent increase for a value, there are actually several different ways that this task can be accomplished. Choose *just one* of the following methods to perform this calculation:

    a. One way to calculate a percent increase is to add the original value to a secondary formula that multiplies the original value by the percent of increase. So, if the original value is in cell B16 and the percent of increase is in cell G2, then one possible final formula for the increased value would be =**B16 + (B16 * $G$2)**.

    b. Another way to calculate this percent increase is to add the percent of increase to the whole number 1 (which represents 100%.) Then, multiply this new percentage by the original value. So, if the original value is in cell B16 and the percent of increase is in cell G2, then the second possible final formula for the increased value would be =**(1 + $G$2) * B16**.

Whichever method you choose, the final result for the first payroll date in July should show that for the Day Shift, a 2% increase has been added to the last payroll amount from June.

14. Now, you can use the fill handle in that cell to drag that formula over to the Evening Shift and the Night Shift to calculate their pay raises for the first pay date in July.

15. For the second pay date in July, this will be a simple relative cell reference to the first pay date in July. Complete the second pay date in July for all three shifts.

16. Once the second pay date in July is completed, you can use those three cells' fill handle to drag down the payroll for the rest of the year.

17. Now you are ready to fill in the rest of column E by selecting the last completed total in that column and then use its fill handle to fill in the rest of the Cumulative Payroll.

18. Make any final necessary adjustments to ensure readability and correctness of your work. Then, once you are sure that everything is correct, you should save your work and then submit it in accordance with your class instructions.

	A	B	C	D	E	F	G
1			Planning For Possible Mid-Year Raise				
2			Bi-Week Payroll - All Shifts			Planned	2.0%
3	Payroll Date	Day Shift	Evening Shift	Night Shift	Cumulative Payroll	Mid-Year Raise	
4	1/12/2018	$11,517.95	$ 12,093.85	$12,577.60	$ 36,189.40		
5	1/26/2018	$11,517.95	$ 12,093.85	$12,577.60	$ 72,378.80		
6	2/9/2018	$11,517.95	$ 12,093.85	$12,577.60	$108,568.20		
7	2/23/2018	$11,517.95	$ 12,093.85	$12,577.60	$144,757.60		
8	3/9/2018	$11,517.95	$ 12,093.85	$12,577.60	$180,947.00		
9	3/23/2018	$11,517.95	$ 12,093.85	$12,577.60	$217,136.40		
10	4/6/2018	$11,517.95	$ 12,093.85	$12,577.60	$253,325.80		
11	4/20/2018	$11,517.95	$ 12,093.85	$12,577.60	$289,515.20		
12	5/4/2018	$11,517.95	$ 12,093.85	$12,577.60	$325,704.60		
13	5/18/2018	$11,517.95	$ 12,093.85	$12,577.60	$361,894.00		
14	6/1/2018	$11,517.95	$ 12,093.85	$12,577.60	$398,083.40		
15	6/15/2018	$11,517.95	$ 12,093.85	$12,577.60	$434,272.80		
16	6/29/2018	$11,517.95	$ 12,093.85	$12,577.60	$470,462.20		
17	7/13/2018	$11,748.31	$ 12,335.73	$12,829.15	$507,375.39		
18	7/27/2018	$11,748.31	$ 12,335.73	$12,829.15	$544,288.58		
19	8/10/2018	$11,748.31	$ 12,335.73	$12,829.15	$581,201.76		
20	8/24/2018	$11,748.31	$ 12,335.73	$12,829.15	$618,114.95		
21	9/7/2018	$11,748.31	$ 12,335.73	$12,829.15	$655,028.14		
22	9/21/2018	$11,748.31	$ 12,335.73	$12,829.15	$691,941.33		
23	10/5/2018	$11,748.31	$ 12,335.73	$12,829.15	$728,854.52		
24	10/19/2018	$11,748.31	$ 12,335.73	$12,829.15	$765,767.70		
25	11/2/2018	$11,748.31	$ 12,335.73	$12,829.15	$802,680.89		
26	11/16/2018	$11,748.31	$ 12,335.73	$12,829.15	$839,594.08		
27	11/30/2018	$11,748.31	$ 12,335.73	$12,829.15	$876,507.27		
28	12/14/2018	$11,748.31	$ 12,335.73	$12,829.15	$913,420.46		
29	12/28/2018	$11,748.31	$ 12,335.73	$12,829.15	$950,333.64		
30							

Proposed Mid-Year Raise ⊕

Figure DA_6-2_Completed

At the completion of this directed assignment, your final work should look very similar to Figure DA_6-2_Completed found here. Please note, that if you chose a different starting date (for a different year) in step 3 of this assignment, then your dates will definitely be different and your totals *may* also be different as well.

DA 6-3. For this directed assignment, you will be using the student data file named **DA_6-3.ods** to complete the required information. This file is in LibreOffice Calc version 4.2 or newer format and should open in any contemporary spreadsheet program.

Required student data file: *DA_6-3.ods*

In this workbook we are creating a hypothetical Sales Incentive worksheet just to verify that we can set up the sheet properly. Once everything is set up and working properly with some random sales numbers, then we will be able to clear out the hypothetical data and use real data with the completed spreadsheet.

Your task will be to complete this spreadsheet following the instructions below.

1. Open the student data file named **DA_6-3.ods**.
2. Immediately save a copy of this file using the following specifications:
   a. File name: Rename this file using the filename ***YourName_DA_6-3***
   b. File location: Place this file in any location you choose, but make a note of the location as you will need it later.
   c. File format: Because this file will be sent in to your professor, you must check with him or her to see what format ***he or she*** will want this file to be saved in. Don't just assume that the original file format or the default file format for your own computer will be acceptable!
3. For several steps below, we will be reviewing basic tasks that have already been covered in detail in previous chapters. Therefore, the instructions for these first steps will be more abbreviated. If you need to, refer to the previous chapters to review how to complete any individual step that you may have forgotten. For new material from this chapter, more detailed instructions will be given.
   a. Use the fill handle with cell A2 to fill 10 hypothetical sales people in column A.
   b. In cell B2, you will create a nested function that nests a RAND() function and calculation inside of the ROUND function. The RAND function will be **RAND() * 10000** and this will become the first parameter of the ROUND function. The ROUND function will then round this result to two decimal positions. Therefore, the final calculation in cell B2 will be as follows:
      =ROUND(RAND()*10000,2)
      Remember to format this cell like money or currency.
   c. Fill all of the cells in the range B2:E11 with this formula.
   d. Create a Totals column in column F with appropriate SUM functions in cells F2:F11.
   e. Create a Totals row in row 12 with appropriate SUM functions in cells B12:F12.
   f. Create an Averages column in column G with appropriate AVERAGE functions in cells G2:G11.
   g. Create an Averages row in row 13 with appropriate AVERAGE functions in cells B13:F13.
   h. In cell A14 enter the label "Overall Average".
   i. In cell B14 calculate the overall average of all of the values in the range B2:E11.
4. Now we are ready to add a column to determine if each salesperson should receive a bonus or not. To determine this, we will say that if the salesperson's individual average is at least 500 dollars above the overall average, then that salesperson will get a $500 bonus. Otherwise the salesperson will get no bonus. To accomplish this, complete the following tasks:
   a. Add a label to cell H1 that says "$500 Bonus?"
   b. In cell H2, enter an IF function using the following parameters:
      i. The first parameter, the ***logical_test***, will make a comparison to see if the relative reference to Sales Person 1's average sales (G2) is greater than (>) the calculation of an absolute reference to the overall average ($B$14) plus 500. This first part of the IF function will look like this: **=IF(G2 > ($B$14 + 500),** Notice the ending comma that represents that this is the end of the first parameter of the IF function.
      ii. The second parameter, the ***value_if_true***, will give the sales person the bonus of $500. This parameter is the simple literal value of **500**. Don't forget to add the comma after the 500 to represent that this is the end of the second parameter of the IF function.
      iii. The third and final parameter, the ***value_if_false***, will give the text message of **"No Bonus"**. Don't forget that literal text values must be surrounded with quotations marks. Also don't forget that to end the IF function, you must enter the final closing parenthesis.

So, putting all three pieces together, the final IF function in cell H2 will look like this:

=**IF(G2 > ($B$14 + 500), 500, "No Bonus")**

c. Using whatever method you prefer, repeat the function in cell H2 for all of the other Sales People in cells H3:H11.

5. Merge cells F14 and G14 and then enter the label "Total Bonuses".

6. In cell H14 insert a SUM function to add up all of the bonus that will be paid.

7. Add conditional formatting to the cells H2:H11 so that the $500 bonuses are highlighted in green and the "No Bonus" indicators are highlighted in red.

8. Make any final necessary adjustments to ensure readability and correctness of your work. Also, feel free to add any additional coloring or highlighting to help make the spreadsheet easier to read. Then, once you are sure that everything is correct, you should save your work and then submit it in accordance with your class instructions.

At the completion of this directed assignment, your final work should look very similar to Figure DA_6-3_Completed found here. Please remember, that this hypothetical spreadsheet uses random numbers to calculate each sales person's quarterly sales. If this were going to be used now in a real environment, then the labels in cell A3:A12 would be cleared out and replaced with real sales people's names. Then the range B3:E12 would also be cleared out to allow for the data entry of the actual sales figures for each sales person. By using random numbers

	A	B	C	D	E	F	G	H
1				Sales Incentive Planning				
2	Sales People		Quarterly Sales			Totals	Averages	$500 Bonus?
3	Sales Person 1	$4,256.95	$4,192.88	$5,047.72	$3,712.14	$17,209.69	$4,302.42	No Bonus
4	Sales Person 2	$4,015.60	$6,211.19	$8,597.93	$7,312.46	$26,137.18	$6,534.30	$500.00
5	Sales Person 3	$426.42	$3,174.50	$129.77	$1,989.33	$5,720.02	$1,430.01	No Bonus
6	Sales Person 4	$6,058.43	$1,576.45	$7,885.24	$7,972.10	$23,492.22	$5,873.06	$500.00
7	Sales Person 5	$7,345.43	$3,989.65	$6,308.38	$3,096.97	$20,740.43	$5,185.11	No Bonus
8	Sales Person 6	$957.05	$740.86	$6,442.27	$3,114.35	$11,254.53	$2,813.63	No Bonus
9	Sales Person 7	$5,863.62	$1,275.66	$7,396.19	$5,812.81	$20,348.28	$5,087.07	No Bonus
10	Sales Person 8	$4,975.42	$7,697.70	$4,646.53	$1,208.57	$18,528.22	$4,632.06	No Bonus
11	Sales Person 9	$2,212.85	$6,523.73	$8,773.93	$3,759.87	$21,270.38	$5,317.60	No Bonus
12	Sales Person 10	$7,608.48	$7,343.02	$8,464.56	$4,704.75	$28,120.81	$7,030.20	$500.00
13	Totals	$43,720.25	$42,725.64	$63,692.52	$42,683.35	$192,821.76	$48,205.44	
14	Averages	$4,372.03	$4,272.56	$6,369.25	$4,268.34	$19,282.18		
15	Overall Average	$4,820.54					Total Bonuses	$1,500.00
16								
17								

Sales Incentives

Sheet 1 / 1   Default   Sum=0

Figure DA_6-3_Completed

in this manner, you can create the *shell* of a spreadsheet even if you don't have all of the *real* values yet. This is a very common use of spreadsheets – to work ahead for the purposes of planning.

DA 6-4. For this directed assignment, you will be using the student data file named **DA_6-4.xlsx** to complete the required information. This file is in Microsoft Excel version 2007 or newer format and should open in any contemporary spreadsheet program.

Required student data file: *DA_6-4.xlsx*

For this assignment, you have been asked to come up with some creative but simple Halloween costumes for some kindergarten children. You've decided to try to let your spreadsheet program help you create some characters that they could use.

Your task will be to complete this spreadsheet following the instructions below.

1. Open the student data file named **DA_6-4.xlsx**.

2. Immediately save a copy of this file using the following specifications:

   a. File name: Rename this file using the filename *YourName_DA_6-4*

   b. File location: Place this file in any location you choose, but make a note of the location as you will need it later.

   c. File format: Because this file will be sent in to your professor, you must check with him or her to see what format *he or she* will want this file to be saved in. Don't just assume that the original file format or the default file format for your own computer will be acceptable!

3. This file has been pre-loaded with some alliterative descriptors in column A, and a list of some common Halloween characters in column B. The goal will be to come up with some random combinations of these two lists to create 10 possible costumes for 10 students. Let's start out by adding in the very simple things we've already done many times before. In cell A16, enter the label "Student #1" to serve as the first placeholder.

4. Use the fill handle in cell A16 to drag this content down until you have 10 students.

5. The next things we need are a couple of COUNTA functions. In cell C3, enter a COUNTA function to count up all of the descriptors in the range A3:A14.

6. Then, copy the formula from cell C3 to D3. These two numbers will be used to be the upper bounds of the RANDBETWEEN function in the next steps.

7. Now, in cell C16, use the RANDBETWEEN function to calculate a random integer having a lower bounds of 1, and having an upper bounds of the **mixed cell reference** of cell C$3. By having this mixed reference, we will be able to effectively copy this cell both across as well as down and still have the correct cell references!

8. Copy cell C16 to cell D16 first, then copy both C16 and D16 down to the range of cells C17:D25.

9. Now, here comes the slightly more complex part of this assignment. For this part you are going to create the first generated Halloween Character for Student #1 in cell B16 by entering several nested functions. This single cell will include an outer PROPER function, which contains two INDEX functions and the & operator to join several text pieces together. The end result of this function will be the proposed Halloween Character name for the Student #1. To accomplish this, you will complete the following tasks:

   a. Begin the function by entering the first part of the PROPER function: =**PROPER(**

   b. Next, on the inside of this function, enter the first nested function, which is an **INDEX** function to look up the correct descriptor for Student #1 by using the **absolute** reference to the range of descriptors ($A$3:$A$14) and the relative index position reference, which is the random number for descriptors in cell C16. This part of the overall function will look like: **INDEX($A$3:$A$14,C16)**

   c. Next, use the **&** operator symbol followed by " " (a quoted blank space) to tell the function to concatenate a blank space onto the information calculated thus far. This part of the overall function will look like: **& " "**

   d. Next, use the **&** operator symbol once again to concatenate the final function. The final function will be another **INDEX** function to look up the correct Halloween Character for Student #1 by using the **absolute** reference to the range of Halloween Characters ($B$3:$B$14), and the relative index position reference, which is the random

number for characters in cell D16. This part of the overall function will look like: **&
INDEX($B$3:$B$14,D16))** Notice the extra closing parenthesis at the end of this section – this is the closing parenthesis for the PROPER function that was begun in step a.
above. The final nested function that should end up in cell B16 will look like the following:
=PROPER(INDEX($A$3:$A$14,C16) & " " & INDEX($B$3:$B$14,D16))

10. Finally, use the fill handle in cell B16 to drag this complex formula down to cell B17:B25. If you
have properly constructed the functions with the appropriate use of relative, absolute, and mixed
cell references, then you will see all of the 10 students now have a randomly generated Halloween
Character name!

11. Make any final necessary adjustments to ensure readability and correctness of your work. Also,
feel free to add any additional coloring or highlighting to help make the spreadsheet easier to
read. Then, once you are sure that everything is correct, you should save your work and then submit it in accordance with your class instructions.

At the completion of this directed
assignment, your final work
should look very similar to
Figure DA_6-4_Completed found
here. Please remember, that this
spreadsheet uses random numbers to calculate each student's
character name. Your specific file
will most probably have different final answers. Also remember
that you can always regenerate
new random numbers by simply
pressing either the function key
F9 or the key combination of the
control key and the function key
F9 depending on your spreadsheet program.

Also please remember that we
have a very small sample of
descriptors and starting characters. As a result, it is very possible
that more than one student might
end up with the same character
name. To lessen the odds of this
occurring, you would need to add
additional rows in between rows 3

	A	B	C	D
1	Random Halloween Character Generator			
2	Descriptors	Halloween Characters	Count of Descriptors	Count of Characters
3	A snoozy, sleepy	Dracula	11	8
4	A sniffling, sneezing	Frankenstein		
5	A hilariously happy	Werewolf		
6	A wildly wicked	Witch		
7	A creepy crawly	Spider		
8	A spooky, scary	Ghost		
9	A disturbingly dusty	Mummy		
10	A frighteningly furry	Pirate		
11	A fully fabulous			
12	A totally tough			
13	A silly stumbling			
14				
15	Student Names	Halloween Character	Random Number for Descriptors	Random Number for Characters
16	Student #1	A Snoozy, Sleepy Spider	1	5
17	Student #2	A Creepy Crawly Pirate	5	8
18	Student #3	A Spooky, Scary Werewolf	6	3
19	Student #4	A Hilariously Happy Frankenstein	3	2
20	Student #5	A Sniffling, Sneezing Mummy	2	7
21	Student #6	A Snoozy, Sleepy Spider	1	5
22	Student #7	A Spooky, Scary Frankenstein	6	2
23	Student #8	A Snoozy, Sleepy Ghost	1	6
24	Student #9	A Hilariously Happy Pirate	3	8
25	Student #10	A Sniffling, Sneezing Dracula	2	1
26				

Random Halloween Costumes   ⊕

Figure DA_6-4_Completed

and 14 to enter additional values in both columns A and B. The formulas and functions would automatically adjust to accommodate these extra entries. This is also a very common technique used
in spreadsheets: planning the spreadsheet well and entering in the formulas and functions, with
intentional detail to the types of cell references, so that the spreadsheet can be easily expanded as
necessary.

DA 6-5. For this directed assignment, you will be using the student data file named **DA_6-5.ods** to complete the required information. This file is in LibreOffice Calc version 4.2 or newer format and should open in any contemporary spreadsheet program.

Required student data file: *DA_6-5.ods*

In this workbook we will be exploring a ***very common*** calculation that is used in both spreadsheets and databases all the time. It is the calculation of deriving a person's age if you are given their date of birth. But in this assignment, we will be doing this single calculation – twice. The first time, we will perform the calculation using five total steps to derive the final desired outcome. Each of these steps will become intermediary calculations for the subsequent steps to use. Then when we redo the calculation the second time, we will nest all of the functions together into a single step after the initial data entry.

Your task will be to complete this spreadsheet following the instructions below.

1. Open the student data file named **DA_6-5.ods**.
2. Immediately save a copy of this file using the following specifications:
   a. File name: Rename this file using the filename ***YourName_DA_6-5***
   b. File location: Place this file in any location you choose, but make a note of the location as you will need it later.
   c. File format: Because this file will be sent in to your professor, you must check with him or her to see what format ***he or she*** will want this file to be saved in. Don't just assume that the original file format or the default file format for your own computer will be acceptable!
3. In cell A3, enter your own birth date and format the cell as a short date.
4. In cell B3, enter the TODAY() function to get today's system date.
5. In cell C3, enter the simple subtraction formula to subtract your birth date from today's date. This will calculate your age in days.
6. In cell D3, we need to see how many years are represented by those number of days in cell C3. So, the next question is: How many days are there in a year? If you answered **365.25** you are spot on! Remember, every year has 365 whole days and one quarter-day (.25), which we typically lump together every four years and call it a ***leap year*** and we celebrate this extra ***leap day*** on February 29 every four years. So, how many days are there in a year? Answer: 365.25! Therefore, in cell D3, calculate your age in years by dividing your age in days (C3) by the number of days in the year (365.25).
7. We're getting closer, but typically, we don't describe ourselves as having a fractional portion of a year as being part of our "age". So now we need to throw away the fractional part of the last calculation. To do this, we will use the ROUNDDOWN function in cell E3 to round the age down to the whole years only.
8. So let's take a break and look at all of the calculations in row 3. Here you can see that you started with a known value (your birth date) entered in cell A3. From there, you proceeded to perform four more individual calculations to finally derive your age from your birthdate. Next you will perform the same calculations but this time by using ***nested functions***. Let's start by reentering your birthdate into cell A6 and make sure that it is formatted as a short date.
9. Next in cell C6, you will create a single calculation that includes nested functions to calculate your age as we normally describe ourselves. To achieve the desire results, perform the following steps:

a. Enter the first part of the function by entering the **outermost** function of all of the nested functions. For this calculation, that will be the ROUNDDOWN function. The first part of this calculation will therefore be as follows:
=ROUNDDOWN(

b. Next, for the first parameter of the ROUNDDOWN function, we need to calculate the entire age as it is derived from the other calculations. So the next part of this calculation will be: **((TODAY() – A6) / 365.25)**
Notice that there is an extra set of parenthesis surrounding the nested TODAY() function and the subtraction of cell A6. Remember, this is necessary to force the correct **order of operations.** The concept of "order of operations" was discussed in Chapter 2. Without these extra parenthesis, the spreadsheet would have calculated A6 / 365.25 *first* and then subtracted *those results* from the results of the TODAY() function. This would have been the wrong answer!

c. Finally, to complete the nested function, we need to supply the second parameter of the ROUNDDOWN function, which will be **0** to show no decimal places. The last part of the calculation will therefore be: **,0)** Notice that the comma signifies that this is the next parameter in the ROUNDDOWN function. Also notice that the function has to end with a closing parenthesis. The final nested function that should end up in cell C6 will look like the following:

=ROUNDDOWN(((TODAY() – A6) / 365.25),0)

	A	B	C	D	E
1	Age Calculation Using Intermediary Steps				
2	Date of Birth	Today	Age in Days (Using Date Math)	Age In Years (Includes Fractional Part of Current Year)	Age In Years (Rounded Down as We Do)
3	10/29/63	06/01/18	19939	54.5900068446	54
4	Age Calculation Using Nested Functions				
5	Date of Birth		Age in Years (Rounded Down as We Do)		
6	10/29/63		54		
7					

Nested vs. Non-Nested Functions

Figure DA_6-5_Completed

10. Make any final necessary adjustments to ensure readability and correctness of your work. Also, feel free to add any additional coloring or highlighting to help make the spreadsheet easier to read. Then, once you are sure that everything is correct, you should save your work and then submit it in accordance with your class instructions.

At the completion of this directed assignment, your final work should look very similar to Figure DA_6-5_Completed found here.

Some additional final thoughts about nested functions: As you can see in this assignment, by using nested functions, you can reduce the total number of columns or rows that you need to complete a calculation. But with that being said, it is also true that nested functions are often considered more difficult to review and to troubleshoot if there is a problem with your spreadsheet. So, as with everything else, just because you **can** nest a whole bunch of functions together, this doesn't necessarily mean that you **should** do that kind of excessive function nesting.

A good rule to keep in mind is that it may be someone else who has to come behind you to review your spreadsheets. Be considerate of what they will need to work with in the future!

DA 6-6. For this directed assignment, you will be using the student data file named **DA_6-6.xlsx** to complete the required information. This file is in Microsoft Excel version 2007 or newer format and should open in any contemporary spreadsheet program.

Required student data file: *DA_6-6.xlsx*

In this workbook you are creating a spreadsheet that will show you the true costs of paying off a credit card. For this assignment, we will assume that you start with an opening balance and, while paying off this credit card, you make no new purchases on this card. This exercise is just to discover how much it costs to pay off a credit card with high credit card interest.

Your task will be to complete this spreadsheet following the instructions below.

1. Open the student data file named **DA_6-6.xlsx**.
2. Immediately save a copy of this file using the following specifications:
   a. File name: Rename this file using the filename ***YourName_DA_6-6***
   b. File location: Place this file in any location you choose, but make a note of the location as you will need it later.
   c. File format: Because this file will be sent in to your professor, you must check with him or her to see what format ***he or she*** will want this file to be saved in. Don't just assume that the original file format or the default file format for your own computer will be acceptable!
3. First, let's fill in the easy parts. The following entries are the very simple ones that won't take much effort at all:
   a. Let's assume that the credit card has an original balance of $5000. Enter 5000 into cell A3. Make sure this is formatted as currency or money.
   b. Let's use the average APR for credit cards, which is 18.9%. Fill that value into cell B3. Make sure this is formatted as a percentage with two decimal places.
   c. Enter a simple formula to calculate the monthly interest rate in cell C3. Make sure this is formatted as a percentage with 4 decimal places.
   d. Enter 0 in cell D3 for the moment – we will be changing this later on. Make sure this is formatted as currency or money.
   e. Enter a simple cell reference in cell A5 to reference the original balance in cell A3.
4. Well that's all of the *easy* parts. From here on, some of the calculations will be more difficult and some may be fairly complex! So let's continue.

   The minimum payment for a credit card payment is a fairly involved calculation that says there is a minimum payment due, which is **one of three possible values**. The first value that is considered is 4% of the balance that is owed. If this value is greater than a minimum amount of $15, then this value is used as the minimum payment due. But, if 4% of the balance due is less than $15 and the actual balance due is greater than or equal to $15, then the minimum amount of $15 is used as the minimum payment due. But if the remaining balance on the card is greater than $0 but is less than $15, then the minimum payment is just the final balance that is due on the card.

   Whew!

   So, with this complicated set of rules, how does this get reduced to a spreadsheet calculation? To accomplish this complex calculation, you will need to perform the following steps:

a. In cell B4, you will end up entering **_two nested IF functions_**. The first part of the first if statement tests to see if 4% of the current balance is greater than 15. Enter:

=IF((0.04*A5)>15,

Notice that there are two sets of open parenthesis after the IF function name. The first open parenthesis is for the IF function, while the second open parenthesis is to control the order of operations to make sure that the multiplication happens first, before the comparison to the literal value of 15. Also, notice the comma that represents the end of the first part of the IF function!

b. Continue this function by entering the **_value_if_true_** portion of the IF function, which is the actual calculation of 4% of the current balance. Enter: (0.04*A5),

Notice once again the ending comma that indicates the end of that parameter in the IF function.

c. Continue this function by entering the **_value_if_false_** portion of the IF function. Here, however, is where we are going to **_nest_** an additional IF function. The reason is because if we are at this point in the calculation, we know that 4% of the balance is less than $15, so now we need to see if the remaining balance itself is greater than or equal to $15. If it is, then the minimum payment will be precisely $15. Otherwise, the balance that is left must be less than $15, so the minimum payment will be the remaining balance. The entire second nested IF function will be entered as follows:

IF(A5>=15, 15, A5))

Notice how the end of this entry has a second closing parenthesis. This second closing parenthesis is to complete the original IF function that was begun in step a. up above. To double-check your work, the final nested function in cell B5 should look like:

=IF((0.04*A5)>15,(0.04*A5),IF(A5>=15,15,A5))

d. Don't forget to format this cell as currency or money.

5. The next fairly complex calculation is calculating your actual monthly payment. This calculation will also be an IF function. The question you are asking yourself at this point is this: "Is the minimum payment that I am being asked to pay **_plus_** any additional amount I _want_ to pay less than or equal to the balance that is left?" If the answer to this question is true, then you will pay the minimum payment due plus the extra amount you have indicated. If the answer to this question is false, then you will simply pay off the remaining balance. The function that should be entered in cell C5 is the following:

=IF(B5 + $D$3 <= A5, B5 + $D$3, A5)

Notice that this function has both relative and absolute references! Make sure the reference to the extra amount that you will be paying each month above the minimum payment due (cell D3) is referenced with an **_absolute reference_**. Also remember to format this cell as money or currency.

6. The next calculation is an easy one. In cell D5, calculate the New Balance by subtracting your payment in cell C5 from the current balance in cell A5. Remember to use relative references here.

7. This next calculation in cell E5 is also an easy one. To calculate the new interest that will be added to your balance, simply multiply the new balance in cell D5 with an **_absolute reference_** to the monthly interest rate in cell $C$3. Make sure this value is properly formatted as currency or money with only two decimal places.

8. The next calculation in cell F5 is also an easy one. To calculate the new final balance, simply add the new interest in cell E5 to the new balance in cell D5. Make sure these are both relative references.

9. In cell A6, you need to show that the current balance in this row is now the new final balance from the previous row. Therefore, in cell A6 enter a simple relative reference to cell F5.

10. For the rest of the entries in row 6, you can simply copy-and-paste or use the fill handle to pull the corresponding formulas from row 5 down into this row.

11. Now that row 6 is complete you can use this entire row to fill in all of the desired rows beneath row 6. To accomplish this, select the range A6:F6. With this range selected, use the fill handle and then drag these calculations down until you reach row 200! You may be asking, "why would we want that many rows?! That's an awful lot of monthly credit card payments!" and you would be right! The issue is, depending on how you pay your credit cards off, it could potentially take that many payments (which is **over 15 years** – Gulp!)

But even though you have dragged these calculations from row 6 down to row 200, as you look at the data, you see that you actually have paid off this credit card on row 139! That's some good news! So now, let's add some calculations the top of the sheet to see how much total interest you have paid, how many months it took to pay off the credit card, and how much you have paid back totally including the original balance and the interest.

12. In cell E3, this will be a simple SUM function to sum up the total new interest that was charged by using the range E5:E200.

13. In cell F3, you will use the COUNTIF function to conditionally count up how many actual payments were made in order to pay of this credit card. To use the COUNTIF function, the first parameter will be the range of your payments (C5:C200). For the second parameter of the COUNTIF function, which is the **criteria** parameter, enter the following: **">0"** Don't forget to use the quotation marks to signify that this is the criteria that should be used to determine if the cell will be counted.

14. For cell G3, you have one final simple calculation. This will be the simple addition of the original card balance in cell A3 with the total interest paid in cell E3.

15. Make any final necessary adjustments to ensure readability and correctness of your work. Then, once you are sure that everything is correct, you should save your work and then submit it in accordance with your class instructions.

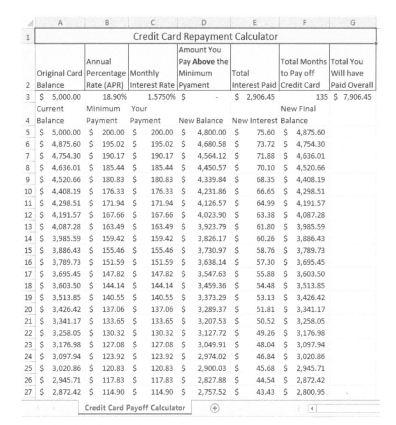

	A	B	C	D	E	F	G
1			Credit Card Repayment Calculator				
2	Original Card Balance	Annual Percentage Rate (APR)	Monthly Interest Rate	Amount You Pay **Above** the Minimum Pyament	Total Interest Paid	Total Months to Pay off Credit Card	Total You Will have Paid Overall
3	$ 5,000.00	18.90%	1.5750%	$ -	$ 2,906.45	135	$ 7,906.45
4	Current Balance	Minimum Payment	Your Payment	New Balance	New Interest	New Final Balance	
5	$ 5,000.00	$ 200.00	$ 200.00	$ 4,800.00	$ 75.60	$ 4,875.60	
6	$ 4,875.60	$ 195.02	$ 195.02	$ 4,680.58	$ 73.72	$ 4,754.30	
7	$ 4,754.30	$ 190.17	$ 190.17	$ 4,564.12	$ 71.88	$ 4,636.01	
8	$ 4,636.01	$ 185.44	$ 185.44	$ 4,450.57	$ 70.10	$ 4,520.66	
9	$ 4,520.66	$ 180.83	$ 180.83	$ 4,339.84	$ 68.35	$ 4,408.19	
10	$ 4,408.19	$ 176.33	$ 176.33	$ 4,231.86	$ 66.65	$ 4,298.51	
11	$ 4,298.51	$ 171.94	$ 171.94	$ 4,126.57	$ 64.99	$ 4,191.57	
12	$ 4,191.57	$ 167.66	$ 167.66	$ 4,023.90	$ 63.38	$ 4,087.28	
13	$ 4,087.28	$ 163.49	$ 163.49	$ 3,923.79	$ 61.80	$ 3,985.59	
14	$ 3,985.59	$ 159.42	$ 159.42	$ 3,826.17	$ 60.26	$ 3,886.43	
15	$ 3,886.43	$ 155.46	$ 155.46	$ 3,730.97	$ 58.76	$ 3,789.73	
16	$ 3,789.73	$ 151.59	$ 151.59	$ 3,638.14	$ 57.30	$ 3,695.45	
17	$ 3,695.45	$ 147.82	$ 147.82	$ 3,547.63	$ 55.88	$ 3,603.50	
18	$ 3,603.50	$ 144.14	$ 144.14	$ 3,459.36	$ 54.48	$ 3,513.85	
19	$ 3,513.85	$ 140.55	$ 140.55	$ 3,373.29	$ 53.13	$ 3,426.42	
20	$ 3,426.42	$ 137.06	$ 137.06	$ 3,289.37	$ 51.81	$ 3,341.17	
21	$ 3,341.17	$ 133.65	$ 133.65	$ 3,207.53	$ 50.52	$ 3,258.05	
22	$ 3,258.05	$ 130.32	$ 130.32	$ 3,127.72	$ 49.26	$ 3,176.98	
23	$ 3,176.98	$ 127.08	$ 127.08	$ 3,049.91	$ 48.04	$ 3,097.94	
24	$ 3,097.94	$ 123.92	$ 123.92	$ 2,974.02	$ 46.84	$ 3,020.86	
25	$ 3,020.86	$ 120.83	$ 120.83	$ 2,900.03	$ 45.68	$ 2,945.71	
26	$ 2,945.71	$ 117.83	$ 117.83	$ 2,827.88	$ 44.54	$ 2,872.42	
27	$ 2,872.42	$ 114.90	$ 114.90	$ 2,757.52	$ 43.43	$ 2,800.95	

Credit Card Payoff Calculator   (+)

Figure DA_6-6_Completed

At the completion of this directed assignment, your final work should look very similar to Figure DA_6-6_Completed found here.

Once this spreadsheet is completed, you should explore what happens when you change some values. For instance, change the amount of extra payment that you might make in cell D3. Notice that by paying just $100 extra per month, you will change the total number of payments from 135 down to only *32!* And more importantly, this change would *save nearly $1900* in interest! This is why we use spreadsheets – to help us get a better understanding of the types of calculations that can have a real impact on our lives!

Creative Projects

CP 6-1. Your friend is in a fraternity and has been asked by the Philanthropy Committee to help plan for their upcoming tele-thon where they will be making calls to raise money in the fight against cancer. Your friend knows a little about spreadsheets and has started by creating a shell for this project, but needs your help to complete some formulas and functions that they don't know how to complete yet. For this creative project, you will use this spreadsheet to plan for the event and to estimate the number of donations (by number of calls and by amount) that each one of the 10 fraternity members should make to reach their overall goal of $7000. Your friend has told you that there will be three parts to the worksheet; the first part will be the tele-thon plan; the second part will track their *actual* calls and donations; and then the third part will show the new counts of what is remaining as they work through the tele-thon. This file is in Microsoft Excel 2007 or newer format and should open in any contemporary spreadsheet program.

Required student data file: *CP_6-1.xlsx*

When you open this file, you should immediately save a copy of this file with the name *YourName_CP_6-1* in the file format as instructed in your class.

Here is some of the information that you will need to complete this file:

✦ The top section will be for the plan for the tele-thon. Some items you will update in this section include:

- In the range B4:G9, many of the cells will be blank but only one cell in each row will have a calculation. In that cell, the calculation will divide the absolute reference to cell $I$2 by a mixed reference to the correct corresponding values from row 3. This will calculate how many donations at each donation level would be needed to meet the goal. So for example, in row 4, we are imagining receiving all $500 donations. If this were the case, then there would be no entries at all in cell B4:F4. But in cell G4, this cell would have the calculation of =**$I$2/G$3**. Then, this cell can be copied-and-pasted to the cells F5, E6, D7, C8, and B9.

- In the range B10:G10, you need to make your own estimates of how many *typical* donations in total you think they can expect for each denomination of donation. Your goal here is to come up with the total goal by having some combination of different donations.

- In cell H4, you will use the SUMPRODUCT function which uses two ranges as its two parameters. The first range will be an absolute reference to the range $B$3:$G:$3. The second range will be a relative reference to the range B4:G4. This cell can then be copied down to the range H5:H10.

✦ In the middle section, here are some of the items you will be updating:

- The names of the frat volunteers who are working the phones. We have planned on 10 volunteers, but we also know that sometimes, people don't always show up! So your spreadsheet should be able to handle a minimum of 1 volunteer all the way up to 10 volunteers. Their names would go in the cells A13:A22.

- In cell I5, we need to calculate the goal for each individual member. Since the actual count of how many volunteers show up is unknown at this time, this function should use a COUNTA function to count the number of actual names that exist in the range A13:A22 and then divide this count into the overall goal in $I$2.

- In the range B13:G22, here is where you would actually update the counts of the number of each kind of donation that each frat member collects.

- In the range H13:H22, these cells will also use a SUMPRODUCT calculation similar to those that you used in the range H4:H10.

- In the cell range I13:I22, you need to add an IF function that tests to see if the individual volunteer has collected more than the individual goal per member. If so, then the cells should display the message "GOAL REACHED". Otherwise, the cells should show the message "calling . . ." Also add some conditional formatting in this cell range that highlights any individual who reaches the individual goal.

- Finally in this section, you want to create some totals in row 23. The range B23:G23 should be simple sums of the counts of donations collected. The cell H23 should be the sum of all total donations collected in the range H13:H22. Here also, add some conditional formatting in this cell that highlights if the overall total exceeds the overall goal.

- In cell I23, add an IF function that tests to see if the overall donations collected have exceeded the overall goal in cell I2. If so, then the cells should display the message "GOAL REACHED". Otherwise, the cells should just show an empty cell. A cell can be set to an empty text value by entering an open quotation mark followed immediately by a closing quotation mark with nothing in between (""). Use conditional formatting to format this cell the same as you did in cell H23.

✦ The last section shows calculations that determine the number of new donations that are still needed (based on the actual donations already received) in order to meet the final goal of $7000. Here are the items that need to be updated in this section:

- In cell I24, calculate the balance that is left to go by subtracting the total donations received in cell H23 from the overall goal in cell I2.

- In the range B27:G32, use the ROUNDUP function to divide the balance that is left to go using an absolute reference to cell $I$24 by the appropriate value from the cells in row 26 just like you completed in the first section. By using the ROUNDUP function with a 0 as the second parameter, you will discover the minimum number of donations at that specific denomination that would be required to meet the final goal.

- In the cell range H27:H32, these cells will also use a SUMPRODUCT calculation similar to those that you used in the ranges H4:H10 and H13:H22.

Figure CP_6-1_Sample shows a *possible* version of the completed project. Your own project may vary with different calculations, call counts, and other values, etc.

Figure CP_6-1_Sample

Remember to check your final work for spelling, grammar, and overall correctness and then submit your file in the manner prescribed for your class.

CP 6-2. For this creative project, you have just been hired at a small, local credit union. They hired you in a large part because of your friendly and engaging personality but, to a smaller degree, for your skills and ability to work with spreadsheet programs!

Required student data file: None: Start with a new, blank workbook file and name the file *YourName_CP_6-2*.

The first thing that the boss wants you to work on while she is on a business trip is a spreadsheet to create an amortization schedule for our new car buyers. The boss knows that you don't have much experience working in finance and loans, so she has decided to help you out by giving you a little sketch of what she is thinking about. She sent you the sketch via email and then she told you that she would meet with you after she returned to go over the details.

Figure 6-13 is the picture that she sent to you via email to help you get started.

After reviewing the sketch you met with her to clarify what she wanted and this is what you took away from the conversation:

✦ She wants some type of headings at the top of the spreadsheet that says that this is a loan amortization schedule and that the next section of information is the specific loan information for this client.

✦ Then she wants information about the amount borrowed, the term of the loan, the APR, the monthly payment amount, and the first payment date for this particular loan. That part constitutes the heading section of the spreadsheet and the next part constitutes the detailed section of the spreadsheet.

✦ In this section, there are multiple lines that represent each of the payments for the entire life of the loan. In the various columns we will see the payment number, the date of the payment, the payment amount from above, the principal amount for that particular payment, the interest amount for that particular payment, and then the final loan balance at the end of that payment.

✦ These detail lines will then continue down for all of the payments until the last payment where it shows that the final balance is zero dollars.

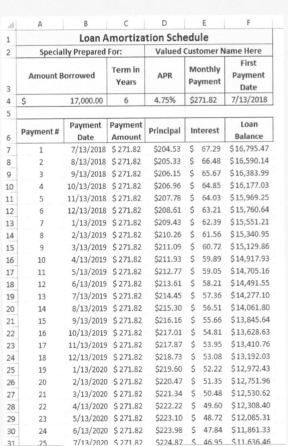

Figure_6-13

✦ For the calculations for this loan, you know that you will use the PMT payment function to calculate the basic loan payment. You also know that you can use date functions to calculate all of the needed dates. You also know that there is are the PPMT and IPMT financial functions that will be used for each of the detailed lines.

Figure CP_6-2_Completed shows a *possible* version of the completed project. Your own project may vary as there are several different ways that some of the calculations can be set up.

Remember that the very last payment may not appear to "add up" correctly in terms of the IPMT and PPMT functions and the last amount due. In fact, typically, the last payment of a loan is handled as a special "Loan Payoff" transaction that simply pays the final balance due. Do not worry if your final payment line appears to be over or short of the actual payment amount by some small factor.

Now, for an extra challenge (optional), see if you can make it so that this same spreadsheet can be used whether the loan term is for 1 year or for 30 years (which is usually the longest term for home loans.) Hint: To make this work, in all of your detail rows, you will have to nest all of the functions that you came up with inside of some IF function that first tests to see if this row is actually part of the number of total payments for the life of the loan. There are several ways to do this as well.

Remember to check your final work for spelling, grammar, and overall correctness and then submit your file in the manner prescribed for your class.

	Loan Amortization Schedule				
	Specially Prepared For:		Valued Customer Name Here		
	Amount Borrowed	Term in Years	APR	Monthly Payment	First Payment Date
	$ 17,000.00	6	4.75%	$271.82	7/13/2018

Payment #	Payment Date	Payment Amount	Principal	Interest	Loan Balance
1	7/13/2018	$ 271.82	$204.53	$ 67.29	$16,795.47
2	8/13/2018	$ 271.82	$205.33	$ 66.48	$16,590.14
3	9/13/2018	$ 271.82	$206.15	$ 65.67	$16,383.99
4	10/13/2018	$ 271.82	$206.96	$ 64.85	$16,177.03
5	11/13/2018	$ 271.82	$207.78	$ 64.03	$15,969.25
6	12/13/2018	$ 271.82	$208.61	$ 63.21	$15,760.64
7	1/13/2019	$ 271.82	$209.43	$ 62.39	$15,551.21
8	2/13/2019	$ 271.82	$210.26	$ 61.56	$15,340.95
9	3/13/2019	$ 271.82	$211.09	$ 60.72	$15,129.86
10	4/13/2019	$ 271.82	$211.93	$ 59.89	$14,917.93
11	5/13/2019	$ 271.82	$212.77	$ 59.05	$14,705.16
12	6/13/2019	$ 271.82	$213.61	$ 58.21	$14,491.55
13	7/13/2019	$ 271.82	$214.45	$ 57.36	$14,277.10
14	8/13/2019	$ 271.82	$215.30	$ 56.51	$14,061.80
15	9/13/2019	$ 271.82	$216.16	$ 55.66	$13,845.64
16	10/13/2019	$ 271.82	$217.01	$ 54.81	$13,628.63
17	11/13/2019	$ 271.82	$217.87	$ 53.95	$13,410.76
18	12/13/2019	$ 271.82	$218.73	$ 53.08	$13,192.03
19	1/13/2020	$ 271.82	$219.60	$ 52.22	$12,972.43
20	2/13/2020	$ 271.82	$220.47	$ 51.35	$12,751.96
21	3/13/2020	$ 271.82	$221.34	$ 50.48	$12,530.62
22	4/13/2020	$ 271.82	$222.22	$ 49.60	$12,308.40
23	5/13/2020	$ 271.82	$223.10	$ 48.72	$12,085.31
24	6/13/2020	$ 271.82	$223.98	$ 47.84	$11,861.33
25	7/13/2020	$ 271.82	$224.87	$ 46.95	$11,636.46

Amortization Schedule ⊕

Figure CP_6-2_Completed

Source: Edward V. Weber

CP 6-3. For this creative project, your friend has just inherited $10,000 and has asked you to help her invest the money in the stock market. She says that if you can help her make some additional money (any amount of profit) that she will give you 10% of the profit for your efforts!

Required student data file: None: Start with a new, blank workbook file and name the file *YourName_CP_6-3*.

Here is some of the information that you might want to consider tracking in this file:

✦ Appropriate headings (both spreadsheet and columns)
✦ The original amount to be invested ($10,000).
✦ A detailed matrix of the assets that you will invest in. Much of this information can be looked up online. Some of the information that you will want to track here includes:

   ● Stock or asset name (online)
   ● Ticker symbol (online)
   ● Purchase price (online)
   ● Quantity purchased (your call)
   ● Starting Market Value (calculation)
   ● 52-week low price (online)
   ● 52-week high price (online)
   ● Price she should sell for a loss (calculation based on your own formula – you may want to use the information regarding the current price and the 52-week low price to help you set this price)
   ● Price she should sell for a gain (calculation based on your own formula – you may want to use the information regarding the current price and the 52-week high price to help you set this price)
   ● Target sell price (you can play "what-if" here)
   ● Projected Ending Market Value (calculation)
   ● Profit or loss (calculation)

	Company	Stock Symbol	Price	Quantity Purchased	Starting Market Value	Low52	High52	Price to Sell for Loss	Price to Sell for Gain	Target Sell Price	Projected Ending Market Value	Profit or Loss
	Investment of Friend's Money								**Original Investment Amount**			**$10,000.00**
3	Google	GOOG	$1,119.50	0	$0.00	$894.79	$1,186.89	$1,031.87	$1,382.39	$0.00	$0.00	$0.00
4	Apple	AAPL	$190.24	10	$1,902.40	$142.20	$190.37	$175.79	$233.59	$220.00	$2,200.00	$297.60
5	Microsoft	MSFT	$100.79	10	$1,007.90	$68.02	$100.86	$90.94	$130.35	$110.00	$1,100.00	$92.10
6	Oracle	ORCL	$47.35	16	$757.60	$43.74	$53.48	$44.43	$56.12	$55.00	$880.00	$122.40
7	IBM	IBM	$141.95	10	$1,419.50	$139.13	$171.13	$132.35	$170.75	$150.00	$1,500.00	$80.50
8	Disney	DIS	$99.36	15	$1,490.40	$96.20	$113.19	$94.26	$114.65	$95.00	$1,425.00	-$65.40
9	Facebook	FB	$193.99	10	$1,939.90	$144.56	$195.32	$178.76	$239.67	$220.00	$2,200.00	$260.10
10	Snapchat	SNAP	$11.63	13	$151.19	$10.50	$21.45	$8.35	$21.49	$10.00	$130.00	-$21.19
11	Twitter	TWTR	$36.65	16	$586.40	$15.67	$36.80	$30.31	$55.67	$50.00	$800.00	$213.60
12	Cisco	CSCO	$43.66	17	$742.22	$30.36	$46.37	$38.86	$58.07	$40.00	$680.00	-$62.22
13				Totals	$9,997.51				Ending Portfolio Value		$10,915.00	
14				Uninvested Funds	$2.49					Total Profit or Loss		$917.49
15										10% Commission		$91.75

Figure CP_6-3_Sample

Then, below this matrix of assets, you should have appropriate totals representing the current balance of the portfolio (calculation of the sum of nonsold assets) and the current profit or loss totals (calculation of the sum of all profits and losses). Finally, you should have a calculation that shows whether or not you get your 10% commission and what the actual amount is that you earned.

Figure CP_6-3_Sample shows a *possible* version of the completed project. Your own project may vary with different stocks, different prices and values, different quantities, etc.

Remember to check your final work for spelling, grammar, and overall correctness and then submit your file in the manner prescribed for your class.

CP 6-4. For this creative project, you have been given an extract file from a donor database containing a list of names of donors who have been invited to a celebration reception. This database extract has four columns that include the person's honorific (e.g. Mrs., Miss, Mr., Ms., Dr.), their first name, their middle name (if provided), and their last name. Your goal is to bring all of these fields together into a single field so that the person's full name can be printed on some fancy place setting cards for the dinner.

Required student data file: *CP_6-4.xlsx*

When you open this file, you should immediately save a copy of this file with the name ***YourName_ CP_6-4*** in the file format as instructed in your class.

Here is some of the information that you will need to complete this file:

+ The final goal is to have a single entry for each person that shows the person's full name. This can be completed in one large nested function, which has several text functions contained within it or it can be accomplished with multiple intermediary calculations; you get to decide.

+ Some of the considerations you will need to remember and handle:
  - Not every person has an honorific field.
  - The committee doesn't want to use the person's full middle name; they thought that sounded too stuffy. So, instead, they want you to calculate a middle initial for each person. You remember that you can use the LEFT text function to help you out with this requirement.
  - You know you need to bring the honorific, the first name, the middle initial, and the last name all together in the final full name. You remember that you can use the CONCATENATE text function or the **&** operator to perform this requirement.
  - You remember that you will need a literal space separation character (" ") between each part of the person's name. So you can either concatenate or join that character into the results wherever it is needed.
  - You also know that you don't want extra, unnecessary spaces in the final name. So you remember that you can use the TRIM text function to remove those pesky extra spaces.

The final file does not need any special highlighting or formatting. This file will be used in a mail-merge process, which will bring the person's full name that you created and place the name onto a specially formatted word processing document to print up as dinner place cards.

Double-check your final work for overall correctness and then submit your file in the manner prescribed for your class.

Chapter 7

Sorting, Filtering, Tables, Pivot Tables, and Charts

Source: Shutterstock, Inc.

You might be thinking, "Sorting and Filtering" sounds like something that you do with your candy or your laundry. What can this possibly mean in a spreadsheet program? And also, are "Pivot Tables and Charts" real things or are you just making terms up?

LEARNING OBJECTIVES

In this chapter, we will explore these learning objectives:

Sorting Spreadsheet Data

Filtering Spreadsheet Data

Table Concepts within Spreadsheets

Creating Pivot Tables and Charts

Issues of Compatibility with More Advance Concepts

To be certain, "Pivot Tables and Charts" are, in fact, very real things. We will be looking at those in the last two sections of this chapter.

But the concepts of "Sorting and Filtering" are two of the most important concepts that you will work with in a spreadsheet after you have mastered the basic topics that we have already covered in the previous chapters.

As we have mentioned several times before, it is very typical to work with large collections of data in a single spreadsheet. In most of our examples so far in this text, we have only had around 10 to 20 lines of data in each sample spreadsheet (with one or two exceptions). But these sample files do not really represent the "real world". More often, you may find yourself working with hundreds, thousands, or even tens of thousands of rows of data in a single spreadsheet! When spreadsheets start getting this large, it becomes more and more important that the data is organized in a way that makes finding information easier. This is where *sorting* comes in.

Additionally, sometimes with that much data, it makes sense to create a subset of the data so you can focus on just a smaller portion of the whole information. This is where *filtering* comes in.

Key Terms

- ascending order
- converting a table to a range
- descending order
- extending the sort selection
- filter types
- filtering
- hiding/unhiding rows
- order of actions
- pivot chart
- pivot table
- selecting data to sort
- sort by...
- sort header row
- sort levels
- sort on...
- sort order
- sorting data
- spreadsheet table

In this chapter we will be looking at sorting, filtering, tables within spreadsheets, creating pivot tables and charts, and some compatibility issues with these more advanced topics across diverse spreadsheet programs.

LO 7.1   Sorting Spreadsheet Data

When working with small and large amounts of data in a spreadsheet, it is common that there will be times when you want to see the data in some sequence other than the original sequence in which the data was entered or brought into the spreadsheet. This is called *sorting* the data. Sorting data is the act of specifying the order in which entire rows of data will be presented. While there are some shortcuts to sorting data, we will discover later on that there are some limitations to these shortcuts as well. For now, we will look at a step-by-step approach to the task of sorting data.

The first step to successfully sorting your data is to make sure that you have correctly selected all of the related information that you will need to keep together to make the sort work correctly. Properly Selecting Data to Sort includes selecting the header row for your data and all of the details rows that are to be sorted. Additionally, you must make sure that you necessarily **exclude** any total rows from the selection.

To help visualize this first selection process, please review the selection that is highlighted in Figure 7-1. In this example, we want to sort the data so that the names and addresses of these people are in order by last name.

In this example, we see that all of the data in the header row (row 1) was selected as well as all of the data in the detail rows (2 through 15) was selected. But also notice that the total row (16) was intentionally **not** selected!

This would be the correct selection for sorting this data.

Now, you may be thinking to yourself, "But if I only want to sort the data by the last name, shouldn't I only need to select that data in column C?"

Depending on your version of spreadsheet program, if you only select the column that you want to sort **by**, then the spreadsheet program may incorrectly assume that what you have selected is the **only** data that you want to sort. And if that happens, you will end up sorting all of the last names only but then leaving all of the rest of the data in its original place! The end result will be that you have mixed up and mismatched the data! The last names would all be sorted, but the rest of the individual's data (like their first name and address, etc.) would all still remain in their original locations! This would be quite a mess!

In other spreadsheet programs, however, if you incorrectly select only a portion of the

	A	B	C	D	E	F
1	Honorific	First Name	Last Name	Address	Donation Count	Donation Amount
2	Miss	Russell	Reilly	P.O. Box 401, 1767 Donec Av.	5	$ 9,300.00
3	Mrs.	Griffin	Mcguire	3255 Mus. Street	9	$ 3,700.00
4		Evan	Henry	P.O. Box 826, 2977 Lobortis Rd.	2	$ 3,500.00
5	Mrs.	Chaney	Fuentes	Ap #439-7117 Aliquam Street	3	$ 6,900.00
6	Ms.	Jordan	Wiley	P.O. Box 325, 2840 Proin Av.	4	$ 1,200.00
7	Dr.	Ryder	Spence	P.O. Box 106, 2059 Molestie Ave	3	$ 3,300.00
8	Miss	Hammett	Roth	5639 Egestas, Av.	9	$ 3,000.00
9		Alan	English	Ap #265-8011 Vitae, St.	5	$ 7,300.00
10	Ms.	Walter	Wilkinson	1449 Non St.	10	$ 10,000.00
11	Mrs.	Mufutau	Ochoa	982-9078 Et Rd.	3	$ 7,200.00
12	Prof.	Rae	Fox	7151 Aliquam Rd.	10	$ 10,000.00
13	Hon.	Genevieve	Hinton	2788 Tellus Avenue	5	$ 4,300.00
14	Miss	Brandon	Vazquez	Ap #370-1138 Ipsum Road	7	$ 4,800.00
15	Ms.	Jackson	Parsons	9994 Turpis Av.	3	$ 5,900.00
16	Totals				78	$ 80,400.00
17						

Figure 7-1

data and then attempt to perform a sort activity, then the program may prompt you with this error and ask if you want to extend the sort selection. Extending the Sort Selection is an automatic process that some spreadsheet programs will do if they notice that you have selected an insufficient amount of data before attempting to perform a sort activity. But once again, not all spreadsheet programs will help you out in this way! That is why it is important for you to make sure you have selected all of the appropriate data first before attempting to perform the sort.

Once you have the correct data selected and you are ready to sort your data, there are a number of different ways that you can initiate the sorting process (depending on the program you are using.)

Figure 7-2 shows some of the toolbars and the menu locations of where you can initiate the sorting process in several of the more popular contemporary spreadsheet programs.

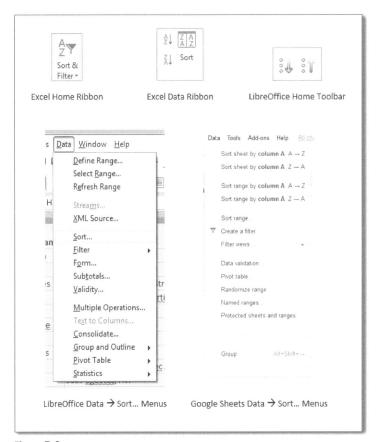

Figure 7-2

In this figure, the top icons are found on the ribbons and toolbars in their respective programs. However, before just clicking on one of these tools, you should make sure you know what the tool is going to do for you.

This is because some of the sorting tools will perform a sorting "shortcut" that may not deliver the results you want.

The sorting shortcuts, also called a quick-sort, will sort all of the data you have selected in either ascending or descending order ***based on the data found in the* FIRST COLUMN** *of the selected data!* Now, if you wanted to sort your data based on the data in the first column, then these tools are very handy indeed!

But what about in our example from Figure 7-1? We wanted to sort this data by the Last Name column which is ***not*** the first column! If we used the shortcut tools or quick-sort tools, we would end up sorting our data by the Honorifics of the person. In other words, we would not have sorted the data in the way that we intended.

These are some more of the limitations of the special tool helpers that some programs have provided and which we have discussed in previous chapters.

We should not fret, however, because all of the programs do have a way that will allow us to accomplish our sorting goals. Instead of using these shortcut tools, we will instead initiate the **Sorting Dialogs**, which will allow us to specify all of the details about the sorting process that we want to undertake.

The sorting dialogs are accessed usually through the menu commands in a program and the specific look of each dialog will typically be different, but their intended functionality is the same.

Figure 7-3 shows the sort dialog for the Microsoft Excel program, the LibreOffice Calc program, and the Google Sheets program. As we continue our discussion on the sorting procedures, please refer back to this figure to see how each program will accomplish the same tasks but use different ways of specifying the options that you choose.

As we have already discussed, the purpose of sorting is to rearrange the selected data in the spreadsheet into a particular order. This is called the sort order of your data. The Sort Order of your data may be described as either ascending or descending order. Ascending Order goes from the smallest value to the largest value as determined by the data type. So, if you're sorting by text-based data, this data will ascend from "A" to "Z".

Numeric data, on the other hand, will ascend from 0 to 99999, etc. Descending Order goes from the largest value to the smallest value as determined by the data type. So, text-based data descends from "Z" to "A". Likewise, numeric data will descend from 99999 to 0, etc.

Both the quicksort tools and the sorting dialogs in all of the programs will tend to represent the sort order with either the actual terms "***Ascending***" and "***Descending***" or they will use the graphic arrows pointing in the desired direction of "A → Z" for ascending or "Z → A" for descending.

Once you are in the sort dialogs, there are several decisions that you will need to make:

Microsoft Excel Sort Dialog

LibreOffice Calc Sort Dialog

Google Sheets Sort Dialog

Figure 7-3

First, you must specify which column *or columns* you want to use to sort the data. This concept of being able to sort by multiple columns is called sort levels. Sort Levels are the various primary and secondary (and tertiary, and others as required) sorting that each program can accomplish. If you specify multiple sort levels, the spreadsheet programs will sort all of the data first by the primary sort level. Then after that, while maintaining that primary sort level, the program will continue to sort by the secondary level that you specify. If you specify a third or more sort levels, the program will continue to sort while maintaining the previous sort levels.

This is important because imagine that you had two people with the same last name of "Smith". Which one should come first and which one should come second in your sorted list? Since they have the exact same last name, the order of the records would become unpredictable!

By adding a secondary sort level that uses the *first name* field, the record with the person named Bob Smith would be sorted before the person with the name Susie Smith.

When specifying each sort level, you must also specify whether the sort order will be ascending or descending as previously discussed. Additionally, in some programs you can specify whether the sorting will occur on the *values* of the data in the cells or on some other attribute. This is called the Sort On... option in some of the programs' sort dialogs. These programs will allow you to sort by the *format* of the cells or perhaps by the *color* of a cell. This comes in quite handy when you use conditional formatting as discussed in the previous chapters.

To further help you in selecting the proper sort columns for each sort level you choose, each program will have a way for you to specify whether or not your data selection includes a header row. The Sort Header Row is typically the first row of your selected data that has the column names for all of the data that has been selected. By telling the sort dialog that your selected data has a sort header row, the dialog will be able to let you specify the columns by name as opposed to simply using a column letter reference.

Whether or not your selected data has header rows, you still will specify which column is to be used for each level of sorting that you need. The Sort By ... field is where you will choose the column that is to be used for each particular sort level.

Once you have filled in all of the appropriate entries in the sort dialog for all of your desired sort levels, you will press the "OK" or "Sort" button and your selected data will then be automatically sorted according to your specifications. And what is important to remember is that this technique will work if you have 20 rows of data *or if you have 20,000 rows of data!* Being able to quickly sort extremely large collections of data is yet another reason why spreadsheets (and those who know how to properly use them) are valued so highly in so many organizations!

LO 7.2 Filtering Spreadsheet Data

As mentioned previously, typical spreadsheet files can have very many rows of data. In fact, it is not uncommon for spreadsheets to have hundreds, thousands, or even tens of thousands of rows of data! With that much data in a spreadsheet, trying to work with all of the data at one time may become impractical or nearly impossible. What is needed, therefore, is some way to create one or more subsets of this large collection of data so that we can work with one subset at a time.

The process of creating subsets of large collections of data in the spreadsheet is known as filtering. Filtering in spreadsheet programs is the process by which you can temporarily hide rows of data that do not meet some particular criteria that you have chosen.

Filtering data in a spreadsheet is accomplished in a similar fashion to the way sorting is accomplished. In fact, most contemporary spreadsheet programs will group the filtering commands right along with the sorting commands.

So just like with sorting, the first technique that you must use in order to begin to properly filter your data is the technique of selecting the header row for the data.

Once this header row is selected, the next step is to turn on filtering for the data. To turn on filtering, you will use one of the filtering tools or menu commands for your particular program. Figure 7-4 shows the filter tools for some of the more popular contemporary spreadsheet programs.

When you have begun the filtering process, you can now specify a multitude of criteria by which the program will filter the data to show you only the corresponding data, which matches your chosen criteria. For example, if column B in your worksheet is a column that has last names in it, and you only want to see the last names that begin with the letter A through G, then you can specify a text filter to say "<H". In this manner,

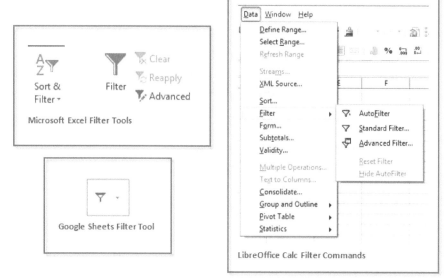

Figure 7-4

the program will now filter all of the data and show only data where the last name is less than the letter "H". All of the other rows of data that do not match these criteria will be hidden within the spreadsheet.

The concept of filtering spreadsheet data brings up this new, interesting topic called "hiding and unhiding data" in a spreadsheet. Hiding/Unhiding Rows or columns in a spreadsheet is the process by which the data is removed from the visual appearance of the spreadsheet, *but not physically deleted* from the spreadsheet. Rather, the row numbers or column letters that surround the data will be changed to a different color or highlight to indicate that there are hidden rows and columns that are not being seen.

This technique of hiding rows and columns allows for data to remain in the spreadsheet physically, but not be visually shown to the viewer while it has been hidden. Additionally, this activity of hiding rows and columns can make it easier to capture a subset of data by copying-and-pasting only the visible rows and columns while the other data remains hidden.

The act of filtering data effectively hides the rows that do not match the criteria of the filter that has been applied.

To see an example of filtering in action, consider Figures 7-5 and 7-6. In Figure 7-5, we see the first 20 or so rows of people's names and addresses. There are, in fact, 100 rows of data in this sample file. That's not really all that much data, but it will be enough to let us see the effects of filtering.

	A	B	C	D	E
1	Honorific	First Name	Middle Name	Last Name	Address
2		Quin	Ingrid	Elliott	215 Morbi Rd.
3	Dr.	Marvin	Colby	Morrow	481-993 Vestibulum, Street
4	Prof.	Sopoline	Lareina	Shepherd	637-7478 Neque. Avenue
5	Ms.	Basia	Hoyt	Manning	8557 Libero. Av.
6	Mr.	Rogan	Lacey	Pitts	219-3171 Elit Ave
7	Mr.	Emerald	Beatrice	Cotton	Ap #358-7660 Parturient Av.
8	Prof.	Boris	Lee	Wagner	P.O. Box 561, 2680 Lobortis Street
9	Dr.	Bell	Levi	Riley	123-8386 Sit Rd.
10	Dr.	Clark	Michelle	Martinez	6507 Urna. St.
11	Mr.	Marshall	Eliana	Moran	302-4440 Ullamcorper Road
12	Hon.	Alisa	Thomas	Buck	638-1850 Nunc Rd.
13		Noelani	Camilla	William	1808 Morbi Rd.
14	Mr.	Jacqueline	Nelle	Spears	693-5663 Ornare Ave
15	Prof.	Wallace	Emerald	Warner	P.O. Box 427, 5202 Enim, Street
16	Hon.	Zachary	Oliver	Sears	388 Ante. Av.
17		Jamalia	Kiona	Hurst	P.O. Box 207, 7368 Nunc Av.
18	Hon.	Yuli	Clare	Dunlap	P.O. Box 802, 2498 Cubilia Rd.
19	Ms.	Kermit	Beatrice	Moreno	P.O. Box 282, 1474 Odio. Av.
20	Mr.	Anika	Lionel	Galloway	P.O. Box 455, 8844 Risus. Street
21	Mr.	Uriel	Lila	Horne	P.O. Box 101, 7709 Vestibulum. St.
22	Miss	Talon	Upton	Jennings	8570 Malesuada. Rd.

Figure 7-5

Now let's suppose that we notice just in the first 20 or so records that there are a number of people who have P.O. boxes for their addresses. Also, you notice that some people have an apartment number listed as the first part of their address. Now, let's imagine that we are trying to send some new marketing literature to only the homeowners in this list. We may decide that anyone on this

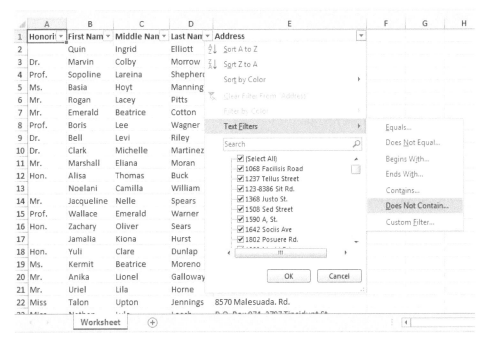

Figure 7-6

list who has an address which includes a P.O. box or which has an apartment number is actually *not* our target audience. So what we effectively want to do with this list is **filter out** those addresses that include either P.O. boxes or apartments.

To accomplish this task, we first select the header row and then turn on filtering for this spreadsheet. You will always know that filtering is turned on because the header row of your data will now have little drop-down arrows in each of the header row cells. You use these arrows to set the filter criteria for each desired column.

As we can now see in Figure 7-6, we can apply pretty much any imaginable filtering criteria on our data.

We could select specific, individual data values and only show those rows. We could set a filter where the values are equal to some other specific value. In fact, we can use any of the various criteria that are listed in this figure!

For our example we used a custom filter to specify that we wanted to filter the rows where the address "*does not contain*" the value "P.O. Box" **and** "*does not begin with*" the value "Ap #". Figure 7-7 shows the custom filter being created.

In this customer filter dialog box, we can use the drop-down list to discover all of the myriad ways that the data can be compared.

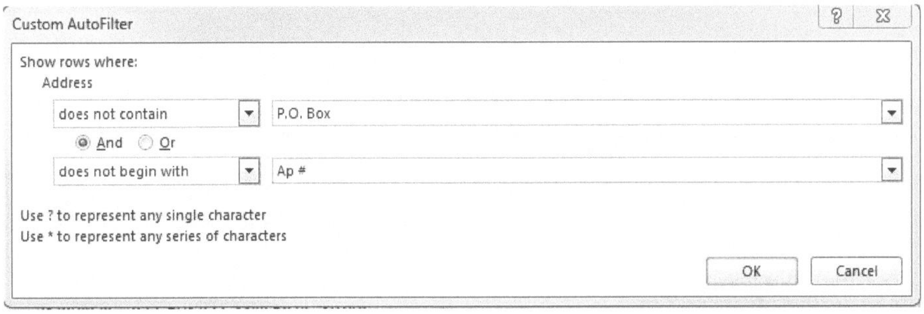

Figure 7-7

There are many types of comparison options that can be specified for filtering data values including:

- equals...
- does not equal...
- is greater than...
- is greater than or equal to...
- is less than...
- is less than or equal to...

- begins with...
- does not begin with...
- ends with...
- does not end with...
- contains...
- does not contain...

And these are only the filter types that can be applied to the text-based data for this column!

Filter Types are the specific kinds of comparisons that can be made on a column of data based upon the type of data that is stored in the column. If the data in the column is text-based data, then the filter types that will be allowed will be the text-based filter types. If the data in the column is numeric data, then the filter types that will be allowed will be the numeric filter types. Likewise, there are Date and Time filter types as well.

Looking back at our example, once this filter is applied, we notice some interesting changes in the spreadsheet data. Figure 7-8 shows the sample spreadsheet after the filter has been applied. First, in the header row of the spreadsheet we see that all of the column headers have the little down-arrow signifying that filtering is turned on for this data. But we also notice that there is another little funnel now showing in the filter indicator in cell E1. This is showing you that there is an active filter being applied in this column.

The next item you should notice is the row numbers. You will notice that all of the data rows are now colored blue, which also indicates that filtering has been applied.

	A	B	C	D	E	F
1	Honori ▾	First Nam ▾	Middle Nan ▾	Last Nan ▾	Address	⫪
2		Quin	Ingrid	Elliott	215 Morbi Rd.	
3	Dr.	Marvin	Colby	Morrow	481-993 Vestibulum, Street	
4	Prof.	Sopoline	Lareina	Shepherd	637-7478 Neque. Avenue	
5	Ms.	Basia	Hoyt	Manning	8557 Libero. Av.	
6	Mr.	Rogan	Lacey	Pitts	219-3171 Elit Ave	
9	Dr.	Bell	Levi	Riley	123-8386 Sit Rd.	
10	Dr.	Clark	Michelle	Martinez	6507 Urna. St.	
11	Mr.	Marshall	Eliana	Moran	302-4440 Ullamcorper Road	
12	Hon.	Alisa	Thomas	Buck	638-1850 Nunc Rd.	
13		Noelani	Camilla	William	1808 Morbi Rd.	
14	Mr.	Jacqueline	Nelle	Spears	693-5663 Ornare Ave	
16	Hon.	Zachary	Oliver	Sears	388 Ante. Av.	
22	Miss	Talon	Upton	Jennings	8570 Malesuada. Rd.	
24	Mr.	Ezekiel	Octavius	Fitzgerald	1237 Tellus Street	
25		Dolan	Reese	Snow	1802 Posuere Rd.	
26		Carl	Kadeem	Anthony	1642 Sociis Ave	
27	Mr.	Cooper	Vivian	Hines	239 Gravida Rd.	
29	Ms.	Charles	Owen	Skinner	394-6428 Lectus St.	
32		Perry	Gil	Garza	1068 Facilisis Road	
33	Mr.	Dustin	Brett	Cooper	441-6394 Ut Rd.	
34	Dr.	Melvin	Cara	Schwartz	8973 Dictum Street	

Worksheet (+)

Ready   50 of 100 records found

Figure 7-8

Additionally, as you scan your eyes down the row numbers, you will begin to notice that some of the row numbers are "missing" and there are double-line row separators wherever there are "missing" rows. This is the way that the spreadsheet programs show you that there are currently filtered rows that **did not match** the filter criteria and, therefore, are currently being hidden in the spreadsheet. The rows are still there; they are just not visible when the filter is applied!

Now that the data is filtered, you could copy the filtered data and then paste this data onto its own worksheet. By doing so, you will have created a subset of the entire spreadsheet that represents just the data that you want to focus on!

The combination of ***sorting*** and ***filtering*** is a "one-two punch" that really lets you take control over those really big spreadsheet files that have hundreds or thousands of rows of data.

LO 7.3 Table Concepts within Spreadsheets

In earlier sections and previous chapters we have discussed that many of the very basic functions of spreadsheets haven't changed all that much since they were first introduced in the earliest spreadsheet versions. In fact, the simple formulas and functions have been around since the very beginning and continue to work the same way as they always have.

But with each new version of spreadsheet programs, additional new functionality has been added by the different vendors over time. Some of these new features are simple extensions of the basic functions that were always around.

One of these features that was added along the way is the concept of having a *table* inside of a spreadsheet.

Now, as you may recall, we have already discussed how spreadsheets are basically an extension of the word processing tables in which the ability to perform calculations was added and this is what basically makes spreadsheets most significantly different from word processing tables. So at first glance, it might seem that the spreadsheet programs were actually taking a step *backwards* when the programs decided that they would try to introduce the concept of a *table* as something that could be embedded into a workbook that was already an extension of an existing *word processing table*.

But the "tables" in spreadsheet programs have additional properties that make them different than just any other simple table.

To help understand why tables were created in spreadsheets let's think about a scenario where you are working with a very large collection of data – let's say about 5000 rows are so. In order to properly work with this data we have learned in this chapter that we will probably need to both *sort* and *filter* this data to get the data into a workable order. Then, before we can do any meaningful calculations on the data, we may have to break the data into smaller subsets that are more manageable.

There is a specific Order of Actions that you will want to take whenever you are working with these large collections of data.

1. First, remove any filtering that has been set.
2. Next, sort the data in the most appropriate sort order for your task at hand.
3. Next, apply any appropriate filters to limit the data down to just the data set you are interested in.
4. Next, copy the filtered data and paste it onto its own sheet so you can work with it independently of the other hidden rows.
5. Repeat this entire process for as many different subsets of the data as you might need.
6. Then, with each subset, perform the desired calculations.

As you can imagine, by working with this specific order of actions, you can fairly quickly slice-and-dice a very large collection of data and turn it into manageable chunks that can be processed independently.

This type of processing has been available in spreadsheets since the earliest versions. But several vendors decided that this process itself was still too "manual". That is where tables come into play in spreadsheets. Spreadsheet Tables are a specific range of cells that have been formatted to be a table using the Insert Table tool or the Format as Table tool or commands in your spreadsheet program.

The process of creating tables in a spreadsheet is as simple as selecting all of the data that you are interested in (no matter how big it is) and then applying the table tool in your spreadsheet program. This action *converts the basic range* of data into a defined table space. Once the data has been converted into a table, there are now new, additional functions that are available that will only work on data that is in a table in a spreadsheet.

Tables allow you to easily insert subtotals or sub-averages or several other sub- calculations, to selected groupings of rows of data that are all controlled by the table definition itself.

But once you convert a range to a table so that you can use the specialized table functions, you must also be aware that there are some functions that **cannot work** with data when it is in the table format. Rather, if you attempt to use a function that cannot work with table data, the program will inform you that you must exercise the command to convert the table back to a range. Converting a Table to a Range is a necessary activity in order to use certain tools and functions in the spreadsheet.

Some additional consideration you should know about spreadsheet tables: Nearly all of the things you can do with a spreadsheet table can also be accomplished *without* using spreadsheet tables – just by using the tools and techniques you have already learned so far!

Also, not all spreadsheet programs support *spreadsheet tables*. Those programs that *do* have them do not necessarily implement the tables in the exact same way. Therefore, tables that behave one way in one program may not actually behave the same way in another program. We will discuss this issue in more detail in Learning Objective LO 7.5.

LO 7.4   Creating Pivot Tables and Charts

In the last section, we learned that most spreadsheet programs have some sort of *table* that can be used to make some common tasks with large selections of data easier to implement. We also learned that there are some limitations and concerns with spreadsheet tables that will be discussed in more detail in Learning Objective LO 7.5.

Another collection of advanced functionality that exists in most contemporary spreadsheet programs is the concepts of Pivot Table and Pivot Charts. A Pivot Table is a secondary table that is created from an original data table and allows for the cross-tabulation of large lists of data. Pivot Tables are used for quickly organizing and summarizing typically large rows and columns of data. Pivot Tables allow the user to quickly apply many of the functions that have been previously discussed in the earlier chapters. Functions like sorting, grouping, averaging, counting, and summing data across the specified groups are easily accomplished with just a couple of clicks in a Pivot Table.

Pivot Tables allow the user to very quickly change the parameters of the summarized data without directly manipulating the original, main data. In other words, Pivot Tables create a way in which a user can accomplish numerous manual spreadsheet steps with just a few clicks.

Creating a Pivot Table is the exact same as creating a basic spreadsheet table. Simply select the **all** of the data (header rows and detail rows) and then click the Insert Pivot Table tool for your spreadsheet program.

Once the Pivot Tool has been initiated, the program will provide a Create Pivot Table dialog for you to complete. Figure 7-9 shows one example of a Create Pivot Table dialog.

Here the table or range that you had previously selected will already be filled in for you. You can manually change this reference if necessary.

Notice that you can also use an external data source for your Pivot Tables. We will be learning about working with external data in Chapter 8.

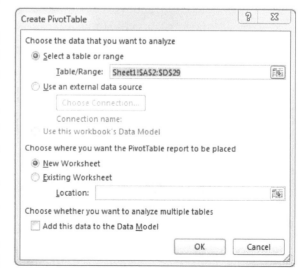

Figure 7-9

Also, notice that you can choose where the Pivot Table will be placed within your workbook. Typically, Pivot Tables and Pivot Charts are placed on their own worksheets. This is because these tools are typically used to summarize **very large** collections of data that is already completely filling up its own original worksheet. Therefore, placing Pivot Tables and Pivot Charts on their own worksheets will keep the summarized data neatly away from all of the overwhelming and voluminous raw data.

Once the Pivot Table is created, new views and new toolbars become available to you, which will help you work more directly

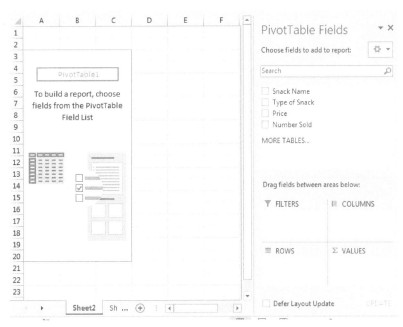

Figure 7-10

with the Pivot Table. Figure 7-10 shows a "blank" pivot table before the settings have been entered.

Here, we see the four column headers are listed as PivotTable fields, which can be turned on and turned off.

These fields can also be dragged to any of the four boxes in the lower right column of this dialog. This allows you to quickly set the rows, columns, filters and summary or aggregate calculations (such as sums, counts, averages, etc.) simply by dragging the fields wherever you want them to be used.

As you can see, PivotTables effectively combine about 20 or more unique spreadsheet activities and functions into 1 single activity. This is a **very powerful** spreadsheet functionality.

Figure 7-11 shows the final Pivot Table in action with several fields selected for rows and columns and several aggregate calculations being performed (average and sum). The Pivot Table in this example shows essentially the same results as the Directed Assignment DA 7-3 found at the end of this chapter. In that assignment, you will derive these same results by simply using the tools

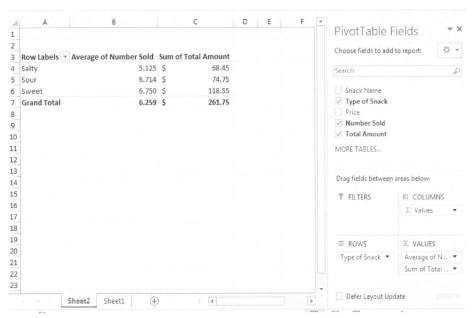

Figure 7-11

and techniques already learned in previous chapters. Here we are discovering that Pivot Tables and charts accomplish the same tasks that you are already capable of performing.

Once a Pivot Table is completed, you may decide that you would like to create a chart based on the Pivot Table data. This is called a Pivot Chart. Pivot Charts are just like regular charts but they have the added benefits of being able to be easily manipulated just like Pivot Tables. In other words, with just a couple of clicks you can filter the underlying data for the chart, and you can turn on and off different chart components, and so on. It's basically like you can keep rebuilding the chart over and over without having to start from scratch each time!

Adding Pivot Charts are as simple as adding regular charts with the same basic steps:

1. First, make absolutely sure that the data is correct – because the chart doesn't care! It will simply chart whatever data it sees.

2. Next simply initiate the Insert Pivot Chart Dialog. Here again, the program will prompt you with some suggested charts based on the data you already have in the Pivot Table. But you can choose your own charts as well.

3. Next, you will make any adjustments to the chart that was created and place the Pivot Chart in an appropriate place in the workbook.

Figure 7-12 shows that a combo column and line Pivot Chart has been added to our example.

Figure 7-12

You will find that working with Pivot Tables and Pivot Charts can be very rewarding! They can help you quickly sort, summarize, and thoroughly analyze very large collections of data in your spreadsheets.

And if you are working on this data by yourself and simply need the answers that can be delivered from using these tools, then Pivot Tables and Charts are the tools for you!

But just as in the previous sections, there is a catch. As previously discussed, not all spreadsheet programs implement the advanced features in the same ways. There are numerous differences and discrepancies between different spreadsheet program versions in the ways that they create, maintain, and interpret Pivot Table and Pivot Chart definitions and data structures. As a result, a Pivot Table or Chart that is created in one version of one program *may not work correctly or appear correctly* in another program that can nonetheless read and process all of the rest of the information in the file.

In the next section, we will discuss these limitations and their implications in greater detail.

LO 7.5   Issues of Compatibility with More Advance Concepts

As we have seen in some of the earlier chapters and more directly within this chapter, there are several areas where different spreadsheet programs start to exhibit issues of incompatibility with their peer, contemporary programs and even with other versions by the same vendor. For example, there are increasing instances where the file format of an online version of a spreadsheet program will be incompatible with the desktop version of the spreadsheet program from the same vendor!

The further we delve into the more advanced functionalities in any particular spreadsheet program, the higher the probability that those more advanced functions *will not* be fully compatible with other programs. Part of this is, unfortunately, absolutely by design!

In the earliest days of spreadsheet programs, new versions were released periodically because there were many new functions being added to the programs and many of the bugs and kinks were being worked out of the programs as well. But after a decade or so of ongoing development, the core functionality of spreadsheet programs became exceptionally stable and predictable. As a result, there were fewer and fewer differences between different vendor's versions of the "standard spreadsheet program". Likewise, there were fewer and fewer reasons why anyone would need to "upgrade" to a newer spreadsheet program.

So, when new versions were introduced, these new versions often changed very little to the underlying, basic spreadsheet concepts. Instead, the new versions added new "bells-and-whistles" which, often times, were just minor enhancements which would attempt to reduce a 2- or 3- or 4-step process down to a 1-click tool or solution.

In fairness though, as we discussed in Chapter 5, as graphics processing has continued to improve over the years, several new versions of spreadsheet programs have included significant enhancements in their charting and graphing capabilities. This trend has not abated. The newest versions of several spreadsheet programs have introduced unique and enhanced charts with innovative chart types and new ways of *really* visualizing larger and larger datasets.

Also, some additional functionality does continue to be introduced in newer spreadsheet versions. The Pivot Tables and Charts that we covered in this chapter are the "spreadsheet-based forerunners" of the whole field of Data Analytics. And as that field continues to grow and churn out new ways of thinking about and looking at data, spreadsheet programs are looking to bring some of those new data analytics concepts *back into the spreadsheet programs themselves.*

So that's the good news! You can expect that as we continue moving forward, spreadsheet programs will continue to include newer and more visually appealing charts. They will also continue to add shortcuts and toolbars which contain 1-click solutions to some proclaimed 3-click problems. They also will continue to add functionality that is becoming part of the standard toolbox for data analysts of all types. But there's a catch . . .

It took quite a number of years for spreadsheet program vendors to work toward harmony with each other with regards to compatibility – both in file formats and in overall spreadsheet functions and processing. And after many years, there is today a very high cross-platform compatibility of spreadsheet programs.

But for various reasons, some vendors appear to be stepping away, once again, from the harmony of compatibility and are beginning to try to force distinctiveness. If that happens, you will find yourself having to learn multiple programs to be able to know the strengths and weaknesses of each and to decide which program you want to use and under which circumstances.

One of the main goals of this text was to help you achieve proficiency in the **Spreadsheet Fundamentals** – the things that are *nearly universal or ubiquitous across* **ALL** *spreadsheet programs*. As we approach the more advanced concepts and topics, we must constantly be aware that interprogram compatibility drops off with the use of the higher level functionality.

Therefore, if you can complete your work using the most common techniques and functions, you will have the greatest probability of maintaining compatibility with any other spreadsheet user with whom you might need to collaborate.

As a further note, Chapter 10 of this text will look at the concepts of Macros. As we will see in that chapter, macro creation, development, maintenance, and usage are almost ***never*** compatible between vendor programs and may not even be compatible between program versions from the same vendor. As such, you really must have a firm understanding of who is going to be using your macros before even spending any time developing them. As a general premise, it is best to assume that macros will **not** be compatible with any other program besides the one that was used to develop them.

In closing this section, you should know that the intent is not to have you swear off the more advanced versions of spreadsheet programs or the more advanced functionality and shortcuts and graphics that they bring to the table. Rather, it is just to help you understand that with just the spreadsheet fundamentals that you have already mastered in these first several chapters, you can accomplish pretty much anything you need to do ***and*** have confidence that your work will still be compatible and accessible to anyone else who also has mastered spreadsheet fundamentals – no matter which program they choose to use.

Chapter 7 – Assignments and Projects

Directed Assignments

DA 7-1. For this directed assignment, you will be using the student data file named **DA_7-1.xlsx** to complete the required information. This file is in Microsoft Excel 2007 or newer format and should open in any contemporary spreadsheet program.

Required student data file: *DA_7-1.xlsx*

In this workbook you will be working with the sample data that was introduced in the beginning of the chapter. This data is an extract of some donor information from a donor database. The purpose of this spreadsheet is to allow you to sort the data in two different ways. First, you will sort the data by Donation Amount so we can see who has given us the most donations. You will then take a screenshot of the way the data looks sorted that way and place a copy of the screenshot directly into the spreadsheet. Then, you will re-sort the data into order by last name so that you can use the list to help check the people in when they arrive for the event.

Your task will be to complete this spreadsheet following the instructions below.

1. Open the student data file named **DA_7-1.xlsx**.

2. Immediately save a copy of this file using the following specifications:

   a. File name: Rename this file using the filename ***YourName_DA_7-1***

   b. File location: Place this file in any location you choose, but make a note of the location as you will need it later.

   c. File format: Because this file will be sent in to your professor, you must check with him or her to see what format ***he or she*** will want this file to be saved in. Don't just assume that the original file format or the default file format for your own computer will be acceptable!

3. First, select all of the data that you will want to sort. This includes the header rows and data rows but excludes the total rows. Select the range A2:F16.

4. Next, initiate the sort dialog in your program to set the sort order for this first sort. For the first sort, set the sort by column to "Donation Amount" and set the sort order to descending or "largest to smallest".

5. Once the data is sorted, you notice that there are two people who have donated $10,000. You now decide that you want to re-sort the data so that there is a secondary sort by last name. Therefore, you will now repeat steps 3 and 4 above, but this time, you will add a secondary sort level to sort by the column "Last Name" in ascending sort order.

6. Now that the data is properly sorted for the first task, take a screenshot of the cell range A2:F17 and paste that screenshot into the location G2:L17. This will stay as a static picture of the way the data was sorted at this particular moment in time. Then, when you re-sort the data in a different sort order later, you will still have a "picture" of what the data looked like when it was sorted in the current manner.

7. Now that you have a screenshot to show the way the data looked when it was sorted by donation amount, you can re-sort the actual data in the other way that it is needed to be sorted. Once again, select all of the data that you will want to sort. This includes the header rows and data rows but excludes the total rows. Select the range A2:F16.

8. This time, initiate the sort dialog in your program to set the sort order for this next sort. For this last sort, remove any secondary sort levels and then set the primary sort level to be by the column "Last Name" and set the sort order to ascending or "A to Z".

9. Once the data has been re-sorted, let's update the main label in cell A1 to describe how we have just sorted the data. Select cell A1 and update the cell to say, "Donor Information from Database Sorted By Last Name".

10. Make any final necessary adjustments to ensure readability and correctness of your work. Also, feel free to add any additional information that you think might help make the spreadsheet easier to read. Then, once you are sure that everything is correct, you should save your work and then submit it in accordance with your class instructions.

At the completion of this directed assignment, your final work should look very similar to Figure A_7-1_ Completed found here.

Figure DA_7-1_Completed

DA 7-2. For this directed assignment, you will be using the student data file named **DA_7-2.ods** to complete the required information. This file is in LibreOffice Calc version 4.2 or newer format and should open in any contemporary spreadsheet program.

Required student data file: *DA_7-2.ods*

In this workbook you are working with the local animal shelter's current list of shelter "residents". This lists all of the animals that are still currently living in the shelter. When you open up this spreadsheet, you notice that there are currently 100 animals in the shelter of different species, ages, and colors. And some of the animals have been residents in the shelter for a number of months! The young couple who you are working with today would like you to help them to find that "perfect little someone" to take home today.

Your task will be to complete this spreadsheet following the instructions below.

1. Open the student data file named **DA_7-2.ods**.
2. Immediately save a copy of this file using the following specifications:
   a. File name: Rename this file using the filename *YourName_DA_7-2*
   b. File location: Place this file in any location you choose, but make a note of the location as you will need it later.
   c. File format: Because this file will be sent in to your professor, you must check with him or her to see what format *he or she* will want this file to be saved in. Don't just assume that the original file format or the default file format for your own computer will be acceptable!
3. The first person you speak with says that they are looking for a puppy or kitten, but only if they are black or gray. But then the other partner in the couple says that they would also consider an older dog if they have been "stuck" here in the shelter for more than 3 months. You tell them that you will need to apply a couple of different filters to the data to see if you have any animals in the shelter that match either of these two criteria. To accomplish these tasks, you will need to first select the range A2:E2 and then turn on filtering in your particular spreadsheet program.
4. Use the filter tools to filter the species down to just Dogs and Cats.
5. Next, since they said that they were looking for a "puppy" or a "kitten", you should now use the filter tools to filter the approx. age field to just those rows that have a 1 or a 2 for this value.

6. Next add a final filter that limits the colors to just black and gray.

7. Take a screenshot of this filtered data and place that screenshot directly to the right of the actual filtered data. That way you will have a copy of the data that was found with the first set of criteria.

8. Add a label above the screenshot that you just placed so that you can remember what filters were applied.

9. Now you are ready to begin the next set of filter criteria. You must first clear all of the current filters so that you make sure you aren't filtering the data using the previous set of criteria.

10. Next you remember that the couple said that second possible adoptees would be any "older" dogs that have been in the shelter for at least 3 months. So, set the first new criteria to be species that are Dogs only.

11. Add the next filter that shows only 4- or 5-year old dogs.

12. Finally, add criteria that show only those dogs that have been residents for at least 90 days.

13. Take a screenshot of this filtered data and place that screenshot directly under the other screenshot you took in step 7 above.

14. Add a label above this second screenshot so that you can see what filters were applied this time as well.

15. Remove all filters from the original data to unhide all of the hidden rows of data.

16. Make any final necessary adjustments to ensure readability and correctness of your work. Also, feel free to add any additional information that you think might help make the spreadsheet easier to read. Then, once you are sure that everything is correct, you should save your work and then submit it in accordance with your class instructions.

At the completion of this directed assignment, your final work should look very similar to Figure DA_7-2_Completed found here.

Intake #	Species	Approx. Age	Color	Days in Shelter		Intake #	Species	Approx. Age	Color	Days in Shelter
\multicolumn{5}{c}{**Current Shelter 'Residents' - June 02, 2018**}		\multicolumn{5}{c}{**Only Puppies or Kittens that are Black or Gray**}
12032	Dog	1	Gray	117		12032	Dog	1	Gray	117
12059	Reptile	1	Brown	47		12262	Cat	1	Gray	143
12070	Reptile	2	Black	128		12772	Cat	1	Black	122
12074	Rodent	1	White	163		12427	Cat	2	Gray	175
12137	Dog	3	Gray	1		13103	Dog	2	Black	96
12117	Reptile	5	Gray	47		13330	Dog	2	Black	25
12242	Cat	3	Spotted	94		13417	Cat	2	Black	158
12195	Dog	4	Black	5						
12316	Dog	4	Spotted	176		\multicolumn{5}{c}{**Older Dogs that have been with us > 90 Days**}
12171	Cat	5	Yellow	52						
12262	Cat	1	Gray	143		Intake #	Species	Approx. Age	Color	Days in Shelter
12231	Rodent	1	White	128		12778	Dog	5	White	154
12201	Bird	2	Spotted	154		13550	Dog	5	Brown	157
12448	Bird	3	White	100		13174	Dog	5	Yellow	144
12375	Rodent	1	Spotted	14						
12536	Cat	5	Green	33						

Figure DA_7-2_Completed

DA 7-3. For this directed assignment, you will be using the student data file named **DA_7-3.xlsx** to complete the required information. This file is in Microsoft Excel 2007 or newer format and should open in any contemporary spreadsheet program.

Required student data file: *DA_7-3.xlsx*

In this spreadsheet, you will find information about the sales that have occurred over the past 4 weeks for the main vending machine in your business lobby. You want to do some analysis on the type of snacks that are being sold out of that machine including which ones seem to be more popular and which ones seem to be more profitable.

Your task will be to complete this spreadsheet following the instructions below.

1. Open the student data file named **DA_7-3.xlsx**.
2. Immediately save a copy of this file using the following specifications:
   a. File name: Rename this file using the filename ***YourName_DA_3-1***
   b. File location: Place this file in any location you choose, but make a note of the location as you will need it later.
   c. File format: Because this file will be sent in to your professor, you must check with him or her to see what format ***he or she*** will want this file to be saved in. Don't just assume that the original file format or the default file format for your own computer will be acceptable!
3. Select the range A2:D29 so that you can sort the data.
4. Use the sort tool in your spreadsheet program to sort the selected data with two levels of sorting: The first sort level will be ascending order by snack type. The secondary sort level will be descending order by price.
5. After the data has been sorted, with the same range still selected (A2:D29), use the tool in your program to insert a spreadsheet table. This will convert the selected range to a spreadsheet table. This may also change the default styling of the data. You can update the styling to your own desires as you see fit.
6. Now, use the filters to change the display so that only the Salty snacks are shown and all of the other snacks are hidden.
7. After the data has been filtered, in cell F1 add the label "Salty Snacks Total Sales".
8. In cell G1, use a SUMPRODUCT function to calculate the total sales for the salty snacks. The first parameter for this function will be the range of snack prices that are shown. The second parameter for this function will be the range of the number sold that are shown.
9. Next change the filter to show only Sour snacks.
10. In cell H1, add the label "Sour Snacks Total Sales".
11. In cell I1, use a SUMPRODUCT function to calculate the total sales for the sour snacks. The first parameter for this function will be the range of snack prices that are shown. The second parameter for this function will be the range of the number sold that are shown.
12. Finally, change the filter to show only Sweet snacks.
13. In cell J1, add the label "Sweet Snacks Total Sales".
14. In cell K1, use a SUMPRODUCT function to calculate the total sales for the sour snacks. The first parameter for this function will be the range of snack prices that are shown. The second parameter for this function will be the range of the number sold that are shown.

15. In cell F2, enter the label "Average # of Salty Snacks Sold".

16. In cell H2, enter the label "Average # of Sour Snacks Sold".

17. In cell J2, enter the label "Average # of Sweet Snacks Sold".

18. Next, you will filter the data just as you did in steps 6, 9, and 12, and each time, you will calculate the average of the number of snacks sold for each category. These calculations will be placed in cells G2, I2, and K2 respectively. Format these numbers to have three decimal places of precision.

19. Finally, remove any filtering on the main data and then add some highlighting and coloring to appropriate group of cells in the range F1:K2 to help separate the information about each snack type to make the data easier to see as groups of information.

At the completion of this directed assignment, your final work should look very similar to Figure DA_7-3_Completed found here.

	A	B	C	D	E	F	G	H	I	J	K
1	Main Vending Machine Sales					Salty Snacks Total Sales	$ 68.45	Sour Snacks Total Sales	$ 74.75	Sour Snacks Total Sales	$ 118.55
2	Snack Name	Type of Snack	Price	Number Sold		Averge # of Salty Snacks Sold	5.125	Averge # of Sour Snacks Sold	6.714	Averge # of Sweet Snacks Sold	6.750
3	Prickles	Salty	$ 1.95	5							
4	Mumbles	Salty	$ 1.95	10							
5	Goldies	Salty	$ 1.95	1							
6	Wonkies	Salty	$ 1.95	5							
7	Bumbles	Salty	$ 1.75	3							
8	Jazzles	Salty	$ 1.45	5							
9	Bitterbutter	Salty	$ 1.25	4							
10	Huffles	Salty	$ 1.25	8							
11	Picolocos	Sour	$ 1.95	10							
12	Slapples	Sour	$ 1.95	7							

Vending Machine Sales

Figure DA_7-3_Completed

You may have noticed that simply converting the range to a table made some tasks easier than by using the original manual steps that you learned in the earlier chapters. While this may be true in some instances, as we discussed in Learning Objective LO 7.5, the risk of incompatibilities with other programs may be just too great for you to simply ignore. If you are going to need to share your workbook with another person and you aren't 100% sure that they have the same version of spreadsheet program that you are using, you won't be sure that they will see the same thing that you see when they open up your file. All of your hard work may not be accessible to those you need to share your work with. And remember, you can do all of the tasks from this assignment *without* using spreadsheet tables!

DA 7-4. For this directed assignment, you will be using the student data file named **DA_7-4.xlsx** to complete the required information. This file is in Microsoft Excel 2007 or newer format and should open in any contemporary spreadsheet program.

Required student data file: *DA_7-4.xlsx*

In this spreadsheet, you will find information (*fictitious*) from five companies who have chosen to share their employee salary data for analysis. They are interested in topics of salary comparisons across companies as well as gender/pay issues. You have been asked to perform some analysis to compare some aspects of the data including salaries by job type and salaries by gender, etc. They haven't been very specific about the analysis you are to do, so you have decided to create a Pivot Table with the data and see where that leads you. To help you track your analysis, you decide that you will create a separate sheet to show any screenshots of interesting discoveries you make along the way.

Your task will be to complete this spreadsheet following the instructions below.

1. Open the student data file named **DA_7-4.xlsx**.

2. Immediately save a copy of this file using the following specifications:

    a. File name: Rename this file using the filename ***YourName_DA_7-4***

    b. File location: Place this file in any location you choose, but make a note of the location as you will need it later.

    c. File format: Because this file will be sent in to your professor, you must check with him or her to see what format ***he or she*** will want this file to be saved in. Don't just assume that the original file format or the default file format for your own computer will be acceptable!

3. First, rename the original data sheet with the name "Raw Data".

4. Next you will add a PivotTable to the spreadsheet by initiating the Insert Pivot Table tool in your particular spreadsheet program. Place this Pivot Table on its own sheet and name this sheet "Pivot Table" and place it second in the workbook.

5. Next, create a third sheet and name it "Screenshots" and place it third in the workbook. As you work, you will take periodic screenshots of the current values in the Pivot Table and paste them onto this sheet to keep a "log" of your analysis.

6. Now, to start your analysis, the first thing you are curious about is how many people (by gender) work at each company and what their average salaries are. Adjust the Pivot Table to show the company name as a row, the gender as a second row, the count of gender as the first value, and the average of salary as the second value. Remember to format the columns appropriately.

7. Take a screenshot of this and place it as the first screenshot on the appropriate sheet.

8. Next, you decide to add another value to show the average age by gender. Add this to the values section of the Pivot Table. Remember to format this value so that it only has one or two decimal places of precision.

9. Take another screenshot and place it on the appropriate sheet.

10. Now, you are interested in departmental breakdowns. Add the Department as a row between the company and the gender. Once you have done this, you discover that you now have too much data to review in your Pivot Table. So you will need to filter your work down to make it more manageable.

11. Use the drop-down arrow on the Department field in the field list area to only show the Business Development departments in the list.

12. Take another screenshot and place it on the appropriate sheet.

13. Next you are thinking about looking at the data from a department point of view first. So you clear all of the entries in the pivot table configuration and start over by placing the department only in the rows area. Remember to remove the department filtering so that you see all departments in column A.

14. Next you want to see the average salaries of each department (regardless of gender). Add the average salary as a value in the Pivot Table. Format this value as currency.

15. Next you want to see what percent of the overall average each departmental average represents. Add the Salary field to the values area *as a second average calculation* and adjust this value to show the value as a % of the Parent Row Total.

16. Update the column label in cell C3 of the Pivot Table to be "Percent of Average".

17. Take a final screenshot of this area and place it on the Screenshot sheet.

At the completion of this directed assignment, your final screenshot worksheet should look somewhat similar to Figure DA_7-4_Completed found here.

As you work with Pivot Tables, you can quickly see how powerful they are and how they can help you make very significant analyses with very minimal effort! But as we discussed in Learning Objective LO 7.5, you may run into issues trying to save your Pivot Tables into other file formats. Also, if you share your file with someone else who uses a different program, they may end up seeing unpredictable results. And depending on the program, some adjustments may allow the Pivot Table to work. But some of these advanced functions may simply remain incompatible with the other spreadsheet programs.

	A	B	C	D	E	F	G	H	I	J	K
1	Row Labels	▾	Count of Gender	Average of Salary		Row Labels	▾	Count of Gender	Average of Salary	Average of Years	
2	⊟Corinthial Intl		186 $	73,057.76		⊟Corinthial Intl		186 $	73,057.76	8.1	
3	Female		93 $	73,601.30		Female		93 $	73,601.30	8.4	
4	Male		93 $	72,514.23		Male		93 $	72,514.23	7.7	
5	⊟Forestent Inc		200 $	73,906.39		⊟Forestent Inc		200 $	73,906.39	7.8	
6	Female		113 $	72,188.13		Female		113 $	72,188.13	8.0	
7	Male		87 $	76,138.15		Male		87 $	76,138.15	7.6	
8	⊟Rempel LLC		206 $	72,461.27		⊟Rempel LLC		206 $	72,461.27	7.9	
9	Female		101 $	71,564.29		Female		101 $	71,564.29	7.8	
10	Male		105 $	73,324.08		Male		105 $	73,324.08	7.9	
11	⊟Spinka Group		205 $	71,522.90		⊟Spinka Group		205 $	71,522.90	8.0	
12	Female		95 $	70,252.97		Female		95 $	70,252.97	8.1	
13	Male		110 $	72,619.66		Male		110 $	72,619.66	7.9	
14	⊟Weimann Inc		203 $	73,768.60		⊟Weimann Inc		203 $	73,768.60	8.1	
15	Female		94 $	75,317.39		Female		94 $	75,317.39	8.1	
16	Male		109 $	72,432.94		Male		109 $	72,432.94	8.0	
17	Grand Total		1000 $	72,934.26		Grand Total		1000 $	72,934.26	7.954	

	A	B	C	D	E	F
3	Row Labels	▾T	Count of Gender	Average of Salary	Average of Years	
4	⊟Corinthial Intl		11 $	114,251.09	10.1	
5	⊟Business Development		11 $	114,251.09	10.1	
6	Female		6 $	119,038.17	11.2	
7	Male		5 $	108,506.60	8.8	
8	⊟Forestent Inc		21 $	109,129.67	7.5	
9	⊟Business Development		21 $	109,129.67	7.5	
10	Female		13 $	106,202.23	6.8	
11	Male		8 $	113,886.75	8.6	
12	⊟Rempel LLC		10 $	111,637.40	9.4	
13	⊟Business Development		10 $	111,637.40	9.4	
14	Female		6 $	110,347.67	10.0	
15	Male		4 $	113,572.00	8.5	
16	⊟Spinka Group		14 $	105,195.93	6.2	
17	⊟Business Development		14 $	105,195.93	6.2	
18	Female		6 $	107,336.83	5.5	
19	Male		8 $	103,590.25	6.8	
20	⊟Weimann Inc		17 $	113,206.29	10.8	
21	⊟Business Development		17 $	113,206.29	10.8	
22	Female		11 $	113,244.00	11.1	
23	Male		6 $	113,137.17	10.2	
24	Grand Total		73 $	110,439.85	8.7	

Row Labels	▾	Average of Salary	Sum of Salary
Accounting	$	61,307.28	6.89%
Business Development	$	110,439.85	11.05%
Engineering	$	69,037.28	7.38%
Human Resources	$	76,203.57	8.99%
Information Systems	$	83,849.70	11.04%
Marketing	$	57,463.06	6.38%
Product Management	$	129,082.02	17.17%
Research and Development	$	66,950.75	6.98%
Sales	$	55,931.72	5.44%
Services	$	53,125.54	5.39%
Support	$	55,017.46	6.56%
Training	$	49,538.27	6.72%
Grand Total	$	72,934.26	100.00%

Raw Data | Pivot Table | **Screenshots** | ⊕

Figure DA_7-4_Completed

Creative Projects

CP 7-1. For this creative project, you will be analyzing data from a music artist tracking site that lists band names, band genre, song prices, and the number of times that the artist has had a song downloaded within the last 6 months. You will create a worksheet named "Analysis" where you will place several screenshots of your findings.

Required student data file: *CP_7-1.xlsx*

When you open this file, you should immediately save a copy of this file with the name *YourName_ CP_7-1* in the file format as instructed in your class.

Here is some of the information that you will need to complete this file:

✦ Rename the first worksheet to "Original Sorted Data" and then sort this data before working with it. Sort the data with a primary sort level on Band Genre in ascending order and a secondary sort level on Times Downloaded in descending order.

✦ Add a second blank worksheet named "Analysis" for holding your screenshots of your findings.

✦ Use a filter to show only bands that have been downloaded at least 400 times and make a screenshot of your findings.

✦ Select this filtered data (including the headings) and copy-and-paste this information into a new sheet named "Most Expensive". Add calculations to this sheet to capture the total number of downloads and the total revenue that these more popular bands have earned.

✦ Go back to the Original Sorted Data sheet and re-filter the data to show the bands that have been downloaded less than 20 times.

✦ Add a worksheet named "Least Expensive" and repeat the steps described above to copy the appropriately filtered data to this sheet and add the calculations to this sheet to capture the total number of downloads and the total revenue that these least popular bands have earned.

✦ Clear all of the filters from the Original Sorted Data and then re-sort the data first by Song Price in descending order and then by Band Genre in ascending order.

✦ Next, filter the data to show only songs priced at $1.39 *and* songs that have been downloaded more than 350 times.

✦ Take a screenshot of this filtered data and place this picture on the screenshot worksheet.

Make sure that all of your worksheets are well formatted with meaningful labels, appropriate formatting and alignment, etc. Remember to apply all of the techniques you have learned in the previous chapters.

Also remember to check your final work for spelling, grammar, and overall correctness and then submit your file in the manner prescribed for your class.

CP 7-2. For this creative project, you will be creating a spreadsheet that captures data about the size and color of cars that you observe over a short period of time.

Required student data file: None: Start with a new, blank workbook and name the file *YourName_ CP_7-2.*

Using either a real street location or intersection, or using the television (or using completely fictitious data), you will locate yourself where you can view a stream of moving cars over a short period of time.

Your goal is to record in your spreadsheet at least 30 different vehicles and make notes about each car. You will capture three pieces of information about each vehicle:

✦ First, use one column to hold the type of car you observe. Limit the cars that you track to only cars, trucks, or SUVs.

✦ Next, record the color of the vehicle using generic colors. In other words, light green and dark green would just be called "green".

✦ Finally, capture your own estimate if the car is "newer" or "older". Whatever you guess here will be just fine.

✦ Make your list to include the first 30 cars, trucks, or SUVs that you see.

✦ Format this data as a table and then use the table sort functions to sort your table by color first and then by vehicle type.

✦ Convert the table back to a normal range and then resort the data to sort by color only.

✦ Use the Subtotal command to count the number of vehicles (regardless of type) with each vehicle color.

Make sure that all of the columns have meaningful text labels. Also, make sure that there is an overall label for the entire contents of the worksheet and that the worksheet tabs have been properly named. Also, adjust the overall formatting to help highlight specific areas or regions of the spreadsheet that are important.

Remember to check your final work for spelling, grammar, and overall correctness and then submit your file in the manner prescribed for your class.

CP 7-3. For this creative project, you will be creating a spreadsheet that captures some survey data from your friends, family, or classmates, etc. about some of the most popular apps that they use. You will create a Pivot Table to help you analyze your data.

Required student data file: None: Start with a new, blank workbook and name the file *YourName_ CP_7-3*.

For this project, you will interview at least 20 of your family members, friends, or classmates, etc. to see what apps they use most often and how frequently they use each app.

To set up your spreadsheet, you will capture the following data:

✦ In column A, list the names of the people you survey.

✦ In columns B and C, indicate their age and gender.

✦ Then, for columns D through H, add the names of the apps that you think will be most frequently used by the people you will interview.

✦ As you interview people, record the counts of how many times a day they indicate that they use each app. If they say that one of their top 5 apps is one that you don't have listed, simply add that as another column. If they don't use one of the apps you have listed, then enter a 0 for that cell for that person. (In other words, don't leave any cells blank.)

✦ After all of the data is captured, create a Pivot Table with the following characteristics:

  • Use the gender as the rows.

- The first value will be the count of interviewees.
- The remaining values will be the sums of the usage for each app.
- Take a screenshot of this Pivot Table and place that picture on its own sheet called "Screenshots".

✦ Next create a Pivot Chart using the existing data (a clustered column chart might work well!)

✦ Remove the count of gender from the chart so that you just see the sums of app use by gender.

Make sure that all of the columns have meaningful text labels. Also, make sure that there is an overall label for the entire contents of the worksheet and that the worksheet tabs have been properly named. Also, adjust the overall formatting to help highlight specific areas or regions of the spreadsheet that are important.

Remember to check your final work for spelling, grammar, and overall correctness and then submit your file in the manner prescribed for your class

Chapter 8

Importing and Working with External Data

Source: Shutterstock, Inc.

Now that we know most of the Spreadsheet Fundamentals and can create our own spreadsheets for whatever purposes we want, shouldn't that be enough? Why do we need to worry about working with someone else's data. Can't we just make our own spreadsheets based on whatever information we might find "out there"?

LEARNING OBJECTIVES

In this chapter, we will explore these learning objectives:

- Defining External Data Types and Sources
- Referencing (Linking) External Data
- Importing (Embedding) External Data
- Inspecting and Cleaning Up External Data
- Deriving Value from External Data

Well, the short answer is yes, yes you can! But how much do you like to type?! Also, how accurate are you and how well do you pay attention to details? If you were to find some important data on an external site and that data spans multiple pages, do you really feel confident that you will be able to perform complete data entry of that large collection of data and not have any errors?

This is the way spreadsheets were used in the earlier versions, and, well, that didn't work out so well! This is why the spreadsheet programs today all have the ability for you to be able to import and embed external data.

This technique is an extension of the old adage, "Don't reinvent the wheel!"

When you find that some other location has the exact data you need and is willing to share it with you freely (or for a fee) you will probably want to take advantage of that. In this chapter, we will explore the different types of external data and sources, how to reference or import that external data, and then, when necessary, how to inspect, clean, and eventually derive value from that external data.

Key Terms

- broken external references
- cleaning "bad" data
- database connectors and ODBC
- defining "bad" data
- external data file types
- external data sources
- external reference considerations
- finding "bad" data
- linking vs. embedding
- referencing across workbooks
- referencing across worksheets
- referencing vs. copying-and-pasting
- static data vs. dynamic data
- updating external references

LO 8.1 Defining External Data Types and Sources

Throughout this text so far, and in most of the assignments, we have been working with either partially created spreadsheets or completely blank files. In fact, you may have felt a little overwhelmed when an assignment asked you to start with a new, blank worksheet and begin from there. But don't despair!

What you will most likely find when you begin working with spreadsheets on a regular basis is that most data that are used in spreadsheets today are coming in from some other source and are not being "created from scratch." In fact, one of the important premises of effectively working with spreadsheet programs is that spreadsheets allow you to "not have to reinvent the wheel every time."

Most contemporary spreadsheet programs can typically import data from a variety of external file sources. The External Data File Types are the specific files that can be opened and read by a spreadsheet program for the purposes of trying to parse the data into the predictable rows and columns that a spreadsheet program will use. Some of the external file types that most spreadsheet programs can work with include:

+ Other Spreadsheets files (XLS, XLSX, ODT, WK1, QP1, etc.)
+ Databases (too many to name)
+ Web Pages (HTM, HTML)
+ Word Processing Documents (DOC, DOCX, ODF, RTF, etc.)
+ XML (Extensible Markup Language) files
+ CSV (Comma Separated Values) files
+ TXT (Text) files

These external data files can come from many different sources. Some examples of External Data Sources might be a second spreadsheet file, or some data that you download or copy from the internet, or an internal or external database.

But let's not get too far ahead of ourselves. Before we look at importing data into our spreadsheet, we must first make sure that we understand the differences between linking and embedding data in a spreadsheet. While both of these techniques will, in fact, bring external data into your workbook, there are some very significant differences to the behavior of these two techniques that we should explore.

To understand the difference between linking and embedding, we should think of the difference between *referencing cells* and *copying-and-pasting cells*. In Figures 8-1 through 8-4, we will explore the differences between linking and embedding when working in spreadsheets.

	A	B
1	Original Data	
2	Pizza Type	Price
3	Cheese	$ 6.99
4	Pepperoni	$ 9.99
5	Sausage	$ 9.99
6	Veggie	$ 7.99
7	Everything	$ 11.99
8	Avg. Price	$ 9.39

Figure 8-1

Figure 8-1 shows a short pricelist for our five favorite pizzas, their individual prices, and the average price for all of the pizzas. We will proceed to first make a *copy-and-paste* of this list for the Figure 8-2 followed by a *reference* of this list for the Figure 8-3 to explore the differences.

Now, here in Figure 8-2 we see the effects of the simple copy-and-paste action that we have come to know very well. As expected, the cells that were copied from the range A1:B8 show the exact same values when they are pasted into the range D1:E8. The changes in coloring and the label text in cell D1 was performed *after* the paste command was completed to show the distinctions between the two.

	A	B	C	D	E
1	Original Data			Copy-And-Paste	
2	Pizza Type	Price		Pizza Type	Price
3	Cheese	$ 6.99		Cheese	$ 6.99
4	Pepperoni	$ 9.99		Pepperoni	$ 9.99
5	Sausage	$ 9.99		Sausage	$ 9.99
6	Veggie	$ 7.99		Veggie	$ 7.99
7	Everything	$ 11.99		Everything	$ 11.99
8	Avg. Price	$ 9.39		Avg. Price	$ 9.39

Figure 8-2

Next we entered new cell references in the range G1:H8, which were simple relative references back to the original data in the range A1:B8 respectively. Figure 8-3 shows the result of this cell referencing. Once again, the change in coloring and the text label in cell G1 was performed after the cell referencing was completed to show the distinctions between this group of cells and the other two cell groupings.

At this point, you can clearly see that there doesn't seem to be any appreciable difference between the techniques of copying-and-pasting vs. simple cell references. However, as you may have already

	A	B	C	D	E	F	G	H
1	Original Data			Copy-And-Paste			Cell References	
2	Pizza Type	Price		Pizza Type	Price		Pizza Type	Price
3	Cheese	$ 6.99		Cheese	$ 6.99		Cheese	$ 6.99
4	Pepperoni	$ 9.99		Pepperoni	$ 9.99		Pepperoni	$ 9.99
5	Sausage	$ 9.99		Sausage	$ 9.99		Sausage	$ 9.99
6	Veggie	$ 7.99		Veggie	$ 7.99		Veggie	$ 7.99
7	Everything	$ 11.99		Everything	$ 11.99		Everything	$ 11.99
8	Avg. Price	$ 9.39		Avg. Price	$ 9.39		Avg. Price	$ 9.39

Figure 8-3

concluded, that would be an incorrect inference. Referencing vs. Copying-and-Pasting becomes the differences between having static (and possibly stale) data vs. having dynamic (and possibly volatile) data. To see this in action, let's say that our five favorite pizzas have just had a price increase. So to reflect these new prices, we update the values in the cell range B3:B7 so that they show the new values. Figure 8-4 shows the results after changing the original data. **Remember!** *Only the values in cells B3:B7 were manually changed!*

As you probably anticipated, the cells that are simply referencing the range A1:B8 are *immediately updated* with the new values! But the cells that were simply copied-and-pasted *before the price increase* are still reflecting the old prices.

Any cells that are referencing other cells are thought of as being **dynamic** while any cells that are pasted from some original copied source are thought of as being **static.**

Static Data vs. Dynamic Data is a decision that you will need to make many times when working with spreadsheets. Sometimes, you will want to make sure that your data automatically updates anytime there is a change to the underlying source data. In these instances, you will want to have dynamic data that is achieved through cell referencing.

Other times, you know that the underlying source data for your spreadsheet will be constantly changing and you want to show only a specific "snapshot in time" of what the data looked like within a particular set of circumstances. In this case, you will want static data that is achieved by either a copy-and-paste action or by taking a static screenshot of the data.

Both of these techniques, creating static data copies or creating dynamic data references, have their appropriate places in spreadsheet work. However, it is your task to determine specifically which technique is the one you need to use for any given circumstances.

	A	B	C	D	E	F	G	H
1	Original Data			Copy-And-Paste			Cell References	
2	Pizza Type	Price		Pizza Type	Price		Pizza Type	Price
3	Cheese	$ 7.49		Cheese	$ 6.99		Cheese	$ 7.49
4	Pepperoni	$ 10.49		Pepperoni	$ 9.99		Pepperoni	$ 10.49
5	Sausage	$ 10.49		Sausage	$ 9.99		Sausage	$ 10.49
6	Veggie	$ 7.99		Veggie	$ 7.99		Veggie	$ 7.99
7	Everything	$ 12.99		Everything	$ 11.99		Everything	$ 12.99
8	Avg. Price	$ 9.89		Avg. Price	$ 9.39		Avg. Price	$ 9.89

Figure 8-4

LO 8.2 Referencing (Linking) External Data

With the fundamental differences between *copying-and-pasting* and *cell referencing* firmly established in our minds, we can now turn our attention to working with external data. So what do we think of when we say "external data"?

Well, most of the work that we have done so far has been confined to a single worksheet at a time. But now, but consider the possibilities of referencing some cells that are external to the current worksheet we are on. Figure 8-5 shows the second worksheet in the same workbook that was used for our previous examples in Figures 8-1 through 8-4.

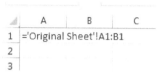

Figure 8-5

Referencing Across Worksheets is the process of having a formula or function in one worksheet referencing cells that are in another worksheet within the same workbook. In Figure 8-5 we see that cell A1 in the second sheet is being set to reference the cell A1 in the original sheet. Note, the original sheet name was renamed to "Original Sheet".

When referencing cells across sheets, there are a couple of techniques that can be used. First, while in the middle of entering a formula or function that needs the external cell reference, you can simply click the other external worksheet to activate it, and then click on the cell or cell range in the external sheet that you want to reference. The spreadsheet program will automatically build the external reference to the secondary sheet by typing in the sheet name surrounded by tic-marks and followed with an exclamation point *before* including the particular cell or cell range that you have selected.

Alternatively, you can simply type in external cell references to other sheets by typing the syntax directly into the cell.

So, thinking once again about the differences between static and dynamic data, here on this second sheet we could have simply copied-and-pasted the information from the original sheet – but that would've created a static copy of the data only. Instead, by creating an external cell reference to the original sheet, we are creating dynamic data that will automatically update whenever the original sheet is updated.

It is important to note that external cell references can also be specified as either relative references, absolute references, or mixed references as was detailed in Chapter 4. Therefore, when you create a relative cell reference to an external worksheet, and then when you copy-and-paste this cell to a new location, the cell references will be automatically updated to the corresponding cell references from the source sheet.

Now that we see that we can reference external data that is on a different worksheet in the same workbook, it is not that large of a leap to see that we can also reference external data that is coming from a completely different workbook!

Referencing Across Workbooks is accomplished very similarly to the way referencing across worksheets is accomplished. The critical difference is that when referencing across worksheets, all of the worksheets are in the same physical workbook file. That means that they will always be available to each other!

But when referencing across workbooks, there is a new consideration that is introduced: Is the source workbook always going to be available and accessible to be used as an uninterrupted reference? We will be exploring this issue in more detail shortly.

To illustrate the relationship between two workbooks using external workbook referencing, we have saved our original pizza list workbook with the name *Chapter8Example.xlsx*. Next, we have created a new, blank, second workbook, which will be used to reference the original data in the Chapter8Example file.

Figure 8-6 shows this second workbook file that is creating an external reference to the original data in the *Chapter8Example.xlsx*.

As we can see in this Figure, the external reference has been updated to include the workbook file name surrounded in square brackets. As described before, this type of referencing can be entered using simple mouse clicks or by typing in the external workbook and worksheet names surrounded by tic-marks, and then followed with an exclamation point *before* the actual cell references.

To help you imagine a situation where referencing cells across workbooks becomes helpful, consider this scenario: You are a mid-level manager in a company and you have six different departments that report to you. Each one of your department managers has created a spreadsheet that has their own departmental budgets for their planned expenses for the upcoming year. You need to create a single, consolidated workbook that will bring together all of the various totals from each of the six departmental worksheets.

Now, you know that you could copy-and-paste the totals from each one of the six departmental workbooks into your own worksheet. The act of copying-and-pasting external data into a worksheet is called **embedding** data.

But you also know that embedding a copy of the data would create a static copy of those totals. You also know that the each of the managers has not completely finalized their budgets just yet. As a result, if you embed copies of their totals before the budgets are finalized, then your copy of the data will be *stale* and will not reflect the actual, final totals for each department!

Therefore, you decide instead to create a dynamic link to each of the six departmental workbooks. The act of creating external workbook cell references is called **linking** data. By creating the external

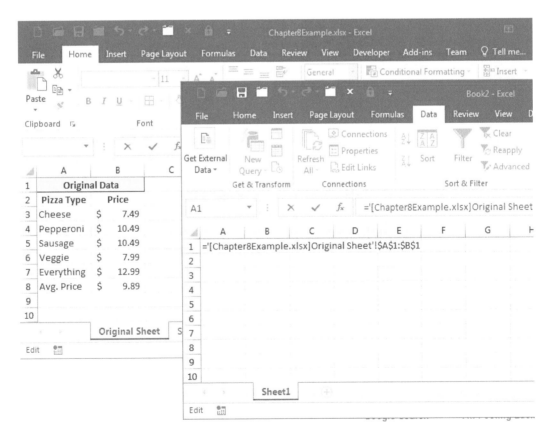

Figure 8-6

data links to the total expenditures from each of those departmental workbooks, you know that as your managers update their budgets and their totals change, your workbook will automatically reflect those changes in a dynamic fashion.

Remember that we mentioned earlier that besides referencing external data from other spreadsheet files, you can also reference external data from various databases. In order to reference data that is in an external database, you will need a database connector such as an open database connectivity (ODBC) connector.

Database Connectors and ODBC allow you to specify the parameters by which you can connect to a database. Some of those parameters include the location of the database, the type of database (vendor-specific descriptors), the name of the database, as well as authorization credentials (e.g. username and password). When creating an external link to a database in a spreadsheet program, you will be prompted for the database connectors or ODBC information.

As you can see, Linking vs. Embedding data from external sources becomes the decision as to whether you need dynamic or static data in *this* spreadsheet. In every instance when you are working with external data, there will be circumstances where either decision may be appropriate. You will make that final determination by considering the needs of the worksheet you are currently working with as well as some of the risks and limitations that come along with each different approach.

For example, there are some External Reference Considerations that you should think about before choosing to link with external data sources:

✦ Will the external data source always have the same physical file name and reside in the same physical location or might it become renamed or moved?

✦ Will the external data source cell references remain consistent or may they move around and, therefore, confound my own required cell references?

✦ Will the dynamic data change so frequently that the two files may become "out-of-sync" too frequently?

✦ Will my destination workbook always have connectivity to the external source workbooks? (e.g. will there be consistent network or Internet connectivity for the two workbooks to talk to each other?)

If you do not have confidence that you will be able to control the external data sources and the considerations that come along with using them, then you should probably consider embedding copies of the external data as opposed to linking to the external data sources.

So now, let's consider what would happen if you have a workbook that is linked to a second workbook as an external data source, and then something happens to that external data source. Perhaps the file got renamed, or moved, or – worse yet – was deleted! A spreadsheet file that cannot locate external file references is said to have Broken External References.

When you attempt to open a spreadsheet that has references to linked external data sources, the spreadsheet program will automatically attempt to reestablish the connections and update the linked cells to their current values. If, for any reason, the program cannot reestablish the link to the external data sources, you will receive an error message alerting you to this fact that the external data is unavailable.

Figure 8-7 shows the message you might receive if an external data source is unavailable.

When responding to this error message, you have several options. First, you can simply continue to work with your existing spreadsheet knowing that some or all of the external links are not currently active. You might choose this option if you think the external file is just temporarily unavailable and will

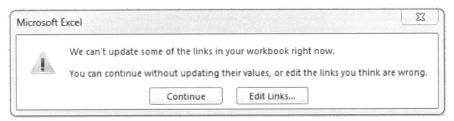

Figure 8-7

be available again in the future. An example of this might be if you are traveling and do not have network connectivity or if your internal network is down for some reason.

You should know that if you choose this option, the data that you will be presented with will be the last known snapshot of the external data from the last time that the link was active. In other words, *you will be looking at stale data*! You probably would not want to make any important decisions based on a spreadsheet that has broken external references due to unlinked external data sources.

Another option would be to edit the links in your active workbook to see if you can locate the file that has been renamed or moved. This process of Updating External References is the way in which you tell the spreadsheet program where the new external data sources are without having to completely rebuild the external data linkages from scratch. In this kind of a situation, you can simply update the links to point to the new file name or the new location.

Oftentimes, when working with external data that you have no control over (e.g. external data that is coming from an internet source), it **will not be advisable** to try to *link* to that external data. The risk is that the data source will change more than just its contents. For example, it could change its name, its location, its connectivity parameters, etc. It is often far too great of a risk to rely on that data being available when your spreadsheet needs it. In the next section, we will look at the activity of importing or embedding external data into your worksheet.

LO 8.3   Importing (Embedding) External Data

As we have seen in previous chapters as well as in the last section, it is very typical for users to create spreadsheets that use data from external sources. Often, these external sources may be websites or external files that were not created directly in a spreadsheet program.

As a result, one of the fundamental skills in working with spreadsheets is the ability to import and embed external data into your spreadsheet so that you can work with it.

Importing (embedding) external data is the process by which you can locate external data, bring it into your spreadsheet program, and then begin the tasks of inspecting and cleaning up that external data so that you can really work with it.

For our examples in this section, we will be using the **National Parks Services Stats** website from the National Park Service/US Department of the Interior. The main address for this site is https://irma.nps.gov/Stats/. Before continuing in your reading of this section, it might be beneficial to go out to that website and browse around a little bit. By becoming more familiar with the site itself, the rest of the reading in this section may become more evident. Figure 8-8 shows this website and the navigation to get to the National Reports page.

From the home page of this site, navigate to the national reports page and then select the report entitled *"Visitation By State and By Park (2017 - Last Calendar Year)."*

On this page of the website, you can see at the top that there are options to change the various parameters that generate the data for the report that you see. If you select all the states and all of the field

Figure 8-8

names, you will discover a massive amount of data! Now, it should be pretty obvious that if you bring down too much data (more than you are willing to actually process) then you will just spend a lot of time deleting unnecessary data. It is better, if it is possible, to limit the data on the website before you attempt to bring that data down to your own worksheets. You should realize, however, that not all websites will provide these kinds of tools for you. For many websites, you have a "take-it-or-leave-it" relationship with the data that you find.

So for our example, we will be picking just three states to compare: Colorado, Maine, and Nevada. Additionally, we will be choosing only three fields to compare: Recreation Visits, Tent Campers, and RV Campers. Figure 8-9 shows a screenshot of this website after running the desired report. The red circled tool that is highlighted on this image shows that this website provides several different ways for you to extract this data to make it available for your own use in your own programs.

One of the options that are available to you is to download this data as an Excel file while another option would be to download this data as a .CSV file. Both of these file types will open up in your spreadsheet program, but as we will see, we will end up with *very* different results.

First, let's download the data using the Excel file option. When selecting this option, the browser automatically begins the download process and opens up your downloaded file in your chosen spreadsheet program. Figure 8-10 shows a screenshot of the data that has been downloaded into the spreadsheet program.

At first glance, you will see that the spreadsheet file that you

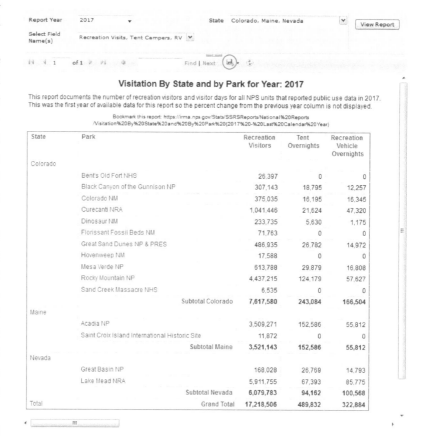

Figure 8-9

would be working with is nearly identical to the data that you saw online! And while this is true and a good thing, there are also some very interesting limitations that you should be aware of.

If you click on any of the subtotal values or the grand total values, you will make an interesting observation:

All of these cells contain ***literal numeric values*** **instead of** ***desired SUM calculations.*** In other words, all you have gotten is raw data and ***everything*** is treated like a data label. There will be ***no calculations*** automatically brought in when you import and embed data from an external source!

Visitation By State and by Park for Year: 2017

This report documents the number of recreation visitors and visitor days for all NPS units that reported public use data in 2017. This was the first year of available data for this report so the percent change from the previous year column is not displayed.

Bookmark this report: https://irma.nps.gov/Stats/SSRSReports/National%20Reports/Visitation%20By%20State%20and%20By%20Park%20(2017%20-%20Last%20Calendar%20Year)

State	Park		Recreation Visitors	Tent Overnights	Recreation Vehicle Overnights
Colorado					
	Bent's Old Fort NHS		26,397	0	0
	Black Canyon of the Gunnison NP		307,143	18,795	12,257
	Colorado NM		375,035	16,195	16,345
	Curecanti NRA		1,041,446	21,624	47,320
	Dinosaur NM		233,735	5,630	1,175
	Florissant Fossil Beds NM		71,763	0	0
	Great Sand Dunes NP & PRES		486,935	26,782	14,972
	Hovenweep NM		17,588	0	0
	Mesa Verde NP		613,788	29,879	16,808
	Rocky Mountain NP		4,437,215	124,179	57,627
	Sand Creek Massacre NHS		6,535	0	0
		Subtotal Colorado	**7,617,580**	**243,084**	**166,504**
Maine					
	Acadia NP		3,509,271	152,586	55,812
	Saint Croix Island International Historic Site		11,872	0	0
		Subtotal Maine	**3,521,143**	**152,586**	**55,812**
Nevada					
	Great Basin NP		168,028	26,769	14,793
	Lake Mead NRA		5,911,755	67,393	85,775
		Subtotal Nevada	**6,079,783**	**94,162**	**100,568**
Total		Grand Total	**17,218,506**	**489,832**	**322,884**

Visitation By State and By Park

Figure 8-10

Additionally, you notice that all of the extra headings and extra blank space is also loaded into your spreadsheet. This may or may not be desirable for you depending on your needs.

Clearly some "clean up" of the embedded data will be in order. We will be discussing the details of inspecting and cleaning up external data in the next section.

Now let's look at the second option that we had available to us for downloading this data: the CSV file.

CSV stands for Comma Separated Values and it is basically a text file where the first row in the text file represents all of the column heading names as values that are separated by commas. Then, each subsequent row is a data row with all of their data values also separated by commas. This is a common text format for importing into spreadsheet programs.

Figure 8-11 shows that this type of imported data is bringing in what appears to be a lot more data! As a matter of fact, this imported spreadsheet has data extending out for 75 columns! What is all of this extra data, you might ask?

	A	B	C	D	E	F	G	H	I	J	K	L
1	Title1	Textbox	Title2									
2	Visitati	This rep	Bookmark this report: https://irma.nps.gov/Stats/SSRSReports/National%20Reports/Visitation%20By%20State%20and%20By%20Park%20(2017%20-%20Last%20Calendar%20Year)									
3												
4	State	Field1	Field2	Textbox	Field4	Textbox	TotalNo	Textbox	TotalRe	Textbox	TotalNo	Textbox
5	Colorad	Bent's C	26,397	-17.38%	3,849	-17.39%	0		46,194	-17.37%	0	
6	Colorad	Black Ca	307,143	29.04%	145,546	9.47%	0		######	9.46%	0	
7	Colorad	Colorad	375,035	-4.10%	107,745	-0.76%	350,601	1.63%	######	-0.76%	175,302	1.63%
8	Colorad	Curecan	######	6.00%	391,391	12.05%	0		######	12.05%	0	
9	Colorad	Dinosau	233,735	3.79%	107,175	-4.65%	540	0.00%	######	-4.66%	540	0.00%
10	Colorad	Florissa	71,763	-2.45%	7,358	-3.13%	0		88,303	-3.14%	0	
11	Colorad	Great Sa	486,935	25.40%	192,361	-1.18%	470	0.00%	######	-1.18%	470	0.00%
12	Colorad	Hovenw	17,588	-6.75%	5,365	2.19%	132	0.00%	64,384	2.18%	24	0.00%
13	Colorad	Mesa V	613,788	5.19%	333,353	-3.36%	9,012	-47.47%	######	-3.36%	9,012	-47.47%
14	Colorad	Rocky M	######	-1.78%	######	-0.97%	8,750	0.00%	######	-0.97%	26,250	0.00%
15	Colorad	Sand Cr	6,535	-4.56%	1,089	-4.56%	0		13,070	-4.56%	0	
16	Maine	Acadia I	######	6.23%	######	2.48%	47,100	0.00%	######	2.48%	47,100	0.00%
17	Maine	Saint Cr	11,872	-14.32%	1,236	-14.35%	0		14,839	-14.33%	0	
18	Nevada	Great B	168,028	16.00%	120,018	-0.12%	748	17.43%	######	-0.12%	374	17.61%
19	Nevada	Lake Me	######	9.84%	######	11.49%	234,026	13.50%	######	11.49%	######	13.50%
20												
21												

	M	N	O	P	Q	R	S	T	U	V	W	X	Y	Z	AA
1															
2															
3															
4	Concess	Textbox	Concess	Textbox	TentOve	Textbox	Recreat	Textbox	Backcou	Textbox	NonRec	Textbox	Miscell	Textbox	State2
5	0		0		0		0		0		0		0		Subtot
6	0		0		18,795	-1.44%	12,257	3.19%	1,708	-11.78%	0		0		Subtot
7	0		0		16,195	-0.04%	16,345	11.94%	407	13.69%	0		0		Subtot
8	0		0		21,624	18.09%	47,320	30.65%	962	31.60%	0	38.59%	1,433		Subtot
9	0		0		5,630	21.15%	1,175	15.42%	23,456	-8.36%	0	-6.80%	2,959		Subtot
10	0		0		0		0		0		0		0		Subtot
11	0		0		26,782	-12.92%	14,972	-14.60%	4,313	-4.33%	0	-24.56%	5,623		Subtot
12	0		0		0		0		0		0		0		Subtot
13	21,822	-18.57%	0		29,879	-33.49%	16,808	39.22%	0		0	-2.79%	279		Subtot
14	0		0		124,179	2.64%	57,627	0.53%	45,194	-0.06%	0	######	13,088		Subtot
15	0		0		0		0		0		0		0		Subtot
16	0		1,657	69.60%	152,586	-0.15%	55,812	19.69%	1,597	20.62%	0	27.16%	10,889		Subtot
17	0		0		0		0		0		0		0		Subtot
18	0		0		26,769	0.10%	14,793	0.31%	403	-62.23%	0	-83.35%	311		Subtot
19	20,289	-11.10%	82,135	-33.33%	67,393	3.45%	85,775	3.45%	70,792	1.82%	0	1.81%	39,517		Subtot
20															
21															

Figure 8-11

In this example the data beginning with column AC and continuing on through the rest of the columns are the data values that you *didn't request* from the website. They have been provided to you and now, you will need to "deal with them."

With the data being imported with this option, we see once again that there is still a lot of "clean-up" work that needs to be completed. Let's explore that topic now in the next section.

LO 8.4   Inspecting and Cleaning Up External Data

As we have just seen in the previous section, data that is imported from an external site (especially websites) will often not be in the most desirable format for you to work with in a spreadsheet. As a result, one of the first tasks you will need to do once you get external data into your spreadsheet is to inspect your data for errors and missing data and other kind of bad data that need to be cleaned up.

Defining "Bad" Data is a task unto itself. For example, one person might go to a website, import some data directly into the spreadsheet, and the end result is *precisely* what the person needs! Another person, however, will go to that exact same website, import the exact same data directly into the spreadsheet, and interpret that a significant portion of the data needs to be removed, some other data that was provided, like subtotals and totals, need to be changed from text values to calculations, and additional data that is not present at all from the website needs to be added. In other words, the source of the data does not know how each possible user will want to use their data. So, some of what defines "bad" data is actually in the eye of the beholder.

With that being said, the task at hand then is to first locate what you consider to be "bad" data and then clean that data so that you can further use the information. When Finding "Bad" Data and Cleaning "Bad" Data, here are some of the very typical things that one might consider to be "bad" data and some of the ways this data may be cleaned:

+ Missing fields – these would be some other needed data that will be required before you can process the rest of the data. This may be found in a secondary external file, which will, itself, need to be imported, and cleaned, and then merged with this data. Another example is possible calculations that were evident on the external source but now appear missing in the downloaded data.

+ Extra fields – these are the extraneous fields that may be present in the external data and which need to be removed. These may also be extra rows of data, like headers and footers, that were important to display on the website but will not be required in your spreadsheet.

+ Combined fields – these are fields that end up in a single column but actually represent two different pieces of information. A common example of this is when a person's full name (honorific, first name, middle name or initial, last name, suffix – like Dr. Susan G. Smith) are all combined into a single cell. This kind of field will typically need to be split into its individual components so that you can filter and sort on the individual fields. This task is commonly known as **parsing the field**. Many of the Text Functions in the spreadsheet programs are available to help in the manipulation of combined fields so that they can be split into their individual columns.

+ Missing data in the fields – sometimes, especially in numeric fields, if the data is missing when you import it into your spreadsheet – will be left as a blank cell. Depending on your needs, you may need those cells to be zeros instead of blanks. This is where the COUNTBLANK and COUNTA and COUNT functions will all come into play to help you find these kinds of fields. Another example of this type of issue is when the first row of the data has some critical fields, but then many of the following rows are all related to the first row. When this happens, some data sources will only show the critical data in that first row and then that data *will not be duplicated* in the subsequent rows. This leaves large gaps of missing data that you may need to fill back in before you can perform other functions and calculations.

✦ Wrong data type – this can occur if the first row has one data type for a field but then subsequent rows have a different data type. An example of this would be if the first row had a dash to signify that there was no value for the field, however the field is actually a numeric dollar amount. When the spreadsheet sees the first row, it will incorrectly assume that that field is a text field and so all of the remaining numeric entries will end up as text entries instead of numeric entries. And as we remember from Chapter 3, you cannot perform mathematical calculations on text fields, so they would need to be converted back to numeric data. Another example of the wrong data type would be how some external data sources will include a label right along with a numeric value. So, for example, a baking ingredient list might show the quantities of items needed in a single column like "2 cups" or "3.5 ounces". When this is imported into the spreadsheet, this will be placed in a single text column. So this single field will need to be split into two fields: the numeric portion and the text portion. Then you will be able to work with the numeric data. The Text functions are most helpful for this task.

✦ Dirty data – data is considered "dirty" when there are nonprintable characters that are part of the data. These nonprintable characters can come from many sources, but many times, they are special characters that are used in websites to help control the overall look and feel of data that is presented on a webpage. They are very helpful to the website, but they are disruptive in a spreadsheet program and must be removed. This is why there are specialized text functions to help with this task.

✦ Inconsistent data – this can be data that is represented one way in some rows but in another way in other rows. Examples of this would be if some of the data showed states as their two-character state abbreviations like CO, ME, and NE while other rows showed the state names fully spelled out like Colorado, Maine, and Nevada. With inconsistent data, your calculations would be much more complex. Here, you would likely use the Sort and Filter commands to isolate the inconsistent data and then change it to be all the same.

As you can certainly see, there is great power and opportunities in being able to reach out and pull down external data, bring it into a spreadsheet, and perform valuable calculations and analysis on that external data. But the true benefits and values of your efforts won't be achieved without your careful inspection of the external data looking for "bad" data to be cleaned up, analysis of your overall needs for the data, and then deploying your fundamental spreadsheet skills to fully derive the value from your external data.

LO 8.5   Deriving Value from External Data

Earlier in this chapter, we explored the National Park Service Stats database and found some external data that we wanted to pull down and work with. Let's wrap up this discussion with deriving some specific value from that data.

As we saw when we imported the data directly into the spreadsheet program using the Excel format, the end result was a spreadsheet that had data in rows and columns but was formatted in a way to look nearly identical to the website itself. There was some cleanup that was necessary including removing blank rows and columns, filling in missing data, converting literal values into formulas that performed calculations, and other activities.

And that might seem like a lot of work if we didn't have a specific purpose in mind. Well, for this example, we just so happened to have that specific purpose right here: it seems that our company is looking to expand our product line to include a new kind of backpack that we think will have high market penetration for the segment of consumers that frequent national parks. To pilot this new product, we have narrowed down our market segment to three different states: Colorado, Maine, and Nevada. We aren't prepared to do full giveaways just yet, but we do want to start to create a buzz by getting some marketing materials out to those three markets.

As the next step in this marketing plan, we need to show the executive management just how great our initial reach will be as we attempt to partner with the National Park Services.

Our plan is to work with the park services' printers so that we can temporarily take over the printing of the cash register receipt tape that all of the parks in those three states will use. We will have these receipt tape rolls printed on the back with images of our new backpack and possibly a coupon or discount for the pack when it becomes available.

By using the external data from the National Park Service, we were able to perform some cleanup and minor manipulation, and then we were able to produce the graphic that you see in Figure 8-12. This image will help show the great potential that this relationship with the National Park Service can bring!

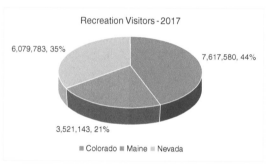

Figure 8-12

Chapter 8 – Assignments and Projects

Directed Assignments

DA 8-1. For this directed assignment, you will be using the student data file named **DA_8-1_Stand1.xlsx** to complete the required information. This file is in Microsoft Excel 2007 or newer format and should open in any contemporary spreadsheet program.

Required student data files: *DA_8-1_Stand1.xlsx*. Also, you will create a new, blank workbook and name the file *YourName_DA_8-1_GrandTotals*.

In this assignment, you have received a spreadsheet file from one of the five concession stand supervisors that contains the weekly soft drink sales for that location. You will be creating a second new spreadsheet file that uses external data references to this first received file and will help you create grand totals for all five of the concession stands that you manage.

1. Open the student data file named **DA_8-1_Stand1.xlsx**.
2. Immediately save a copy of this file using the following specifications:
   a. File name: Rename this file using the filename ***YourName_DA_8-1_Stand1***
   b. File location: Place this file in any location you choose, but make a note of the location as you will need it later.

    c. File format: Because this file will be sent in to your professor, you must check with him or her to see what format ***he or she*** will want this file to be saved in. Don't just assume that the original file format or the default file format for your own computer will be acceptable!

    d. **Keep this file open** as you will need it while you are working on the other file. We will call this file "the original file" in the rest of these instructions.

3. Also at this time, create a new, blank workbook and save this file in the same location and file type as the previous file. Save this blank workbook with the filename ***YourName_DA_8-1_GrandTotals.*** Keep this file open as you will need both files open at the same time. We will call this file "the new file" in the rest of these instructions.

4. In the new file in cell A2, create a relative reference to the cell A2 in the original file.

5. Use the fill handle to drag this relative cell reference down to cell A15.

6. You noticed that cell A15 says, "Total Sold Per Day", which is true for the original file. But in the new file, you only want to see the weekly total. So change cell A15 in the new file to say, "Total Sold This Week".

7. In cell B2 in the new file enter the label "Stand 1".

8. Use the fill handle to fill the series from cell B2 in the new file to cell F2.

9. In the new file in cell B3, create a relative reference to the cell H3 in the original file.

10. Use the fill handle to drag this relative cell reference down to cell A15.

11. In cell G2 in the new file, enter the label "Totals".

12. In cell G3 in the new file, enter a formula that will calculate the SUM for all five stands for the Cola sales in row 3.

13. Use the fill handle to drag this function down to the range G3:G15.

14. Create a merged cell of the range A1:G1 in the new file and enter the label "Weekly Totals for All Stands".

15. Apply appropriate formatting and highlighting and double-check your entries. Make any final necessary adjustments to ensure readability and correctness of your work. Then, once you are sure that everything is correct, you should save your work and then **submit <u>both files</u>** in accordance with your class instructions. Remember, now that these files are linked, both files will be needed in order to function properly!

At the completion of this directed assignment, your final work should look very similar to Figure DA_8-1_CompletedGrandTotals found here.

As you consider this exercise further, you can see that now that the Grand Totals workbook has been set up and the first concession stand's totals have been externally referenced, you are now ready to bring in the other four concession stands just as soon as their files are available. When it is all said and done, you will have your own grand total workbook that has external links to the five independent concession stand files. This is the way that external data is linked into a consolidating workbook.

	A	B	C	D	E	F	G
1	Weekly Totals for All Stands						
2	Beverages	Stand 1	Stand 2	Stand 3	Stand 4	Stand 5	Totals
3	Cola	697					697
4	Diet Cola	959					959
5	Root Beer	642					642
6	Diet Root Beer	734					734
7	White Soda	735					735
8	Diet White Soda	779					779
9	Sweetened Tea	839					839
10	Unsweetened Tea	351					351
11	Lemonade	1090					1090
12	Coffee	938					938
13	Decaf Coffee	758					758
14	Hot Tea	546					546
15	Total Sold This Week	9068					9068
16							

Figure DA_8-1_CompletedGrandTotals

DA 8-2. For this directed assignment, you will create a new, blank spreadsheet and then locate some external data from the Bureau of Labor Statistics and import or embed this data into your workbook.

Required student data file: None: Start with a new, blank workbook and name the file *YourName_DA_8-2*.

1. Create a new, blank workbook using the following specifications:
   a. File name: Rename this file using the filename *YourName_DA_8-2*
   b. File location: Place this file in any location you choose, but make a note of the location as you will need it later.
   c. File format: Because this file will be sent in to your professor, you must check with him or her to see what format *he or she* will want this file to be saved in. Don't just assume that the original file format or the default file format for your own computer will be acceptable!

2. Go to the Bureau of Labor Statistics website (www.bls.gov/data). Here you will find a huge selection of data about countless topics including Employment, Unemployment, Pay & Benefits, Regional Resources, how people spend their time, and so on. Spend some time exploring the various data that is available to you here.

3. Once you have found some data that is interesting to you, bring this data into your spreadsheet program. Depending on the data that you have found, you may be able to click a link to download a spreadsheet file right away. Or, you may find a link where you can download a CSV file or some other acceptably formatted file. These options will be fine as well. However, if there is no direct download link available for you, then you can still simply highlight the data that you see on the screen and then copy-and-paste it into your spreadsheet program. Please note, however, that if you use the method to bring in the external data, there is often a considerable amount of "cleanup" that you will need to undertake to remove codes and extraneous data that may be necessary on the website but just gets in the way in a spreadsheet.

4. Now, you will need to perform a careful inspection of your imported data to seek out any "bad" data and make the necessary adjustments. To document the cleanup effort that you are making here, create a second worksheet in this workbook and name it "Processing Steps". In this sheet, you will create a log of the step-by-step actions that you have taken to create and manipulate the data in this workbook. Some of the cleanup activities that you may need to review and perform are listed in Learning Objective LO 8.4.

5. Once the data is cleaned up, now it is your opportunity to derive some value from this external data by creating some basic calculations to discover unknown data from your spreadsheet. These could be simple SUMs, AVERAGEs, COUNTs, MINs, MAXs, etc. or they could be more intricate calculations – you decide. Make sure that you list the calculations that you chose to add to this worksheet in your processing steps log on the other sheet.

6. Now, after the data has been imported, cleaned up, and meaningful calculations have been added, create some chart about your data and place this chart on its own sheet with an appropriate name. Don't forget to log why you chose to make this particular chart and what the chart is showing us.

7. Once you have completed setting up the worksheet, apply appropriate basic formatting to each of the worksheets and don't forget to give each worksheet its own appropriate sheet name.

8. Remember to check your final work for spelling, grammar, and overall correctness and then submit your file in the manner prescribed for your class.

DA 8-3. For this directed assignment, you will create a new, blank spreadsheet and then locate some external data from a website of your own choosing and copy-and-paste some data into your workbook. For this assignment, we will be seeking a website that will give us an opportunity to work with Text functions to manipulate the copied data.

Required student data file: None: Start with a new, blank workbook and name the file *YourName_DA_8-3*.

1. Create a new, blank workbook using the following specifications:
   a. File name: Name this file using the filename ***YourName_DA_8-3***
   b. File location: Place this file in any location you choose, but make a note of the location as you will need it later.
   c. File format: Because this file will be sent in to your professor, you must check with him or her to see what format ***he or she*** will want this file to be saved in. Don't just assume that the original file format or the default file format for your own computer will be acceptable!

2. Choose a website that has some data that you find particularly interesting. It could be a website about one of your favorite professional athletic teams that you follow. Or maybe you will use a website that has information about one of your favorite hobbies. It could also be a website about some particular form of entertainment that you are interested in, like movies, television, music, etc. You can choose any website you want as long as you can find some data that shows multiple pieces of information about at least 10 or more people. For example you might investigate the roster of a popular sports team. Or you might look up all of the cast members in one season of one of your favorite television show. The idea is that you want to find a listing of multiple people that have shared attributes that can be brought down into your spreadsheet. Also, ensure that your list of people have some numeric values that you could perform some mathematical computations on. These could be salaries, statistics, age values – basically anything that is numeric.

3. Once you see the data on the screen that you want to bring into your spreadsheet, highlight all of the data on the website and then copy-and-paste this information into your blank spreadsheet. Named this spreadsheet "Raw Data".

4. Next, create a blank worksheet and name this worksheet "Cleaned Up Data".

5. Then, create a third blank worksheet and name this worksheet "Processing Steps". On this sheet, you should keep a record of all of the steps that you are taking as you work through this assignment. Some things you should include in this list of steps are:

   a. The location on the web where you found the raw data.

   b. The reason you chose this particular set of data.

   c. The cleanup that you needed to perform to make the data ready to be evaluated.

   d. The actual steps that you did to complete the rest of this exercise.

6. Make a copy of the raw data in its entirety as it is originally, and paste this data into the sheet named "Cleaned Up Data". This is the sheet where you will actually do the work thereby leaving the original data intact – just the way it was brought in from the external site.

7. Perform all of the cleanup steps that you deem are necessary. Remember that some of the cleanup activities that you may need to review and perform are listed in Learning Objective LO 8.4.

8. Create one additional activity of cleanup to further process people's names in this datasheet. If the people's full names are already combined into a single column, then create two or three (or more) columns to hold the individual parts of each person's name. Then use the appropriate text functions to split apart the full name into individual components.

9. But if the people's names are in multiple columns already, then you will do the reverse. Create a single column, in this situation, that will hold the full name as a concatenation of all of the other individual fields.

10. After the names have been manipulated, seek out some additional value from this external data by creating some basic calculations to discover unknown data within your spreadsheet. These could be simple SUMs, AVERAGEs, COUNTs, MINs, MAXs, etc. or they could be more intricate calculations – you decide.

11. Once you are satisfied with the information, apply appropriate formatting to this worksheet to highlight the important information. Also highlight some aspect of the data that you think is particularly interesting and create a chart that helps to visualize why this data is important. Place this chart on its own worksheet and give the worksheet an appropriate name.

12. Don't forget to make log entries in your "Processing Steps" sheet to record what you have accomplished.

13. Remember to check your final work for spelling, grammar, and overall correctness and then submit your file in the manner prescribed for your class.

Creative Projects

CP 8-1. For this creative project, you will create a new, blank spreadsheet and then locate some external data from a website of your own choosing to use as external data for your workbook. For this assignment, you will be nearly completely on your own to capture raw information, clean it up, and derive some meaningful value out of that data.

Required student data file: None: Start with a new, blank workbook and name the file *YourName_ CP_8-1.*

In this workbook, create four worksheets and named them as follows: "Raw Data", "Cleaned Data", "Processing Steps", and "Analysis Chart".

From here, you are pretty much on your own. You need to go seek out some external data that "speaks to you". It should be some data that you find interesting or that you care about. Once you have found the data, extract this data from the website in one of the fashions described in this chapter. Place this raw data in both the "Raw Data" worksheet and the "Cleaned Data" worksheets. Next, clean up the data on the "Cleaned Data" worksheet using the techniques described in this chapter. Create appropriate calculations to derive some interesting, unknown information from this known data. Then create an interesting chart that highlights some aspects of the cleaned up data. Make sure that you keep a detailed log of all of the steps that you did to complete this project.

Good luck!

Remember to check your final work for spelling, grammar, and overall correctness and then submit your file in the manner prescribed for your class.

Source: Shutterstock, Inc.

Creating Templates and Protecting Spreadsheets

So, I just created a spreadsheet that contains a bunch of new recipes that I have been thinking about trying along with all of the ingredients that I would need to buy to make these new dishes. Why on earth would I need to "protect" this spreadsheet?

LEARNING OBJECTIVES

In this chapter, we will explore these learning objectives:

Defining Template Concepts in Various Programs

When to Consider Creating a Template

Planning the Template Layout

Protecting Cells, Sheets, and Files

How and Where to Save Templates

How to Use Created Templates

Well, chances are, you probably do not need to protect *that* particular spreadsheet! In fact, depending on how you use the spreadsheet program, you may never find a need to protect your spreadsheets.

But on the other hand, what if you start using spreadsheets in your new position as a finance manager at a large hedge fund? In that situation, you will probably discover that very many of the spreadsheets that you create will need to be protected! You can't have just anybody looking at your analysis and financial recommendations now, can you? In fact, if you find yourself in a position where you have to protect *any* files, you will probably find yourself protecting *a lot* of files!

In this chapter we will look at the several different ways that you can protect your worksheets and workbooks as well as explore the concepts associated with creating and using template files.

LO 9.1 Defining Template Concepts in Various Programs

The concept of "templates" has been around for a very, very long time. From the earliest days in very many professions, it was discovered that if you want to improve both the quality and the efficiency of

Key Terms

- protecting cells
- protecting workbooks
- protecting worksheets
- template
- template cautions
- template creator
- template file locations
- template file type
- template maintenance
- template user
- using a template

your repetitive work, then you should use a template to help you create your work. So what exactly, then, is a template?

In many other disciplines *besides* computing, a template would be considered any piece of material that could be used as a pattern for repetitive processes such as drawing, painting, cutting, measuring, etc. Templates were used in manufacturing. Templates were used in architecture. Templates were used in sewing. Templates were used in construction. Templates were used in painting and drawing. You may have even used a template in grade school when you are learning to print the alphabet! You can look around the various places that you go and you will probably see templates being used today in many different areas.

So then, when personal computers came onto the scene and office applications were introduced right along with them, it did not take long for the authors of these programs to consider just how valuable the concept of templates could be to help create repetitive documents that would ensure the highest quality and efficiency.

In computing concepts, a Template is a predefined format for a document or file that is used as a starting point for creating a new document that will become preloaded with all of the same aspects of this predefined format. You may have worked with templates in many of the other office applications. Word processors have templates. Presentation programs have templates. Accounting programs have templates. Graphic design programs have templates. And as we are discovering in this chapter, spreadsheet programs also have templates.

Every document that you create today in a contemporary office application is based off of *some* kind of template. If you think about creating a new word processing document, in many programs, when you first start your word processor program, the first thing you see is a blank sheet. You are ready to start typing!

But did you ever really stop to think about that blank sheet? There are already margins set at a particular location for both the top and the bottom of the page as well as for the left and the right edges of the page. How did those margins get set there at those particular spots?

And this blank page also is already set to create paragraphs that are left aligned, have a particular font selected, a particular font size, and default tab-stops at every half-inch. How did this blank document know to set all of that up?

The key point to remember about templates is that every single document that you create in an office application will be based on some template. Yes, even a new, blank document is based on a template that has all of those predefined attributes.

But templates are not just about creating completely blank or empty documents. Templates become extremely valuable when they can help you complete *multiple repetitive documents*. They also allow you to exercise a much greater level of control over how those new, repetitive documents are completed.

So let's now look at the circumstances under which you might consider creating a template for your own work.

LO 9.2 When to Consider Creating a Template

In order to think about the conditions under which templates can become beneficial to you and your organization, it will be helpful to think about the repetitive documents that might be used in your area or department or company.

If you discovered that you are creating essentially the same documents over and over, which have essentially the same layout, format, and some of the same content, then these documents would be candidates to be made into templates.

To help you think about this in more detail, imagine the scenario: You have just created your own company that you are going to be running on the side of your normal job. You have come up with a creative name for your company. You've come up with a very interesting logo that is eye-catching and memorable. You even rented a small space in that new office building, which will be serving as your "corporate headquarters." You are now ready to go!

One of the first tasks that you want to do is to write a letter to all of the members of the Chamber of Commerce to let them know that your new business is open and you are seeking new clients who can use your services. You know just how important it is to make a great first impression, so you decide that you want your introductory letter to be a sharp, professional, eye-catching, and memorable letter.

So you start thinking about creating a letterhead document that will include your new logo, the business address of your new location, your name and title and contact information, and perhaps your company's slogan at the bottom of each page.

Now, you know that it is going to take you some time to set up this document when you first start from a completely blank page. But then it hits you as you stop to consider:

"If I am going to be sending out a hundred letters or so for this first task, I am definitely going to want all of the letters on this same kind of letterhead document. But I sure don't want to have to re-create this layout each time and run the risk of not having it look the same each time. I want my business to show supreme quality and consistency. In fact, I want to ensure that I have an absolutely consistent look and feel to *all* of my business letters when I send them out – not just this first group of letters!"

And there it is! Before you even begin creating that first letter, you have identified that you will need your own, personalized, professional looking letterhead document template that you can use again and again.

So it makes sense to create a template any time you know that you are going to be repeating the task of creating the same kind of document over and over again, which all have many of the same attributes. If you think about it, you create a template one time and then use it many, many times to create the same kind of document any time you need it.

Anyone can be a template creator or a template user but they don't necessarily have to be one and the same person. A Template Creator is a person who is responsible for creating the basic shell of a document that will be used repeatedly – possibly by more than one person – to create other documents that look and behave the same. The template creator is responsible for deciding what pieces and aspects of the document will be predefined and which pieces will be changeable by the end-user. The goal of the template creator is to plan and create the template document in such a fashion so that the end-user does not need to make hardly any changes to the predefined portions of the document.

A Template User, on the other hand, is anyone who would create a new document based on an existing template. Template users will focus primarily on the new or variable data that is being added to the basic shell from the template.

So a template creator might create the letterhead template for a company, but then each template user would create new letters of correspondence using that same letterhead template. The tasks that were required to place the company logo into the top left corner of the letterhead, to set up the name and address and contact information for the company, and to add the company slogan at the bottom of the page, were all tasks that only needed to be created once by the template creator. But from then on, when the template users create new letters using this letterhead template, each and every one of those users gets the benefit of that original work without having to "reinvent the wheel" each time.

Templates increase efficiency, improve quality, and assure consistency of repetitive document creation.

So far, we had been talking about creating templates and have been using the concept of a company's letterhead as our example. This would obviously be a word processing template document. But now it is time to start thinking about spreadsheet templates and what those might look like.

LO 9.3 Planning the Template Layout

Just like when you are planning the layout of a single spreadsheet, the concept of planning the layout of a template is very similar. First, you have to envision the overall layout of the final spreadsheet and ask yourself a number of questions about the nature of those spreadsheets that will be created *from* this template:

✦ What are the general row and column labels that this spreadsheet needs?

✦ Is there any known data in any of the cell ranges that will remain consistent for all of the new spreadsheets that are based on this template?

✦ Are there any calculations that can be predefined so that the user will not have to create them each time?

✦ Is there any overall formatting (general or conditional) that can be configured and set up in advance?

✦ What are the protections that can be configured to make sure that the template user does not inadvertently change information that we don't want to be changed? Learning Objective LO 9.4 will cover the concept of protecting spreadsheet information in more detail.

By answering these questions, you are on your way to starting your template.

Creating a template is exactly the same as creating a regular spreadsheet file with one significant difference: when you have completed the spreadsheet file and are ready to save it, it must be saved with a special file format and in a special location in order for the spreadsheet program to recognize the file as a template and use it properly. We will be covering this in more detail in Learning Objective LO 9.5.

So, now that we have planned the layout for our new template, it is now time to actually create the template file. So let's imagine that the manager of the concession stands for the Community Sports Complex would like to have a consistent spreadsheet document that each one of the 10 concession stand supervisors will be able to use to record their weekly soft drink sales. Figure 9-1 shows this newly created spreadsheet file. It is important to remember that at this point, the spreadsheet file **has not been saved yet** because it will need to be saved in a "special way" to make the file become a template. We will be covering this in more detail in Learning Objective LO 9.5.

So now, let's inspect the layout of this spreadsheet file in more detail. What we are seeing here is that all of the known data and calculations have been set up, just one time, and that the user will not have to worry about doing any of that in the future. In fact we will be protecting this spreadsheet and locking this template down so that the user will only have to fill in the data portion without having to worry about inadvertently changing the rest of the file.

As we look at Figure 9-1 we see that when the template user creates a new weekly sales file, the first thing they will do is perform data entry in cell E2 to enter the concession stand number. Next, the user will perform data entry in cell J2 to enter the week ending date. The cell J2 has already been preformatted to be a date in "short-date" format.

	A	B	C	D	E	F	G	H	I	J
1	Community Sports Complex - Weekly Soft Drink Sales									
2		Concession Stand #				Sales for Week Ending:				
3	Beverages	Mon	Tue	Wed	Thu	Fri	Sat	Sun	Totals	Average Per Day
4	Cola								0	No Data
5	Diet Cola								0	No Data
6	Root Beer								0	No Data
7	Diet Root Beer								0	No Data
8	White Soda								0	No Data
9	Diet White Soda								0	No Data
10	Sweetened Tea								0	No Data
11	Unsweetened Tea								0	No Data
12	Lemonade								0	No Data
13	Coffee								0	No Data
14	Decaf Coffee								0	No Data
15	Hot Tea								0	No Data
16	Total Sold Per Day	0	0	0	0	0	0	0	0	No Data
17										

Weekly Soft Drink Sales ⊕

Figure 9-1

All of the labels in rows one, two, and three as well as all of the labels in column A have already been properly entered, double-checked, formatted, and will be locked down so that the user cannot change them. Likewise, in columns I, J, and row 16, formulas have been created which will automatically calculate the totals, the averages, and additionally shows some conditional formatting if the total per day value for any given day is greater than the overall average. Figure 9-2 shows the actual formulas and functions that are in the various cells. The end user of this template will never get to see those calculations and will not have to worry about them at all. They will just be "in there" doing their tasks. The template user will only have to worry about doing the correct data entry of the counts of soft drinks sold for that week.

And thinking about the template user . . . there will actually be 10 different template users for the 10 different concessions stands. That means each one of the users only has to think about doing the weekly data entry for their own stand and all the rest has been handled for them by the template!

Just looking at this shell of a template file, one might not realize that all of the properties that have been described above are already "in there." But that's the beauty and power of templates!

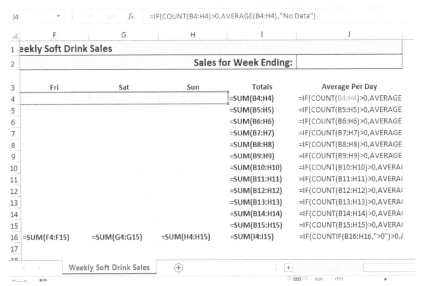

Figure 9-2

LO 9.4 Protecting Cells, Sheets, and Files

Now that the template file is built and ready to be saved, there is just one more task that we need to complete to "lock down" this template file. This task contains three separate but related activities that we will need to discuss: *protecting cells*; *protecting worksheets*; and *protecting workbooks*.

Protecting Cells is a process that changes a cell's status from being "*locked*" to being "*unlocked*" and vice versa. By default, all cells in a new spreadsheet are set to be locked. What this means is that when a spreadsheet becomes protected, all locked cells cannot be changed in any way unless you first unprotect that worksheet.

Likewise, if a cell is said to be unlocked, then when the worksheet becomes protected, that cell remains open and accessible to the user.

To set cells to be locked or unlocked, you simply highlight the cells you want to adjust and then initiate the cell format dialog. Figure 9-3 shows the highlighted cells that we will want to "unlock" so that the template users will be able to perform their data entry into these cells. In Figure 9-3, we see that the cells E2, J2, and the range B4:H15 have all been selected by using the technique of selecting disjointed cells that was described in Chapter 2.

Once you have selected all of the desired cells that you want to unlock, simply initiate the Format Cells dialog. In this dialog, you will see a tab where you can change the protection for the cell. Figure 9-4 shows the cell protection tab in the Format Cells dialog.

You may now recognize that you have been in this dialog many times before. If you plan your work ahead of time, you will become more and more efficient with spreadsheets if you think about setting *all* of a cell's formatting properties at one time when you are in this dialog.

Now, to unlock these selected cells, you simply uncheck the "Locked" option that has been highlighted. By unchecking this box, you are saying to the spreadsheet program that when you protect this worksheet, these selected cells will remain unlocked and accessible to the user.

This concept of locking and unlocking cells and then protecting worksheets and workbooks can be applied to *any* spreadsheet file. It is just a very common thing to do whenever you are building templates.

Now that the template file is fully built and all of the cells that will be used for data entry have been set to be unlocked, it is now time to protect the worksheet.

	A	B	C	D	E	F	G	H	I	J
1		Community Sports Complex - Weekly Soft Drink Sales								
2		Concession Stand #				Sales for Week Ending:				
3	Beverages	Mon	Tue	Wed	Thu	Fri	Sat	Sun	Totals	Average Per Day
4	Cola								0	No Data
5	Diet Cola								0	No Data
6	Root Beer								0	No Data
7	Diet Root Beer								0	No Data
8	White Soda								0	No Data
9	Diet White Soda								0	No Data
10	Sweetened Tea								0	No Data
11	Unsweetened Tea								0	No Data
12	Lemonade								0	No Data
13	Coffee								0	No Data
14	Decaf Coffee								0	No Data
15	Hot Tea								0	No Data
16	Total Sold Per Day	0	0	0	0	0	0	0	0	No Data
17										

Weekly Soft Drink Sales

Figure 9-3

Protecting Worksheets is the process of locking a worksheet file so that the user of the file cannot accidentally or deliberately change, move, or delete the locked data in the worksheet. The location of the command to protect your worksheet will vary by each program so you must locate where the protection options are in your particular spreadsheet program.

Figure 9-5 shows a worksheet protection dialog. You will notice that the very top checkbox allows you to turn on or off worksheet protection for this particular worksheet. Different worksheets that are in the same workbook can be protected and unprotected independently of each other.

Next in this dialog, you see that you can enter an optional password that would be

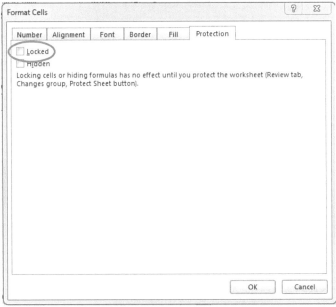

Figure 9-4

required to unprotect the sheet. A word of caution about passwords: don't forget them! A workbook file that has been protected with a password or a worksheet that has been protected with a password will require that password once again to be able to unprotected or unlock it. If you forget the passwords, you may not be able to open up your spreadsheet file to make changes in the future. We will be discussing this in more detail in Learning Objective LO 9.6.

Continuing on with the protect sheet dialog, we see that there are a number of options that you can set that will determine the level of access that you allow the user to experience with this locked sheet. For example with the two top checkboxes marked, the user would be able to select both the locked cells as well as the unlocked cells. What this means is that the user would be able to select the unlocked cell in order to do their data entry, which is what we need them to be able to do.

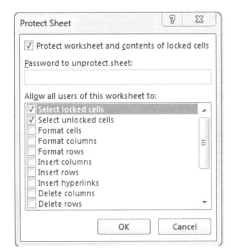

Figure 9-5

But with the first checkbox also showing that the user would be authorized to select locked cells as well, they could select any one of the cells that are locked but they would not be able to change the contents in any way. If you didn't want the user to even be able to see the contents of the locked cells, you would simply uncheck this box.

As you can see, there are a number of ways that you can protect a worksheet so that the end users don't make any undesirable changes to the file.

Once you click OK in this dialog, you have now successfully protected the sheet. The user of this file would only be able to do data entry in the fields that remained unlocked.

The last type of protection that can be enabled in a spreadsheet program is the protection of the workbook file itself. **Protecting Workbooks** is the process of creating a lock on the physical workbook file so that only authorized users will be able to unlock the workbook and work with its contents.

Figure 9-6 shows the workbook protection dialog. In this dialog, you can protect the overall structure of the workbook so that no structural changes (like the adding or removing of worksheets) can be performed without first unlocking the structural changes.

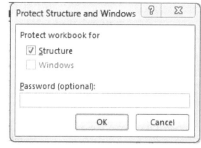

Figure 9-6

Additionally, an optional password can be set for this file's structure. If a password is set for the file's structure, then you will need this password to be able change any of the structural aspects of the workbook.

Additionally, most spreadsheet programs provide the ability to protect the overall workbook file from being accessed or edited in any way whatsoever. When you set a password and encrypt the overall workbook file, then when any user (including yourself!) attempts to open the file, they will be challenged to answer the correct password. If they do not know the password, then the spreadsheet program will not let them access the data at all.

As you can see, the spreadsheet programs have added significant protections to help make sure that only authorized users of the spreadsheet files are able to perform their own, authorized tasks. Additionally, extremely sensitive data can be protected so that only the authorized users can even view those files.

LO 9.5 How and Where to Save Templates

Now that your template file has been created, protected, and locked down, you are now ready to save your template file. Saving the template file is similar to saving a regular spreadsheet file with just a couple of minor differences.

First, you will want to name your template with a name that is meaningful to the template users. So from our previous example, this template might be named "Weekly Soft Drink Sales".

Now, as we remember from our computing fundamentals section, the operating system needs to know three pieces of information in order to properly save a file: the file name; the file location; and the file format or type.

We now have selected a good name for the template file, but what about the other two pieces of information?

In order for templates to work properly within the program, the program needs to know where the template files are stored on the computer. This is called the template file location. Template File Locations are the specifically named file locations where a program will look for any user-defined templates. In the options or settings area of each program, you can look up and/or change the default location where your user-defined templates are stored. You will need to know where this location is in order to store your template in the correct place. If the program doesn't know where to look for a template, then you won't be able to use it in the future.

Most contemporary spreadsheet programs also allow you to specify a *shared* template location. These locations allow multiple simultaneous users to be able to have access to the same, single template file, without having to make multiple copies for each independent user. By choosing the correct template file location, you will be ensuring that all of the authorized template users will be able to locate and use your templates.

The last piece of information that we need to supply in order to properly save the template file is the file type. Each program provides its own, unique Template File Type that must be used in order to specify that this file is going to be a template file and not just a regular workbook file.

By providing these three pieces of information, the spreadsheet program will now be able to properly save the template file in the correct location and it will be ready to be used by any authorized user.

LO 9.6 How to Use Created Templates

Now that the template has been created and stored in the proper location with the proper file type, the template is now ready to be used. There are two different ways that the template file might be used: simply creating a new file based on this template as any template user might do and performing template maintenance on this file to make any required changes or adjustments that the file might need over time.

Using a Template to create a new document is as simple as starting a new file, but instead of picking a blank workbook file, you will choose to create a new file based on this named template. The program will then open up the template to read the file, and then create a new blank document that is based upon the contents of the file. The actual original template file is then closed and is ready to be used by the next template user.

But sometimes, a template file itself will need to be adjusted whenever changes are needed to be made. In this situation, you aren't trying to create a new document based on the template. But rather, you need to tell the program to open the actual template file so that you can make changes directly in the template. This is called template maintenance. Template Maintenance is the process of opening an existing template file so that you can make changes that will then become a part of the revised template and any new document that is based on this updated template.

Finally, there are some Template Cautions that must be shared regarding templates and their use. First, we should reiterate the importance of being very cautious with the use of passwords when locking and protecting spreadsheet files. As was mentioned in the previous sections, if you forget the passwords that you use to protect your worksheets or your workbooks, you may, inadvertently, lock yourself completely out of that file. In that case, you may need to completely rebuild this file from scratch.

Another caution regarding templates is that you cannot simply double-click a template file to open it up for editing like you can with a regular spreadsheet file. When you double-click on a template file, the program creates a new spreadsheet file that is *based on the template file* and opens up that new document for you to edit. If you need to perform maintenance on a template file, you must use the program's File-Open dialog to open a template file for editing.

Another word of caution is that some template files are not valid for any spreadsheet program other than the program that created the template. In other words, template files are oftentimes not cross-program compatible. It is recommended that you build a template file in the same program that the end-user of that template will actually be using.

And finally, there are many websites that purport to offer predefined templates for your use. While this may be very enticing, you need to be extra cautious with these kinds of files. As with anything else that you may download from the Internet, you should make absolutely sure that these files are coming from a reputable source. Malicious software and viruses have been known to be embedded in templates because this can become an easy path to unauthorized access into your systems.

All of these cautions aside, successfully creating and using templates can provide a wealth of efficiency, quality, and consistency in your repetitive spreadsheet tasks.

Chapter 9 – Assignments and Projects

Directed Assignments

DA 9-1. For this directed assignment, you will be using the student data file named **DA_9-1.xlsx** to complete the required information. This file is in Microsoft Excel 2007 or newer format and should open in any contemporary spreadsheet program.

Required student data file: *DA_9-1.xlsx*

For this assignment, you will be updating a file to become a bank deposit template for your company or organization. Your task will be to complete this spreadsheet template by following the instructions below.

1. Open the student data file named **DA_9-1.xlsx**.

2. Immediately save a copy of this file using the following specifications:

   a. File name: Rename this file using the filename *YourName_DA_9-1*

   b. File location: Place this file in any location you choose, but make a note of the location as you will need it later.

   c. File format: Because this file will be sent in to your professor, you must check with him or her to see what format *he or she* will want this file to be saved in. Don't just assume that the original file format or the default file format for your own computer will be acceptable! This file *must be saved in the Template file format for the computer program that your professor specifies!*

3. Use Figure DA_9-1_Completed as a model to make the required changes to this file. Make all of the general formatting changes that you see in the blank template.

4. Update the labels in row 1 and 2 to represent your own real or fictitious organization name and bank name.

	A	B	C	D	E
1		Community Sports Complex Concessions				
2	First National Bank			Deposit Date	6/6/2018
3	Account #	8890756		Deposit Slip	
4		Cash			Checks (listed individually)	
5	Denominations	Qty	Cash Totals	Payor	Amount
6	$500.00		$ -	Joe Johnson	$ 11.00
7	$100.00	1	$ 100.00	Sally Smith	$ 17.00
8	$50.00	1	$ 50.00	Mike Mahoney	$ 10.00
9	$20.00	13	$ 260.00	Julie Jones	$ 9.50
10	$10.00	8	$ 80.00	Pat Pironi	$ 12.75
11	$5.00	22	$ 110.00	Morgan Michaels	$ 18.00
12	$1.00	16	$ 16.00	Chris Callahan	$ 13.25
13	Coins (Enter Total of All Coins)	$ 28.17	$ 28.17	Total from Attached List	$ 215.75
14	Total of all Cash		$ 644.17	Total of all Checks	$ 307.25
15				Total Deposit Amount	$ 951.42
16					
17					
18					

Bank Deposit Slip   ⊕

Figure DA_9-1_Completed

5. Create formulas in the range C6:C12 to multiply the denomination by the quantity being deposited to calculate the cash totals.

6. Cell C13 should be a simple reference to the coin amount that will be entered by the user in cell B13.

7. Cell C14 should be the sum of all of the cash being deposited and cell E14 should be the sum of all of the checks being deposited.

8. Cell E15 should be the some of the total cash and the total checks being deposited.

9. Make sure all of the fields are properly formatted as desired including dates, currency, and text fields.

10. Change all of the data entry cells so that they will remain *unlocked* when you protect the worksheet.

11. Protect the worksheet so that the user can **only select unlocked cells**. Do **not** put a password on the worksheet protection.

12. Before saving the file, try out the data entry to make sure that a completed file will look and perform the way you anticipate. Once everything is behaving properly, then clear out all of the data entry fields to leave the sheet "blank."

13. Save the file as a blank deposit slip template as described above.

Creative Projects

CP 9-1. For this creative project, you will create a new spreadsheet template that could be used as a replacement for any form that you might fill out on more than one occasion. You will recreate the overall look of the form and then add in any known data and any pre-defined calculations that you can. You will then protect the worksheet so that the template user will only be able to perform data entry in the template and will not be able to make any other changes to the form. Then you will save the file as a workbook template.

Required student data file: None: Start with a new, blank workbook and save the file as a template file named *YourName_CP_9-1*.

To complete this project, will first need to locate a form that you might fill out on more than one occasion. This could be a registration form, a financial aid form, a timesheet, a work schedule, etc. Make sure that the form you find has at least some numeric values on it that would require some calculations. Remember, if you aren't performing calculations, then you really don't need a spreadsheet program – you could simply be creating a word processing template.

Once you have chosen your form, then using a new blank spreadsheet, re-create the overall look of the form by using appropriate cell formatting including merging cells, highlighting cells, placing borders around cells, etc.

Add all of the static labels and text to your form and enter any known data that will not change each time the template is used. Also, add any calculations into the cells where needed.

Temporarily fill in the rest of the form just as a user would so that you can set the appropriate formatting for all the cells that the user will use to perform data entry. This way, you are making sure that the new documents that are created by using this template will look right when the user completes them.

Once everything looks correct, select all of the temporary data that you created and clear those cells so that the template once again appears as a blank form. Now the template would be ready for the user to perform data entry.

Next, set the appropriate cell protection attributes so that only the data entry fields remain unlocked for the user to work with. Everything else about the template including the locked cells, and the workbook structure should be protected. Use the password "**secured**" to protect the worksheet and the workbook structure. Use the same password for both protections and make sure that the passwords are in lower-case only.

Save your file as a template file type and make note of the location where the template file was stored. Remember to check your final work for spelling, grammar, and overall correctness and then submit your file in the manner prescribed for your class.

Source: Shutterstock, Inc.

Chapter 10

Working with Macros

I had never heard of the term "macros" before but my friend says that they can be very powerful but they may also be a little complicated to create and use. So why do I need to know about macros as a part of spreadsheet fundamentals?

LEARNING OBJECTIVES

In this chapter, we will explore these learning objectives:

- Defining Macros in Various Programs
- Issues with Macro Compatibility
- When to Consider Creating Macros
- Cautions and Warnings regarding Macros
- How to Create Macros
- How to Edit Existing Macros
- How and Where to Save Macros
- How to Use Macros

Now that you have mastered the fundamentals of working in a spreadsheet program, you will just keep getting better and better from here. The more you use a spreadsheet program, the more proficient you become in that environment and your work will quickly take on a higher quality and you will become more efficient in your daily tasks.

But also over time, you'll discover that there are situations where you will be repeating the exact same spreadsheet steps and processes time and time again. This is where macros come in.

In the last chapter, we saw that certain repetitive spreadsheet tasks, which will end up as nearly identical final spreadsheet documents, can be converted into templates, which will make those repetitive tasks even easier. In this chapter we will explore macros that automate any number of repetitive tasks that can be automatically executed with just a single click or a simple keystroke.

It should be noted that macros may be closer to being considered an advanced spreadsheet concept than a spreadsheet fundamentals concept. Many people become proficient in using spreadsheet programs and never create or use macros at all. This chapter is primarily included to help those who are ready to move on to the next level of spreadsheet proficiency.

Key Terms

- Editing a Macro
- Macro
- Macro Language
- Macro Locations
- Macro Security
- Macro-Enabled File
- Playing a Macro
- Recording a Macro

We will also see in this chapter that macros have some safety and security considerations that must be explored, as well as cross-program compatibility issues, which will be discussed in detail.

LO 10.1   Defining Macros in Various Programs

A Macro is a collection of computer commands and statements that are stored in a document by the user for the purpose of automating repetitive tasks. Macros can simulate a user's keystrokes, mouse clicks, and nearly every kind of action or command that the program can execute. Let's look at how macros can be used in various office applications.

In word processors, macros can be used to automatically type in large, boilerplate verbiage that can be used time and time again without having to be retyped each time. An example of this would be in a law office, where certain paragraphs or clauses are used in many contracts and other legal documents. In this kind of scenario, a macro can be created that would allow the legal professional to type a single keystroke or click a single tool and have multiple pages of text automatically show up in the document.

In a graphic design program, macros can be used to perform complex, multistep processes that are typically executed in the exact same sequence. For example once a graphic object is selected, a macro can be executed that will automatically create a frame around the object, create a dropped shadow effect for the object, and reduce the opacity of the object by 50% to turn the object into a watermark object.

In an email program, macros can be set up to perform routine mailbox maintenance such as automatically processing mailbox rules, automatically archiving emails that are older than six months, and compacting mailbox folders to ensure the program's efficiency.

And just the same as macros can be executed in those other programs, macros can be created and executed for spreadsheet programs as well.

LO 10.2   Issues with Macro Compatibility

Before diving too deeply into the creation and using of macros in spreadsheet programs, we should explore some of the issues of macro compatibility across the various spreadsheet programs.

One of the major themes of this entire text has been that if you understand all of the spreadsheet fundamentals, then you can work in any spreadsheet program and be highly productive, efficient, and produce exceptional quality work with very little re-training to get use to each different spreadsheet program. When it comes to spreadsheet fundamentals, all of the spreadsheet programs perform effectively the same way.

When it comes to macros, however, compatibility becomes a significant issue. Generally speaking macros will only be compatible with other programs that share the same macro language. A Macro Language is the programming language that is used by an application program to record and process the specific keystrokes and commands within that program. Two of the more common macro languages are Visual Basic for Applications (VBA) and LibreOffice Basic.

Most of the time, if a macro was written in one language, it will not be automatically converted to the other language. As a result, macro-enabled workbooks typically can only be shared with others who have the same spreadsheet program.

Additionally, the security settings of the end user of a macro-enabled worksheet will determine whether or not the macro performs as it was designed. This can become a compatibility issue even with two users who have the same version of the same spreadsheet program. We will look at some of these security issues in more detail in Learning Objective LO 10.4.

LO 10.3   When to Consider Creating Macros

So if there are significant compatibility issues with macros, when should you consider creating or using macros?

Macros are often created by "power users" of spreadsheets and other office programs to automate routine tasks that may not be especially difficult, but rather that are simply time consuming. No matter what office environment you may work in, once you discover that you are performing the exact same task for the second time, you should stop and ask yourself this question: "How many times in the future do I think I will perform this exact same task?"

If your answer to this question is "more than just a few times", then you have identified a task that is right for being turned into a macro. In this regards, you may use macros quite frequently on your own machine, and for your own repetitive tasks.

Additionally, if you find yourself in the role of being a creator of workbooks and templates for other people to use, then you may also discover that creating macros for those end-users can help them automate their day-to-day tasks as well. Examples of this can be found in companies where spreadsheet templates like expense reports or time sheets have been created for everyone to use that have macros within them to help automate the document processing.

LO 10.4   Cautions and Warnings regarding Macros

There are several additional areas of concern that you should consider before creating and using macros in your spreadsheet workbooks. As mentioned previously, there are issues of compatibility that may come into play, which may affect your decision to create or use macros. Additionally, there are a number of concerns with regard to the security and the use of macros.

Because macros are built using a complete programming language, macros can essentially assume control of the computing environment in which they are run. As a result, malicious software (malware) can be coded within a macro language for the purposes of infecting a computer with a virus or performing some other unauthorized tasks.

Because of this reality, application programs have added elaborate macro security to help protect the user's computing environment. Macro Security involves the configuration of your application environment to identify various sources of trusted files and locations, the level to which certain macro commands may be processed, and options to completely prohibit all macro processing.

Macro processing is typically set, by default, to be prohibited in most programs. Users can, however, override these default settings and allow macro-enabled spreadsheets to run. Appropriately setting up the security parameters to allow your macros to execute is a task unto itself. Not only does your own machine need to be properly configured, but also every end-user's machine that will use the macros must have appropriate security settings configured.

A final issue that must be considered when creating and working with macros will be the location in which the macros are stored. The location of where a macro is stored will be discussed in detail in Learning Objective LO 10.7.

LO 10.5   How to Create Macros

When you decide you are ready to create your first macro, the easiest way to get started is to allow the program to do most of the work for you. Each spreadsheet program has a method for you to create a new macro by simply having the program record each step as you complete them.

Depending on your spreadsheet program, you may need to "turn on" or "enable" the specific tool-bars or locations where macros are processed. You will need to investigate specific ways in which your spreadsheet program allows you to enable macro recording.

Recording a Macro begins when you click the tool or menu command to initiate the Record Macro dialog. Figure 10-1 shows the record macro dialogs from two popular spreadsheet programs.

You can quickly begin to appreciate that both programs take different approaches to the way macros are processed. In Excel, the dialog wants you to provide a name for the macro, a possible keyboard shortcut to acti-vate or run the macro, the location where the macro will be stored, and an optional description of what the macro will accomplish. Once you

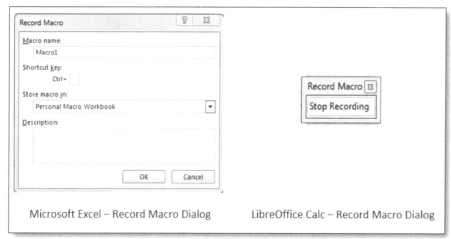

Figure 10-1

enter all of this information and click OK, your macro is now in the process of being recorded and every single step that you take, from then on out, will be recorded until you click the "Stop Recording" button.

In LibreOffice, there is no Record Macro dialog . . . at least not yet! When you click the "Record Macro" command from the menu, the program immediately starts recording your action and then just gives you the single button to immediately *Stop Recording* your macro. You get the opportunity to con-figure the other options about the macro later on through a completion process.

But the effects of these two endeavors are the same: A macro is being created and recorded, which will produce a step-by-step sequence of commands that matches every single activity that you take in this spreadsheet until you click the "Stop Recording" button.

Let's say, for example, that you want to create a macro that will place your organization's name in cell A1 and then merge the cell range A1:G1. Then, it will type the label "Date" in cell H1, and enter the Today function in cell I1. Finally, the macro will add your standard formatting to these cells.

Figures 10-2 and 10-3 show the desired end results in each of the two respective programs. As you can see, in both programs, the recorded steps ended up with nearly identical results.

Once a macro has been recorded, you can use it again and again. Running or playing existing mac-ros will be detailed in Learning Objective LO 10.8.

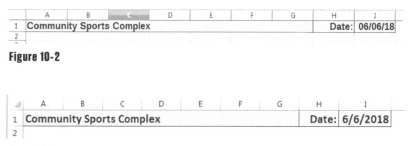

Figure 10-2

Figure 10-3

LO 10.6   How to Edit Existing Macros

Now, let's take a look behind the scenes at the actual macros that were created in each program. From time to time, you may need to make a change to the basic behavior of a previously recorded macro. This is called editing a macro.

Editing a Macro consists of opening up the macro in the programming language editor that is available in your spreadsheet program. Figure 10-4 shows the beginning portion of the macro code that was recorded in Excel and Figure 10-5 shows the beginning portion of the macro that was recorded in LibreOffice.

As you can quickly see, these two macro programming languages are significantly different and that is why macros are not considered to be compatible across different spreadsheet programs.

But if you look carefully in the two code examples, you can see the line of code where the label for the organization name was typed into the cell. If, for example, the organization was to change its name from "Community Sports Complex" to "Little-League Sports Complex", you could simply update the literal value in this code window and then save the macro once again. The actual programming macro steps haven't changed, just the value that would be used changed.

Very often, unless you are the programmer type, it may be just as easy to recreate a macro than it is to edit a macro. But you should know that both of these options are available to you.

```
Sub Heading()
'
' Heading Macro
'
' Keyboard Shortcut: Ctrl+Shift+H
'
    Range("A1").Select
    ActiveCell.FormulaR1C1 = "Community Sports Complex"
    Range("A1:G1").Select
    With Selection
        .HorizontalAlignment = xlCenter
        .VerticalAlignment = xlBottom
        .WrapText = False
        .Orientation = 0
        .AddIndent = False
        .IndentLevel = 0
        .ShrinkToFit = False
        .ReadingOrder = xlContext
        .MergeCells = False
    End With
    Selection.Merge
    With Selection
        .HorizontalAlignment = xlLeft
        .VerticalAlignment = xlBottom
        .WrapText = False
        .Orientation = 0
        .AddIndent = False
        .IndentLevel = 0
        .ShrinkToFit = False
        .ReadingOrder = xlContext
        .MergeCells = True
    End With
    Range("H1").Select
    ActiveCell.FormulaR1C1 = "Date:"
    Range("H1").Select
```

Figure 10-4

```
REM  *****  BASIC  *****

sub Main
rem ----------------------------------------------------------------
rem define variables
dim document    as object
dim dispatcher as object
rem ----------------------------------------------------------------
rem get access to the document
document    = ThisComponent.CurrentController.Frame
dispatcher = createUnoService("com.sun.star.frame.DispatchHelper")

rem ----------------------------------------------------------------
dim args1(0) as new com.sun.star.beans.PropertyValue
args1(0).Name = "ToPoint"
args1(0).Value = "$L$15"

dispatcher.executeDispatch(document, ".uno:GoToCell", "", 0, args1())

rem ----------------------------------------------------------------
dim args2(0) as new com.sun.star.beans.PropertyValue
args2(0).Name = "ToPoint"
args2(0).Value = "$A$1:$G$1"

dispatcher.executeDispatch(document, ".uno:GoToCell", "", 0, args2())

rem ----------------------------------------------------------------
dispatcher.executeDispatch(document, ".uno:ToggleMergeCells", "", 0, Array())

rem ----------------------------------------------------------------
dim args4(0) as new com.sun.star.beans.PropertyValue
args4(0).Name = "StringName"
args4(0).Value = "Community Sports Complex"

dispatcher.executeDispatch(document, ".uno:EnterString", "", 0, args4())
```

Figure 10-5

LO 10.7   How and Where to Save Macros

An important aspect of working with macros is knowing a macro's location. Macro Locations are the various possible places where macros can be stored and executed. Depending on your spreadsheet program, your macros can be stored in the local workbook file only, or they could be stored in a template file, or they could be stored in a generic location that could be a shared macro location.

As previously discussed in Learning Objective LO 10.5, each program will ask you to specify the location where this macro should be stored at different times in the process. For Excel macros, the dialog asks you for the location before you even start recording. For LibreOffice macros, the process waits until the macro has been completely recorded and then the program asks you where you would like to store the macro.

The main concept here is that it is important to understand where your macros will be stored. If you want this macro to be available to more than just this individual spreadsheet workbook, then you must make sure that you save the macro into a shared location and not just within the confines of this single workbook.

Power users of spreadsheets will often create a single workbook file whose sole purpose is to be the repository of all the macros that they create and use on a repetitive basis.

But specifying the location of the macros is not the only consideration here. Additionally, because of the security concerns mentioned previously, you must also tell the program that the file that contains the macros is a macro-enabled file. A Macro-Enabled File is any file that contains user-defined macros that can be run. By saving a workbook or template file as a macro-enabled file type, it alerts the program that there are macros present so that the enhanced security features can make sure that the user's computer remains protected. Both regular workbook files and template files can be saved as macro-enabled files so you must make sure that you choose the correct file type when saving your files.

LO 10.8   How to Use Macros

When it comes to running or playing a macro, you will have several different options depending on the spreadsheet program you are using. Playing a Macro is the process of telling a spreadsheet file that you want to run a pre-recorded macro. Macros can be run by using the macro menu and then selecting the macro by name and then by pressing the "run" or "play" buttons.

Additionally, macros can have keyboard shortcuts assigned to them. This is, in fact, the most common way that macros are typically set up. By assigning a keyboard shortcut to one of your own user-defined macros, you can create a situation where, with a simple keystroke, you can perform a multitude of spreadsheet operations with perfect accuracy and minimal effort.

One final way that macros can be run is by binding the macro to a toolbar or menu and giving the macro its own icon. By doing so, your custom macro becomes just a single mouse click away.

Chapter 10 – Assignments and Projects

Directed Assignments

DA 10-1. For this directed assignment, you will create a new, blank spreadsheet and then record, edit, save a macro, and then run the macro in a second sheet.

Required student data file: None: Start with a new, blank workbook and name the file *YourName_ DA_10-1*.

1. Immediately save this blank file using the following specifications:
   a. File name: Name this file using the filename *YourName_DA_10-1*
   b. File location: Place this file in any location you choose, but make a note of the location as you will need it later.
   c. File format: Because this file will be sent in to your professor, you must check with him or her to see what format *he or she* will want this file to be saved in. Don't just assume that the original file format or the default file format for your own computer will be acceptable! *Remember that this file* MUST *be saved as a Macro-Enabled Workbook.*

2. Initiate the "Record Macro" dialog in your spreadsheet program.

3. When prompted, either at the beginning of macro recording or at the end depending on your spreadsheet program, you will use the name "AddNamesAndDate" (without spaces) for your macro name. Also, you will store this macro in this workbook file whenever prompted.

4. Next, while the macro is recording, perform the following steps in your blank workbook:
   a. Merge the cell range A1:E1 and type "Your Name Goes Here" as the label and align the cell to the left.
   b. Merge the cell range F1:G1 and enter the label "Date:" and align it to the right.
   c. In cell H1, enter today's date by simply typing in today's date directly and format the cell as a short date.
   d. Select the range A1:H1 and format the range to be 14 point font size, bold, with a solid border around all cells, and a lightly shaded background color.
   e. Stop recording the macro and, if necessary, complete the remaining "Record Macro" dialogs.

5. Now that you have the macro recorded, create a new blank worksheet in this workbook and run the macro and see if it performs as you expected.

6. If the macro did *not* perform as you expected, you can either attempt to edit the macro to make the necessary changes, or you can simply delete the macro and recreate it using the steps outlined above.

7. Once the macro is performing as expected, edit the macro to replace the literal "Your Name Goes Here" with your own name.

8. Save the edited macro and test one final time on another blank sheet.

9. Once you know the macro is working correctly, add one more final, blank worksheet and then remove all the rest of the worksheets leaving just this one, single, blank worksheet.

10. Finally, in the cell range A3:H8 in this blank worksheet, merge and center this range and then wrap the text for this new block. Then, type a short message that describes the macro you created, its name, and how the user should run the macro in your spreadsheet.

11. Double-check your work for spelling and grammar and then submit your file in the manner prescribed for your class.

Creative Projects

CP 10-1. For this creative project, you will create a new, blank spreadsheet and build a macro to perform some series of spreadsheet tasks.

Required student data file: None: Start with a new, blank workbook file and name the file *YourName_CP_10-1*.

The very nature of a macro is that it can automate any multistep, repetitive tasks to ensure accuracy and completeness, and to add efficiency. But as we learned in Chapter 9, if the *entire* worksheet is to be repeated often, it is probably a candidate to be made into a template rather than simply building a macro to create or rebuild an entire spreadsheet on each occasion.

For this project, create a macro that includes a number of spreadsheet activities (e.g. entering some labels, adjusting the format of cells or cell ranges, entering formulas) to perform some task that you yourself or some other user might want to perform on a regular basis.

Record and edit the macro as necessary and test the macro to make sure it performs as you expect.

Once the macro has been created, store this macro within this workbook.

Remove all other worksheet from this workbook but then create a single blank worksheet in this workbook where you can type a description of the macro, what the macro achieves, the name of the macro, and how the user would run the macro.

Remember that the workbook must be saved as a "Macro-Enabled" workbook.

Also remember to check your final work for spelling, grammar, and overall correctness and then submit your file in the manner prescribed for your class.